FEMINISMS AND DEVELOPMENT

Disrupting taken-for-granted assumptions, this expert series redefines issues at the heart of today's feminist contestations in a development context. Bringing together a formidable collective of thinkers from the global South and North, it explores what it is that can bring about positive changes in women's rights and realities.

These timely and topical collections reposition feminism within development studies, bringing into view substantial commonalities across the countries of the global South that have so far gone unrecognized.

Series editor

Andrea Cornwall

Forthcoming titles

Voicing Demands:
Feminist Activism in Transitional Contexts
Sohela Nazneen and Maheen Sultan

Feminisms, Empowerment and Development:
Changing Women's Lives
Andrea Cornwall and Jenny Edwards

Changing Narratives of Sexuality:
Contestations, Compliance and Women's Empowerment
Charmaine Pereira

About the Editor

Mulki Al-Sharmani is an Academy of Finland research fellow and lecturer in the Study of Religion Unit, Faculty of Theology, University of Helsinki. She is also a member of Musawah, the Global Movement for Equality and Justice in the Muslim Family. Al-Sharmani has researched and published on transnational migration and Somali diaspora(s), child protection and social welfare policies in Egypt, gender and Muslim family laws in Egypt, and Islamic feminism. After completing a PhD in cultural anthropology at the Johns Hopkins University in 2005, Al-Sharmani worked as a researcher and taught at the American University in Cairo from 2005 to 2010, and was a research fellow at Helsinki Collegium for Advanced Studies from 2010 to 2011.

Feminist Activism, Women's Rights, and Legal Reform

edited by
Mulki Al-Sharmani

Zed Books
LONDON & NEW YORK

Feminist Activism, Women's Rights, and Legal Reform was first published in 2013 by Zed Books Ltd, 7 Cynthia Street, London N1 9JF, UK and Room 400, 175 Fifth Avenue, New York, NY 10010, USA

www.zedbooks.co.uk

Designed and typeset in Monotype Bembo by Kate Kirkwood
Index by John Barker
Cover design: www.alice-marwick.co.uk
Printed and bound by TJ International Ltd, Padstow, Cornwall PL28 8RW

Distributed in the USA exclusively by Palgrave Macmillan, a division of St Martin's Press, LLC, 175 Fifth Avenue, New York, NY 10010, USA

A catalogue record for this book is available from the British Library
Library of Congress Cataloging in Publication Data available

ISBN 978 1 78032 963 5 hb
ISBN 978 1 78032 962 8 pb

Contents

Acknowledgements

....

This work would not have been possible without the support of a number of colleagues and institutions. First, I would like to extend my thanks to the Pathways of Women's Empowerment research programme, which supported both the book project and the research for the chapters on Egypt, Bangladesh, and Brazil. My special thanks to Andrea Cornwall, the coordinator of the Pathways project, for offering insightful feedback on the manuscript as well as writing the preface. My thanks are also due to Jenny Edwards, the programme administrative coordinator at Pathways, for assisting with the editing and formatting of the manuscript.

Special thanks also to Ziba Mir-Hosseini, independent legal anthropologist, professorial research associate at the Center of Islamic and Middle Eastern Law at the School of Oriental and African Studies, University of London, and co-founder of Musawah, the Global Movement for Equality and Justice in the Muslim Family. I am grateful to Ziba for reading the manuscript and offering thorough and insightful comments.

I would also like to thank the Social Research Center at the American University in Cairo (AUC) and its director, Hoda Rashad, for the support and assistance I received for my research on family law reform in Egypt while employed at the Center. Special thanks go to my colleague Hania Sholkamy, associate professor of anthropology in the Social Research Center at AUC and the coordinator of the Middle East hub in the Pathways project. I thank Hania both for inviting me to take part in Pathways, and thus giving me the opportunity to research family law reform in Egypt, and for her helpful input in that research. I am indebted to my colleagues Marwa Sharaf El Din, Egyptian activist, doctoral candidate at Oxford University, and a member of Musawah; to Sawsan Sharif, researcher at the Social Research Center at AUC; and to Fayrouz Gamal, research assistant at the same institution, for their contributions to the research on Egypt.

I thank the Helsinki Collegium for Advanced Studies, University of Helsinki, for awarding me a one-year research fellowship post that provided the time and support to work on this book project.

Last but not least, I would like to thank all the distinguished colleagues who contributed to this volume.

Preface

Andrea Cornwall

Feminist engagements with the law reveal the complex relationships between legal framings and processes, and social domains, practices, and institutions. Law is an instrument that can be used in the pursuit of gender justice. But it is equally an obstacle to the achievement of greater gender equality. The legal arena is, then, both a site of oppression and an important means of social transformation.

Feminist legal scholarship has drawn attention to the nuanced interplay between legal reforms and feminist activism, and strategies, tactics, and struggles that animate the use of the law to create, contest, or challenge social meanings and practices. This book's rich array of case studies from diverse geographical contexts brings these dynamics to life. Focusing on the domain of family and domestic violence legislation, these studies explore newly introduced or proposed laws, setting them in the context of legal and societal debates and contestations, strategies of mobilization of different actors, and the mobilization of meanings in the legal arena. In doing so, they chart the role of law and legal strategies in pathways of women's empowerment.

Feminist Activism, Women's Rights, and Legal Reform forms part of a series, Feminisms and Development, which has grown out of a multi-disciplinary research programme, Pathways of Women's Empowerment. Pathways began in 2006 as a consortium of researchers convened through regional hubs in Africa, Asia, Latin America, and the Middle East, with a cross-cutting focus on global policy processes. The consortium set about a multi-stranded enquiry into the processes of change in women's lives, exploring not only efforts to instigate change through laws, policies, and programmes, but also 'hidden pathways' made possible through more diffuse economic, political, and cultural changes. Inter-regional connections were built through cross-hub working groups on 'work', 'body', and 'voice', giving rise to a number of collective, comparative research projects that provide the basis for this series, with titles reflecting the scope and range of enquiry.

The multi-sited comparative project that produced this insight-ful collection sought to take questions of 'voice' into an enquiry into whether law and legal reform could constitute a pathway of empowerment. Mulki Al-Sharmani brings together in this book studies by Pathways researchers working on law reform and the introduction of new laws in contexts that offer some particularly interesting lessons – from the new family courts in Egypt to the civil society monitoring of the implementation of the landmark 2006 domestic violence law in Brazil; and from the intense contestation that accompanied the passing of domestic violence laws in Ghana to the movement for a uniform family code in Bangladesh. The collection also brings to comparative analysis scholarship in and from Yemen, Iran, Morocco, and Palestine, contexts which are more rarely available to feminist scholars internationally.

This volume does more than analyse the processes of making and shaping these laws and the challenges of implementing them. It delves into the discursive role of law, examining the interplay of social meaning and societal institutions through which norms, values, rights, and responsibilities come to be shaped. As such, it touches on questions of identity, the nature of state–citizen relations, and the role of different kinds of societal and state institutions in defining and producing particular narratives of gender, citizenship, and entitlement. Its conclusions – that feminist activism should extend beyond 'rights' to the complex set of engagements through which gendered identities and relations come to be made and shaped – will resonate more widely with those concerned with creating pathways to greater equality and justice.

INTRODUCTION
Legal Reform and Feminist Activism

• •

Mulki Al-Sharmani

The engagement of Western feminist academic scholarship with law has been multifaceted and diverse.[1] One major question tackled by this scholarship is the gendering and marginalizing role of law (against women), in both its underlying epistemological and philosophical premises and its methodologies and practices. How may legal reform open a pathway of social transformation and gender equality? What are the limits of law (whether as codes, discourses, or practices) in taking into account and enabling the heterogeneity of women's experiences, needs, and desires? How best may women claim agency in the legal domain, whether as activists, litigants, or legal practitioners? And what is the role of the state and its various political projects in shaping, facilitating, or inhibiting processes and outcomes of feminist legal activism?

Whereas some of this scholarship (for example, MacKinnon 1987) asserts the role of law reform (despite the gendered and gendering nature of law) in the political and intellectual pursuit of gender justice, other literature (for example, Smart 1989) is sceptical of the transformative role of legal reform and is wary of the omnipotence of the state in the domain of law and legal reform. One significant insight that most of this scholarship agrees on, however, is that law is neither the only culprit nor the exclusive solution to gender injustice. This is succinctly captured by Susan Boyd:

Law is neither the ultimate oppressor of women nor the ultimate solution to resolve the oppression. Rather it is situated within the complex set of relations that we call state and society, and it is implicated both directly and ideologically in women's oppression and in women's struggles against oppression. (Boyd 1994: 46)

The scholarship on Islamic law and modern Muslim family laws, in particular, vividly drives home the complexity of the relationship between gender and law, by providing rich analyses of different aspects of this relationship. For example, ethnographic studies of courts in Muslim-majority countries highlight the social and cultural embeddedness of law (Rosen 1989, 2000; Bowen 2006). One can infer from these studies that, on the one hand, the social and cultural dimensions of law reinforce its seemingly uniform and dominant power, while, on the other, it is this feature of the law that makes legal interpretation part and parcel of dynamic processes of negotiation and contestation over systems of social norms and meanings. This insight about the socio-cultural nature/role of law is important for the question of gender because it complicates the question of perceiving and constructing law as merely a state mechanism that grants or withholds rights.

Furthermore, an impressive body of literature on Muslim family laws in the past three decades has problematized the notion of legal reform as a state project of pursuing modernity and its assumed attributes of gender equality and democracy (Sonbol 1996, 2003, 2005; Charrad 2001; Welchman 2004; Tucker 2008). This literature has shown that codification of Muslim family laws in the twentieth century and the subsequent legal reforms were neither a linear nor necessarily a favourable march towards the empowerment of women. Rather, processes of codification and reform were embedded in multidimensional and intricate webs of power relations between multiple national actors, and the consequences for women, in terms of claims on and access to legal rights, were mixed and even marginalizing in some cases.

Another important contribution of the scholarship on Muslim family laws has been to shed light on the agency of women (and men) litigants, the complex role of judicial reasoning, and the multiple normative orders that come into play in the dynamic processes of litigation and courtroom interactions (Moors 1995; Hirsch 1998; Tucker 1998, 2008; Mir-Hosseini 2000; Welchman 2000). In particular, these studies have shown that law and its challenges, as well as holding significance for women's rights, go beyond written codes or their religious textual sources (as in the case of Muslim family laws).

In recent years, the scholarship on Muslim family laws has also shed light on a new area of inquiry into law and gender, namely public debates about legal reforms. A number of studies have examined these debates in Middle Eastern and African countries (Buskens 2003; Moors 2003; Schulz 2003; Würth 2003), using them as a lens through which to shed light on various issues such as the processes through which mobilization for particular reforms took place; the alliances that were made and unmade among different actors; and the strategies of advocacy and argumentation styles that were used by different actors. Perhaps the main significance of these studies has been the critique of the binary conceptualizations and depictions of those who push for reform or those who are critical of it.

Legal reform and feminist activism: selected case studies

This volume will also speak to the larger question of law and gender with which the two above-mentioned bodies of scholarship have been concerned – albeit in different ways. The volume aims to provide a nuanced understanding of processes through which legal reforms and feminist activism take place and interplay, and their outcomes for women. Through case studies of reform efforts, successes, and failures in diverse geographical contexts in the Middle East, West Africa, South Asia, and Latin America, the authors identify and analyse multiple factors that enable, hinder, or complicate the role of legal reform as a pathway in seeking gender justice and social transformation.

The book focuses on two areas of law that have been the

subject of reform initiated by feminist movements in the selected countries, namely family and domestic violence laws. The case studies analysed illuminate the complex relationship between legal reform and feminist activism. Shehada, Dahlgren, Al-Sharmani, Nazneen, and Osanloo examine debates about changes in family laws in Palestine, Yemen, Egypt, Bangladesh, and Iran, respectively. Focusing on newly introduced or proposed laws in these countries, the authors identify and analyse the key issues that framed these debates; the goals and strategies of mobilization (and resistance) of different actors and interlocutors; and the underlying assumptions and concerns that drove contestations and struggles between (and within) the proponents and critics of the reforms.

Carlisle, de Aquino, and Manuh and Dwamena-Aboagye focus on the implementation and the monitoring of newly introduced reforms in Morocco, Brazil, and Ghana, respectively. The authors examine diverse implementation challenges and complexities, as well as the difficulties of measuring the success of the new laws in empowering women. The authors also shed light on litigants' strategies and uses of the new laws, judicial reasoning, and various legal and non-legal factors that result in a mixed outcome for women from these reforms. While the specificities of reform processes and feminist activism in each of the case studies are different, the chapters speak to three main underlying questions. I shall outline these main issues, while also providing a brief synopsis of each chapter.

Revisiting binaries and 'uniform' issues

One central question addressed by many of the chapters in this volume is: what is concealed when reform efforts (and the public debates about them) fail to escape conceptualizations and categorizations that are based on binaries and uniform understandings of terms such as 'religious', 'secular' or 'civil', and 'tradition' or 'modernity?' The authors in this volume problem-atize conventional understandings of these categories. They provide multiple answers to the question posed above. What we can take away from their analyses is that it is not simply that these terms do not inherently and always mean opposite things. It is also that the meanings of these terms, and the discourses in which they are articulated, are multiple, diverse, and (most of all) shaped by specific temporalities and socio-political contexts. The significance of this insight is not only that it could facilitate a richer and complex understanding of the ideological frameworks under which feminist legal activism and its opposition take place, but also that it is a call for activists and policy makers to resist seemingly easy but misleading and singular solutions that are yielded by understandings based on oppositional binaries.

Another central point that the authors underscore is that legal reform processes and contestations that concern women and gender rights are often driven and shaped by multiple issues that are related to larger political and social struggles and debates.

In Chapter 1, Shehada analyses the public debate about legislating new Muslim family law in Gaza and the West Bank after the establishment of the Palestinian Authority (PA) in 1994, and the specific efforts of the Palestinian Model Parliament for Women and Legislation (MP) in deliberating and drafting the new code, which took place during the period from 1997 to 1999. Shehada clearly shows that resistance against the proposed changes in the family code cannot be explained away by conceptualizing it as a matter of struggle between those seeking to preserve religious tradition and those seeking modern liberal values of gender equality and modern liberal ways of life. Rather, it was a complex socio-political process that was shaped by the specific historical context of the Palestinian territories at a time in which there were ongoing struggles for liberation and state building; politicization as well as fragmentation of local feminist movements in the midst of a growing globalization of feminist agendas and organizations; and a heterogeneity of religious discourses, whether legitimating or rejecting the proposed legal changes.

For instance, the author explains that the resistance on the part of some MP members (and other sectors in the society) to the proposed abolition of the legal requirement for a male guardian of the bride to be present during the officiating of a marriage contract cannot be justified on religious grounds, since there are diverse legal opinions that sanction as well as prohibit either position in classical Islamic jurisprudence. Rather, the opposition to this proposition had more to do with social norms and practices such as women's keenness on involving their kin families in arranging their marriages so that these new brides can have more leverage and negotiating power *vis-à-vis* their husbands, precisely because of their reliance on their families' support. Again, in deliberating whether to restrict men's right to polygyny in law, the main challenge that confronted MP members who were pushing for this was not whether they could make a valid religious argument for curtailing men's right to take multiple wives; rather, it was the political and cultural price that they might end up paying if they pursued the battle for this particular reform.

In Chapter 2, Dahlgren also deconstructs misleading binaries such as 'tradition' versus 'modernity', 'religious' versus 'secular', or 'modernist' versus 'Islamist' in her analysis of the processes leading to the promulgation of both the 1974 Family Law in South Yemen (with all the gains it brought to women there) and the 1992 Personal Status Law in unified Yemen that abolished the former gender-sensitive family code of South Yemen. Dahlgren engages in what she calls a 'political' analysis of the processes leading to the making of both codes, focusing in particular on the underlying interests of political actors who pushed for the changes introduced by the latter code. In the public discourse about the new law, polarizing religious/modernist terms were used to garner support for the 1992 Personal Status Law, vilify the 1974 Family Law, and silence the voices of critics of the new code. Thus the new code was presented by the drafting committee as 'Shari'a-based', while the 1974 Family Law was referred to as 'void of Shari'a'. Ironically, the author points out, the 1974 Family Law was passed not only because at the time it matched a nationalist state ideology of equal partnership between female and male citizens in the building of South Yemeni society, but also because it was perceived by its drafters and society as being compatible with the principles and doctrines of Islamic Shari'a.

But beneath the surface of these Shari'a arguments, Dahlgren shows that in the case of unified Yemen, gender rights are being reshaped (to the detriment of women) as a result of political struggles for power and national wealth (over land and mineral resources, for example) between, on the one hand, an oppressive and despotic northern state and its supporters of co-opted southern political elites and, on the other, the increasingly marginalized sectors of southern Yemeni society. This political struggle, Dahlgren points out, also has a cultural dimension to it, in which the peoples (and particularly women) of both regions of the unified country are presented in public discourses in polarizing and 'othering' terms such as 'backward' or 'uncivilized *badu*' (for the northerners) versus 'morally loose' or 'unbelievers' (for the southerners).

Al-Sharmani, in Chapter 3, unpacks the religious discourses that were used by different interlocutors in public debates in Egypt (from 2007 to 2010) about proposing a new comprehensive family code. The draft code was meant to introduce wide-ranging changes in marriage, divorce, and child custody laws after a decade of important but piecemeal, and mostly procedural, legal reforms. Al-Sharmani points out that religious-based arguments were a main strategy used by almost all interlocutors in making the case both for and against the proposed reforms. Yet it would be erroneous, she argues, to reduce the contestations in this debate to the issue of disagreement over the religious validity of interpretations used by different interlocutors. Rather, much of the disagreement also had to do with multiple socio-political factors.

For instance, some of the 'religious' opposition to the draft law was driven by a modernist agenda of religio-cultural preservation of a gendered notion of Muslim family against a perceived Western threat, as exemplified by the discourse of an NGO, the International Islamic Committee for Woman and Child (IICWC). Another dimension in the contestation was related to the fragmentation and diversification of the processes through which religious education and knowledge were produced, disseminated, and legitimized. For example, Al-Sharmani points out, some of the opposition from the religious establishment (the Islamic Research Academy of Al Azhar, for example) to the positions of independent religious scholars, such as Gamal El Banna, on gender rights in the family, was driven by the latter's lack of Azhar-based religious education and the perception, on the part of the religious establishment, that the kind of religious knowledge that El Banna produced departed from the foundations of the corpus of mainstream Azhar-based knowledge and scholarship. Opposition to the proposed draft code was also shaped by a rejection of the central role that a corrupt state was playing in the reform process through its monopoly of legal power (I will return to this point in a subsequent section). In fact, there was opposition on the part of some interlocutors to the privileging of the domain of law as a site for gender reform and social transformation over other social institutions connected to the daily lives of people, such as the home, school, and places of worship.

It seems, though, that it is not only religion as a discourse and a framework for guiding or resisting legal reform that is contested, but also other discursive systems such as secularism. The contradictions of secularism as a feminist ideology are well illuminated by Nazneen in Chapter 4. Nazneen documents and analyses the failure of the efforts of feminist movements in Bangladesh to mobilize for the promulgation of a unified Family Code (UFC) in the late 1980s and early 1990s. The goal behind advocating for a UFC was to have one code, based on the principle of gender equality, that would regulate the personal status affairs of all citizens regardless of their ethnic or religious background. The draft law and the discourse that was used to promote it were framed by its proponents within the framework of secular nationalism. In making the case for the new code, the feminist movements steered clear of religion and religious arguments, and invoked the principles of social justice, the constitutional right to equality for all citizens, and the modernist notion of the importance of equal gender rights for the social development of the country. But the proponents of the new law were challenged not only (as expected) by Islamic groups but also (interestingly) by male and female members of ethnic minority groups (such as Hindus). Minority groups who were opposed to the draft law argued that the feminists' pursuit of secularism and equal rights for individual female citizens would come at the expense of the right of minorities to preserve their own cultural and religious identity.

In Chapter 5, Osanloo's analysis of the debate about the amendments to the Iranian Family Protection Act that were passed in 2011 highlights the layered dimensions in the competing discourses lobbying for and against these amendments. Osanloo shows that the debate about this bill, and particularly on the amendments that focused on temporary marriage and polygamy, is not simply about competing visions of the family or women's 'status' as opposed to their rights, but also about the nature of the Iranian state and whether it is to be an 'Islamic government' or an 'Islamic republic', the former being primarily based on establishing a certain Islamic social and moral order, and the latter being concerned with regulating rights of citizens. In other words, the debate and contestations around the new family law amendments in 2011 were driven and shaped by multiple issues that cannot be neatly categorized in oppositional categories.

Moreover, Osanloo also shows that the discursive strategies used in the competing discourses are complex and intermixed. On the one hand, one discourse adopts the language of 'women's status' in the family as mothers and wives to argue for family laws that it sees as protective of the Iranian 'family' and women, while another discourse adopts the framework of women's 'rights' in their capacity as citizens to guide gender-sensitive legal reform. Yet, Osanloo points out, the actors adopting these seemingly polarized discourses draw on each other's discursive strategies to make their claims. For example, women's rights activists lobbying against the amendments made their arguments on the grounds that the proposed new laws were detrimental to the family and its welfare; while conservative actors espousing the amendments also drew on the language of 'women's rights', but their perspective of women's rights is one that is based on a notion of complementary and gendered rights and responsibilities.

Engaging the state: the pitfalls, gains, and limits

The second underlying question guiding this book concerns an old but important aspect of feminist legal activism, namely its engagement with the state. The various chapters tackle this issue through addressing a number of questions. What is gained by feminist activists when they seek and engage with the state and its institutions as the pathway to realizing the goals of gender equality and justice? What are the challenges and drawbacks of this engagement? What other, and perhaps potentially effective, pathways become subordinate and less frequented by feminist activists precisely because of their focus on the state as the agent of social change and gender equality? What are the different ramifications for ordinary women as well as feminist movements in different contexts when gender rights become entangled in political struggles for state control, legitimacy, and access to resources?

In Chapter 7, de Aquino's first goal is to document a success story of the Brazilian feminist movement which sought to address the problem of domestic violence against women through sustained and concentrated engagement with the state. The epitome of this success was the promulgation of the Maria da Penha Law (LMP) in 2006. LMP is a code that stipulates comprehensive (that is, preventive and punitive) measures to deal with the problem of domestic violence. Other achievements of the feminist movements included constitutional amendments in a number of Brazilian states that directly address the issue of domestic violence as well as successful mobilization for the establishment of specialized state institutions that provide different but interrelated services to victims of domestic violence who are seeking legal redress and support. These institutions are the Women's Police Stations and Special Courts for Familial and Domestic Violence against Women.

Interestingly, de Aquino notes that while important factions of Brazilian feminist movements had often been sceptical and even critical of feminists' engagement with the state – seeing the latter as an intrinsic part of the patriarchal order – since the 1980s, the state and its institutions have become the main sites and domains in which feminists rally to address gender inequalities and problems. De Aquino explains that this change in the mode of activism was to a great extent facilitated by the advent of an era of democratic rule and political culture. She points out that since the 1980s a significant tool of mobilization leading to the success of the feminist movements was the adoption of a discourse that conceives of women's rights and gender equality as intrinsic to the protection of human rights in a democratic society. But have these impressive legislative and policy achievements translated into success on the ground? And how do you measure this success? Addressing these questions is the second goal of de Aquino's chapter (on which I comment in the following section). But perhaps the implication of de Aquino's first point is that the success of feminists' engagements with the state is related not only to issues such as the nature and scope of support that the latter is willing to give feminist movements, or whether they espouse the same reform goals, but also to what kinds of state and political culture are most conducive to successful alliances and cooperation between activists and state actors.

However, Dahlgren's case study in Yemen, in Chapter 2, brings to light the excessive power of the state and the effects (good and bad) of such power on the processes and outcomes of reform efforts by feminist movements. In the 1970s, feminist movements in the People's Democratic Republic of Yemen thrived, and their efforts to legislate a just family law succeeded mainly because they matched state ideology of equal partnership for male and female citizens in the development of the country. In the 1990s and after the unification, again it was mainly the political power of the state (in this case oppressive and marginalizing to the southern region of the country) that brought about (this time) a highly regressive family law that was detrimental to women. Dahlgren's analysis shows us the challenges (and sometimes inevitability) of the entanglement of political and gender struggles.

Nazneen, in Chapter 4, also reflects on the challenges of feminist activism when it relies heavily on the state as its main agent of social change, on the one hand, or when feminists lack political power because of disengagement from the state, on the other. In her analysis of the strategies used by different feminist movements in Bangladesh, the author points out how heavy reliance on state mobilization (in the case of Bangladesh Mohila Parishad, for example) led to 'less emphasis on grassroots support building', which then acted as one of the obstacles to the success of their efforts to lobby for the new family code. Yet, at the same time, feminist groups that opted for distance from state institutions (in order not to lose their credibility in civil society) faced the challenge of lacking political influence.

In Egypt, a top-down state-oriented strategy of introducing legal changes had been the main vehicle of reform adopted (since the 1980s) by a coalition of women's rights activists, prominent legal figures, and government officials from the former regime of Mubarak. While diverse women's rights organizations, such as the Network of Women's Rights Organizations (NWRO) among others, were actively involved in debating and mobilizing for the proposed new comprehensive family code, the key actors who had the power (albeit with varying degrees) to influence or take part in the drafting of the proposed code were governmental and semi-governmental bodies such as the Women's Committee within the then-ruling and now-dissolved National Democratic Party, the Ministry of Justice, and the National Council for Women. In Chapter 3, Al-Sharmani points out that this state-centred approach of pursuing gender justice in family laws created further opposition to legal reform not only because it excluded different sectors of the society from taking part in and shaping the reform process, but also (and more importantly) because it was being led by a corrupt, oppressive state whose legitimacy with its people was plunging sharply at the time.

In the Palestinian case study, however, we are presented with a different and quite distinct picture. As Shehada points out in Chapter 1, the MP in Gaza, which led the initiative to draft a new family code, made a conscious effort to involve different sectors of society in its membership and its deliberations, as well as to ensure that 'stronger political actors' such as Fatah and Hamas did not take over the MP's work and agenda. One wonders if this spirit of grassroots-oriented activism was perhaps facilitated by the unique condition of Palestinian society, as one still struggling for its independent country and state, as well as the specific historical context in which the initiative took place (after the Oslo Agreement and the establishment of the PA).

In Chapter 8, Manuh and Dwamena-Aboagye present a case study of successful promulgation of a significant Domestic Violence Act in Ghana in 2007, which nonetheless is facing great challenges in its implementation mainly because of the lack of political will on the part of the state. This lack of will, the authors argue, is manifested in a host of implementation problems arising from a severe lack of funding resources as well as an absence of adequately trained personnel in the different state institutions that have been mandated to formulate a policy and legal framework for the implementation of the new law. On the one hand, the institutional structure that the state established to implement the law seems to reflect state interest (albeit misleading) in tackling the problem of domestic violence. For instance, a Domestic Violence Management Board, including members from civil society, has been entrusted to oversee the implementation of the law; a Domestic Violence Secretariat has been set up to provide technical and administrative support to the management body; under the purview of the Ministry of Women and Children's Affairs, a National Policy Plan of Action has been adopted with the aim of institutionalizing 'a coordinated and integrated approach' towards the law's implementation; and Domestic Violence and Victim Support Units, which function under the purview of several state ministries, have been set up to handle domestic violence cases. On the other hand, the authors show abundantly that these different institutions and other involved agencies that work with them are ill-equipped to implement the law effectively because of lack of coordination, severe shortage in funding and human resources, and lack of the needed training.

One telling example of the state's lack of real political will to create an institutional environment conducive to effective implementation of the law is that state funding of domestic violence work is secured from a small budget set aside by the Ministry of Women and Children's Affairs, which itself is only allocated 1 per cent of the national budget of the country. Hence, since the Act was passed in 2007, external funds from foreign embassies and development agencies have been the main source of funding for the implementation work. But the challenge is that these external funds specify the items that they would fund, which leaves the national institutions that are mandated with the implementation work little freedom in allocating the funds as needed, and accordingly obstructs their work.

It is not only the role played by the state, as enabling or hindering successful legal reform, that the chapters of this book address, but also the discursive role it can play in processes of legal reform and the ramifications of this role. For instance, in Chapter 5, Osanloo argues that the debates about 'women's status' versus 'women's rights' in the contestations around the Iranian family law amendments in 2011 are fundamentally about what kind of 'state' and governance different factions in the society are seeking in their struggles. Interestingly, Osanloo shows that what has actually transpired on the ground several decades after the Iranian revolution is a 'hybrid' state that is neither an 'Islamic government' nor a 'republic'. Moreover, the legal court system and codes that have evolved are also 'hybrid', drawing on Islamic jurisprudence as well as modern civil laws and court systems. Osanloo points out that though the contestations around the family law amendments may seemingly depict these competing discourses as presenting two opposing poles, the hybrid nature of both the state and the family law can create a space for negotiation and progress towards meaningful legal and social change that is supportive of strengthening women's rights.

Implementing legal reforms: the social embeddedness and gendering of legal practices

Our understanding of law as a tool of reform is not meaningful if we do not extend our analysis from the written codes to actual legal practice and its impact on women's lives. This brings us to the third main issue which is raised in this book, namely the question of implementation. Carlisle, de Aquino, and Manuh and Dwamena-Aboagye examine different aspects of this issue and the roles legal practice and the political will of the state play (or fail to play) in bringing about positive changes for women.

In Chapter 6, Carlisle sheds light on the mixed outcomes of the highly significant reforms that were introduced in Morocco's new family code, Moudawana, in 2004. Carlisle focuses on the enforcement of the newly introduced judicial divorce, *shiqāq*, and examines litigants' goals and strategies in such court cases as well as judges' interpretations of this new divorce law. According to Moudawana, either a wife or husband can petition for *shiqāq* divorce if there is a discord between the spouses that renders the continuation of the marriage untenable to either party. The court then appoints two arbiters to attempt reconciliation between the spouses and to investigate the causes of the marital discord. If arbiters' reconciliation efforts fail, the judge grants judicial divorce to the plaintiff and issues a sentence regarding financial settlements owed to or by both parties, based on the arbiters' reports.

Carlisle found that *shiqāq* divorce was becoming the most prevalent form of judicial divorce among Moroccan women and men. On the one hand, this kind of divorce was desirable for women because its evidentiary requirements were relatively easy to meet, unlike the case in other types of judicial divorce. On the other hand, more husbands, interestingly, were resorting to *shiqāq* as an alternative to unilateral repudiation since in the case of the latter they were legally obligated to deposit all financial rights due to their wives with the court at the time when they registered the divorce. But if a husband were to file for a *shiqāq* divorce or push his wife to petition for one, he might gain financially if the judge found the wife to be the cause of the discord. This is because, in such cases, the court orders compensation for the husband or reduces his financial dues to his spouse.

Carlisle also found that 'judges exhibit a spectrum of responses when "thinking through" the implications of the new legislation'. The outcome was not necessarily positive for women in some cases. In fact, Carlisle found that in some cases judges' rulings on financial settlements tended to penalize women if they were persuaded that female disputants did not try to save their marriages even in situations when the latter based their legal claims on the grounds of being subjected to spousal domestic violence. In short, Carlisle's chapter brings to light the social embeddedness, multidimensionality, and complex nature of legal reform. Thus, written laws (such as *shiqāq*) that appear to be gender-neutral – facilitating equal spousal rights and expanding women's legal rights to divorce – actually work in complex and sometimes mixed ways for women in the actual process of interpretation and implementation undertaken by judges and arbiters.

The LMP observatory, which de Aquino discusses in Chapter 7, was set up by a consortium of twelve organizations (research centres and women's rights organizations) in 2007 with the purpose of monitoring the implementation of the new code. Another goal of the observatory was to experiment with the development of original and reliable indicators of success (or failure) of the newly introduced law in addressing the problem of domestic violence.

Hence, the observatory conducted field research on Women's Police Stations and the Specialized Courts for Domestic and Familial Violence. De Aquino's analysis makes two central points. The first is the need for critical re-examination of conventional indicators of success in legal reforms targeting domestic violence. For example, de Aquino notes that the research carried out by the observatory on Women's Police Stations reported a decrease in the number of domestic and familial violence cases filed with these stations in the period from 2006 to 2007. On the surface, this could be construed as an indicator that these stations, which were assigned the responsibility of investigating cases of violence against women, were succeeding in diminishing the scope of this problem. However, another finding of the observatory research showed that the staff members in these police stations were routinely telling victims that punitive measures were going to be adopted against their assailants. This scared off women who did not necessarily want to bring a criminal charge against the perpetrators, but still would have liked to have sought assistance from these stations – hence the decrease in the number of cases of domestic violence filed with the police stations.

The second point is related to the ways in which the understandings held by court personnel of gender norms and relations shape their interpretation of the new law. For instance, de Aquino points out that the LMP was either unenforced or enforced poorly in some of the specialized courts for domestic and familial violence because judges tended to pressure women into reconciling with the perpertrators. Some judges even suggested that female plaintiffs modify some of their behaviours towards their partners so that there would be less cause for friction between them, implying that the women were partly responsible for the violence inflicted against them.

Finally in Chapter 8, Manuh and Dwamena-Aboagye also show that it is not only written laws that matter when it comes to ensuring women's rights and protecting them from domestic violence but also (and more importantly) the social context in which the laws are being implemented – the understandings that agencies and practitioners who are involved in the implementation process have of gender rights, marriage, and what constitutes violence against women. For instance, the authors note that trends have been recorded in the work of the Domestic Violence and Victim Support Units that show failure to prosecute male perpetrators of domestic violence offences because staff members in the units tend either to blame women for the violence; dismiss the gravity of the offence; or choose not to bring charges against husbands because they are assumed to be the breadwinners of their families, and hence their prosecution and possible incarceration are seen as detrimental to their families.

Law reform and gender justice: complex connections?

Through diverse and rich case studies, this book sheds light on the complexity and the contradictions of the roles that legal reform plays in women's lives. Law as a written text is an important mechanism through which states enact policies that can have serious ramifications for women. As such, it is a crucial vehicle through which women's rights are granted or withheld. Thus, the power of law as a state tool is exemplified, on the one hand, in its success in expanding Moroccan women's right to different forms of judicial divorce, or in introducing extensive legal measures to protect women from domestic violence, as in the case of Brazil. On the other hand, the downside of law as a state power is exemplified in the case of South Yemeni women who were instantly deprived in 1992 (after the promulgation of the post-unification Personal Status Law) of many legal rights that they had previously enjoyed.

But law is not simply written texts (whether they are pro- or anti-women) that are legitimized by state power. It is also (and perhaps more importantly) part of social processes in which court personnel and litigants interpret and implement the law in multiple ways, some of which may work against women. Examples of this are some of the Moroccan judges' decisions on financial settlements in *shiqāq* cases, and Brazilian judges' interpretations of what constitutes domestic or familial violence against women and whether or not the court should attempt reconciliation between the parties in such cases. Also, litigants may appropriate new laws for their own agendas that go beyond the intent of these reforms (Moroccan husbands' use of *shiqāq* divorce, for example). Accordingly, implementation and outcomes of even the most ambitious legal reforms that seek to address the problem of gender inequality and injustice against women do not necessarily translate into tangible successes (that is, positive change for women). Similarly, the views that staff members in the Ghanaian Domestic Violence and Victim Support Unit have on gender relations, marriage, and what constitutes violence against women have a negative impact on their work and result in failure to prosecute male perpetrators in domestic violence cases. The lesson to be learned here is that legal reforms that seek gender justice need to be part of a larger and ongoing multidimensional societal project of education, awareness raising, public debates, and alliance building with different sectors of society.

The case studies in this book, furthermore, shed light on the discursive role of law. The authors' analyses suggest that law as a system of meanings that shape gender norms is actualized and shaped through its interplay with other diverse discourses such as those that are concerned with religious knowledge and its place in law making (in Egypt, for example), discourses that centre around issues of national identity as well as cultural and ethnic rights of citizens (as in Bangladesh), or discourses that revolve around the nature of state and governance (as in Iran). In other words, the significance (as well as the challenge) of law is not simply that it is a right-granting mechanism. It is also because it is part of multiple intertwined discourses in which systems of meanings (and subsequently practices) about norms, rights, and identities are created, reinforced, or transformed. Hence the significance of the debates about legal reform and gender rights, such as the ones discussed in this book, is not limited to whether or not they lead to legal changes that grant equal rights to women. More importantly, these debates are meaningful and influential in that they can be part of public discursive processes through which dominant gender norms are reiterated, but also may be destabilized and shifted (Butler 1999).

Finally, the authors' analyses of the complexities and the challenges of legal reform in the different case studies suggest that it is vital (although surely not easy) that activists, policy makers, and researchers complicate their understandings of the notions of 'equality', 'gender neutrality', and 'women's empowerment'. It is noteworthy that the pursuit of 'formal equality', for Bangladeshi women in the family domain was caught up in, and even stopped by, the complexities of reconciling the right to gender equality with the right to cultural and ethnic difference. In Palestine, reformers found that the abolition of dower payment requirements (*mahr*) and the presence of a male guardian for the bride as conditions for a valid marriage contract might work against Palestinian women in the continuing presence of other social structures that privilege men (whether husbands, brothers, or fathers) over women and grant them more power in family relations. Lastly, gender-neutral legal rights may turn out to be (when implemented) very much gendered and with contradictory effects for women, as was the case in some of the court practices of *shiqāq* divorce in Morocco.

The implication of these insights is not that gender equality and legal reform as goals of feminist activism should be abandoned. Instead, what we learn is that there is a further need for extending the focus of feminist activism (and scholarship) from the issue of 'rights' to social realities in which gender norms are made, unmade, or remade through processes of engaging in social relations, interactions, and discourses.

Note

1 See, for instance, MacKinnon 1987; Smart 1989; Mossman 1991; Cornell 1992; Jackson 1993; Boyd 1994; Bartlett 1995; Kapur and Cossman 1996; Chunn and Lacombe 2000; Armstrong 2004; Lacey 2004; Thornton 2004.

References

Armstrong, S. (2004) 'Is Feminists Law Reform Flawed? Abstentionists and

Sceptics', *Australian Feminist Law Journal,* Vol. 20, pp. 43–63.

Bartlett, K. (1995) 'Tradition, Change, and the Idea of Progress in Feminist Legal Thought', *Wisconsin Law Review*, No. 28, pp. 243–303.

Bowen, J. (2006) 'Fairness and Law in an Indonesian Court', in M. K. Masud, R. Peters, and D. Powers (eds), *Dispensing Justice in Islam: Qadis and Their Judgments*, Brill, Leiden and Boston, MA.

Boyd, S. (1994) 'Replacing the State: Family Law and Oppression', *Canadian Journal of Law and Society*, Vol. 39, pp. 39–74.

Buskens, L. (2003) 'Recent Debates on Family Law Reform in Morocco: Islamic Law as Politics in an Emerging Public Sphere', *Islamic Law and Society*, Vol. 10, No. 1, pp. 70–131.

Butler, J. (1999) *Gender Trouble: Feminism and the Subversion of Identity*, Routledge, New York, NY.

Charrad, M. (2001) *States and Women's Rights: The Making of Postcolonial Tunisia, Algeria, and Morocco*, University of California Press, Berkeley, CA.

Chunn, D. E. and D. Lacombe (eds) (2000) *Law as a Gendering Practice*, Don Mills and Oxford University Press, Ontario.

Cornell, D. (1992) 'The Philosophy of the Limit, Systems Theory, Feminist Legal Reform', *New England Law Review*, Vol. 26, pp. 783–804.

Hirsch, S. (1998) *Pronouncing and Persevering: Gender and the Discourse of Disputing in an African Islamic Court*, Chicago University Press, Chicago, IL.

Jackson, E. (1993) 'Contradictions and Coherence in Feminist Response to Law', *Journal of Law and Society*, Vol. 20, No. 4, pp. 398–411.

Kapur, R. and B. Cossman (1996) *Subversive Sites: Feminist Engagement with Law in India*, Sage Publications, New Delhi.

Lacey, N. (2004) 'Feminist Legal Theory and the Rights of Women', http://www.yale.edu/wff/cbg/pdf/LaceyPaperFeministLegal Theory.pdf, accessed 14 May 2013.

Mackinnon, C. (1987) *Feminism Unmodified: Discourses on Life and the Law*, Harvard University Press, Cambridge, MA.

Mir-Hosseini, Z. (2000) *Marriage on Trial: A Study of Islamic Family Law – Iran and Morocco Compared*, I. B. Tauris, London and New York, NY.

Moors, A. (1995) *Women, Property, and Islam: Palestinian Experiences, 1920–1990*, Cambridge University Press, Cambridge.

—— (2003) 'Public Debates on Family Law Reform Participants, Positions, and Styles of Argumentation in the 1990s', *Islamic Law and Society*, Vol. 10, No. 1, pp. 1–11.

Mossman, M. J. (1991) 'Feminism and Legal Method: The Difference It Makes', in M. Fineman (ed.), *At the Boundaries of Law*, Routledge, New York, NY.

Rosen, L. (1989) *The Anthropology of Justice: Law as Culture in Islam*, Cambridge University Press, Cambridge.

—— (2000) *The Justice of Islam: Comparative Perspectives on Islamic Law and Society*, Oxford Socio-Legal Studies, New York, NY.

Schulz, D. (2003) 'Political Factions, Ideological Fictions: The Controversy over Family Law Reform in Democratic Mali', *Islamic Law and Society*, Vol. 10, No. 1, pp. 132–64.

Smart, C. (1989) *Feminism and the Power of Law*, Routledge, New York, NY.

Sonbol, A. (ed.) (1996) *Women, Family, and Divorce Law in Islamic History*, Syracuse University Press, Syracuse, NY.

—— (2003) 'Women in Shari'ah Courts: A Historical and Methodological Discussion', *Fordham International Law Journal*, Vol. 27, pp. 225–53.

—— (ed.) (2005) *Beyond the Exotic: Women's Histories in Islamic Societies*, Syracuse University Press, Syracuse, NY.

Thornton, M. (2004) 'Neoliberal Melancholia: The Case of Feminist Legal Scholarship', *Australian Feminist Law Journal*, Vol. 20, pp. 7–22.

Tucker, J. (1998) *In the House of the Law: Gender and Islamic Law in Ottoman Syria and Palestine*, University of California Press, Berkeley, CA.

—— (2008) *Women, Family, and Gender in Islamic Law*, Cambridge University Press, Cambridge.

Welchman, L. (2000) *Beyond the Code: Muslim Family Law and the Shar'i Judiciary in the Palestinian West Bank*, Kluwer Law, Hague and Boston, MA.

—— (2004) *Women's Rights and Islamic Family Law: Perspectives on Reform*, Zed Books, London and New York, NY.

Würth, A. (2003) 'Stalled Reform: Family Law in Post-unification Yemen', *Islamic Law and Society*, Vol. 10, No. 1, pp. 12–33.

1

Debating Islamic Family Law in Palestine

Citizenship, Gender, and 'Islamic' Idioms

Nahda Shehada

Unlike today's atmosphere in which pessimism prevails, the mood in the Palestinian territories during the second half of the 1990s was optimistic; somehow, Palestinians were confident that they were about to harvest the first *intifada*'s sacrifices. With the establishment of the national authority in 1994, they were hopeful that they would finally be able to focus on their internal 'social' problems, including gender issues. It was in this context that the Palestinian women's movement took the lead in campaigning for family law reform as part of the state-building project anticipated after the signing of the Oslo agreements between the PLO and Israel in 1993, which led to the establishment of the Palestinian Authority (PA).

This initiative of the women's movement triggered various reactions from different political and social groups, which led to a discussion of family law in the public sphere so intense that it came to be recognized as the first major social debate in Palestinian history. In comparison with other Arab and Muslim countries, this focus on family law in Palestine is not unique. In all these countries, the debate has been based on the struggle for power and hegemony. The Moroccan, Egyptian, Iranian, and Yemeni debates of the 1990s focused on the place of Islam, the Shari'a and religion in people's lives, and on determining who could claim the right to exercise *ijtihad* (independent reasoning).[1] They also referred to notions of national and cultural authenticity and the ways in which various expressions of traditionalism and modernism are contested. All these elements are to be found within the Palestinian debates as well.

The debate on family law in Palestine presented certain similarities with those under way in other parts of the Arab world, in that personal status was used by many political actors to further their interests and gain power. For instance, when a project for family law reform was tabled in the Legislative Assembly in 1997, it elicited hostile reactions from the Islamist members. Their discourse, despite contextual differences, showed many resemblances to the Islamist discourses from other Arab countries. Similarly, the religious establishment, fearing to lose influence over Shari'a courts, launched attacks on the women's movement activists, linking them with the 'West' and the 'conspiracy against Islam'. One distinct feature of the debate in Palestine was that it originated in the context of an ongoing struggle for liberation and state building, whereas in other Arab countries it was debated in the context of escalating tension between an already established state and emerging civil society.

This chapter presents the various issues at stake, beginning with a brief discussion of the political context in which the family law debate took place in Palestine. Then I offer a detailed analysis of the Model Parliament for Women and Legislation (MP), which was the climactic event of the debate, and some concluding remarks.

Political context of the debate in Palestine

The process of state building in Palestine counts as one of the most complex experiences in Third World history. The PA lacks independence, sovereignty, and control over its borders and resources. Even in those disconnected areas of the West Bank and Gaza Strip that are formally under its control, the PA's power is largely hampered by Israeli restrictions on the movement of individuals and goods, by the Israeli right – stipulated in the Oslo agreements – to supervise security in most areas, and by the presence of hundreds of thousands of hostile Jewish settlers on Palestinian land, whose numbers continue to increase steadily. Twenty years after the Oslo agreement, the Israeli settlements have expanded to cover 70 per cent of the West Bank land, ending the two-state solution and shattering the Palestinians' dream of independence.

Under these circumstances, the situation has been worsened by the PA's lack of previous experience in governance, the undemocratic political structure, and the presence of a strong Islamist opposition. These deficits are combined with a severe shortage of natural resources and extreme economic dependence on Israel and the international donor community. The hostilities since 2000 show that signing a 'peace accord' on paper without establishing justice on the ground easily enables the iron fist of the powerful to prevail. As Hammami and Hilal (2001) observe, Israel now enjoys control over Palestinian public funds and hampers Palestinian workers' access to the Israeli labour market, while fragmenting the occupied territories into dozens of encircled areas. Thus, it has made the PA's ability to practise self-rule, or even to carry out its assigned task as guarantor of Israeli security, a virtually impossible task.

The debate on family law began during the first years after the Oslo agreements. A central feature of Palestinian politics during that period was that while many Palestinians were enthusiastically debating the laws and challenging their newly established government on the basis of equal citizenship, they were aware of the framework on which their new reality was being constructed, namely agreements that deprived them of their fundamental right to self-determination and independence; that approved and sustained their inequality with Israel; and that, by virtue of being signed by Palestinian representatives and approved by the international community, amounted to a written surrender and acceptance of the unequal relation with the state of Israel.

Furthermore, the PA's discourse since the signing of the Oslo agreements has focused increasingly on negotiation at the expense of resistance, thus delegitimizing the resistance-based discourse of Islamists. The negotiation discourse has portrayed the Israeli abuses of Palestinians' human rights as mere violations of the peace process. Islamists, on the other hand, view the PA as no more than guardians of Israel's security (Sh'hada 1999). Avoiding the discourse of rights, as Welchman *et al.* (2002) argue, weakened the legitimacy of the emerging PA and gave credibility to the Islamists' opposition, based on rights. This influenced the responses of these two players on the gender issue, particularly in the field of family law.

The post–Oslo political circumstances created a contradictory environment for the women's movement.[2] On the one hand, there was a conducive atmosphere; nationalists continued to recognize the role of the women's movement as vital; it was still the most active social movement (Hammami and Johnson 1999: 319). The project of a Palestinian 'state' was still in the making and there was thus room for negotiating gender; laws were being drafted and therefore social groups could lobby for change. However, the PA as an administrative body lacked power and resources – and thus the struggle for independence and self-determination remained the top priority.

The likelihood of political compromises between the strong conservative Islamist movement and the PA at the expense of the gender issue was a real concern. It was these contradictory circumstances that provided the political opportunity for the women's movement to initiate programmes and activities for legal reform, culminating in the Model Parliament for Women and Legislation (Abdulhadi 1998; Welchman *et al.* 2002). It raised issues related to equal citizenship at a time when the nationalist movement was at its 'lowest ebb' (Abdulhadi 1998: 661). The latter's failure to address issues related to social rights, democracy, and freedom of speech was striking (Hammami and Johnson 1999: 319). The nationalist movement had faced severe setbacks abroad since the early 1980s due to the PLO's military defeat in Lebanon, and in the occupied territories it was confronted with the rise of alternative political initiatives in the wake of the *intifada*.[3] More generally, the new international order, after the collapse of the Soviet Union, was a decisive moment for many national movements, including the PLO. The 1991 Gulf War was another breaking point because it altered the international and regional balance of power, putting the PLO in danger of being reduced to nothing more than a disintegrating and destitute bureaucracy located in Tunis. Its only aim was survival and its only claim to legitimacy was that it represented Palestinians (Usher 1995). After 1993, political disputes over the Oslo agreements further impeded the nationalist movement from meeting the expectations of its constituents (Usher 1995).

The women's movement's public appeal reflected a particular political strategy. Instead of grounding its equality discourse on specific, exclusive gender rights, the movement communicated its message in the idiom of nationalism, state building, and democracy, on which no national faction would disagree. Peteet (1999) points out that this strategy emanated from the movement's deliberate attempt to locate its arguments within the human rights and democracy paradigm rather than around issues related to sexuality. The women's movement's ability to enter the 'monopolised public space' (Bishara 1998) with new claims and demands allowed left-wing factions to reassert their presence in the political arena following a a growing demobilization of political activities in the West Bank and Gaza in the wake of the Oslo agreement and the multiplication of security services by the PA (Bishara 1998). In other words, advocating family law reform 'open[ed] up the possibility of new democratic alliance' with these factions (Hammami and Johnson 1999: 337). The same factions that were apologetic *vis-à-vis* the Islamists during the first *intifada* (1987–1991) now became supporters of a Model Parliament for Women and Legislation. It was the social question posed by the MP, which the leftists had long failed to advocate, that made possible a renewed engagement with the 'masses'. One leftist leader commented on the MP campaign, saying that 'the [MP] was like a light and we had to respond' (Zakut 1999, cited in Hammami and Johnson 1999: 335).

Despite the ideological differences and heterogeneity within the women's movement, a common element emerged, namely a shift towards the public questioning of gender relations. This process was paralleled by a gradual institutionalization of the women's movement itself through the establishment of study centres and grassroots organizations focusing on empowerment and awareness as well as the setting up of women's departments within ministries. Further, a number of organizations established programmes reflecting the importance of family law reform and the provision to women of adequate advice and counselling in matters of divorce, child custody, sexual abuse, and violence in the domestic sphere.

The women's movement, while appearing in public as a body unified around the question of family law reform, was in fact subjected to a number of limitations. Power relations developed within it based on differences in locality, access to material resources or publicity, and the expression of divergences with mainstream discourse on family law. Unity *vis-à-vis* others was no more than a mantle hiding divergences of vision and over access to power resources. Such differences were marked by strong criticism and counter-criticism expressed in memos and meetings, but they did not emerge in public. The reasoning behind this consensus on hiding discord was that washing dirty linen in public would give the Islamists further ammunition and thus would not be in the interest of any organization. In this sense, the women's movement had – at least – two facets: one of unity and harmony when encountering other political actors, and the other marked by the exchange of invective within the movement itself.

The Model Parliament for Women and Legislation

The activities and initiatives of the women's movement culminated in the campaign for family law reform known as the Model Parliament for Women and Legislation in 1997–9. The MP project resulted from a four-year review of gender-based laws by a number of women's organizations and human rights centres. Established in 1997, the MP project proposed Palestinian legislation based on equality and human rights. The campaign for family law reform was viewed as the first major social debate in the history of Palestine. It engaged a wide spectrum of political and social groups. For the first time, political actors of diverse backgrounds and interests used Palestinian television stations, radio, newspapers, and posters to communicate a politicized gender discourse.

When the MP project started, its activities were organized in the West Bank by the Women's Centre for Legal Aid and Counselling (WCLAC), which had taken the initiative and obtained funding for the project in both Gaza and the West Bank. However, when the Gazan MP preparatory committee (of which I was a member)[4] received the proposed working manual from the West Bank, written by a Jordanian lawyer familiar with the West Bank legal system and laws (Khadr 1998), which was supposed to review all the gender-based laws implemented in Palestine, the committee found that no Gazan law had been considered. This generated a sense of frustration and anger among the members.[5] The Gaza committee decided to ignore the West Bank manual entirely and design its activities according to what it described as 'Gazan specificity'. It decided to focus on family law only and to leave other less controversial laws to be reviewed by the West Bank group. Not only the women's movement, but all political actors, including Islamists, recognized the special significance of family law.

Further, instead of appealing to human rights conventions and international measures when presenting its proposed reforms, the Gaza committee worked from within the context of the Shari'a. It sought points of leverage by appealing to the principles of *takhayyur* (selection from different schools of *fiqh*), thinking that this would prevent accusations of going beyond the boundaries of the Shari'a. In this sense, the suggestions made were not innovative. The final text included proposals that the minimum marriage age be set at 18 for men and women;

that the institution of guardianship be abolished; that alimony (*nafaqa*) be paid from the date of separation; that legal rights of inheritance be protected by the state; that polygyny be subject to state regulation; that unilateral divorce be replaced by courts making the decisions; that mothers' renunciation of their custody rights be disallowed; and that custody decisions should apply to children up to the age of 18, with the best interests of children being the guiding principle for deciding cases (Nashwan 1998). The reforms proposed by the Gaza MP were in many ways similar to, or even less 'revolutionary' than, the laws already applied in other Arab countries. For example, it was suggested that women should be guaranteed their legally prescribed (and Shari'a-sanctioned) share of inheritance. Concerning the rights of the *wali*, the draft proposed activation of the already specified right of women to initiate their marriage contract as stipulated in the Book of Personal Status Rulings.[6] Further, the MP committee proposed to limit polygyny to exceptional cases, to subject it to the authorization of a judge, and to require that both the first and the second wife be informed in advance (Nashwan 1998). Despite all the efforts to accommodate wider social perspectives, it appeared that the Islamists were not convinced of the MP's sincerity. As one religious scholar put it, 'We know that the MP use the Shari'a as a mask to further their evil project. They use it for public consumption and that is worse than rejecting the Shari'a squarely' (Abu Sibbah, Shaykh 'Atta Allah, Professor of Islamic Studies at the Islamic University of Gaza, during a public discussion, 1998).

The suggestions for reform in Gaza were not top-down initiatives; rather, they were subject to discussion and negotiation within the preparatory committee and then the wider community. Often, certain suggestions for reform would be modified after a few rounds of debate. Even after a document was drafted, the plenary session of the MP in Gaza could modify certain proposals (Nashwan 1998). At the MP, various approaches were repeatedly presented by passionate activists. Some drew on personal experiences and others were inspired by feminist writings. Yet other activists were well-versed in law, *fiqh* or Shari'a. Most had been active during the first *intifada* as members of the nationalist movement. The majority perceived the MP as an exceptional platform for debating gender relations within the wider framework of national aspirations for independence and self-determination. Therefore, the Gazan leadership of the MP did its best to take advantage of the opportunity. For example, seats in the MP's assembly were divided equally between men and women. The number of seats was initially equivalent to that of the Legislative Council members, 88, but was later increased to 120 due to the number of people wanting to participate. In the West Bank, the central session maintained the number of seats at 88. Attention was paid to maintaining social and political plurality so that the composition of the assembly would reflect the wider spectrum of Palestinian society. All political parties, civil society organizations, community figures, imams, Legislative Council members and religious leaders were invited to take part in the debate. During the preparatory meetings, members of Hamas, Jihad and national parties were invited, but the agenda for the meetings was prepared by the MP preparatory committee.

Public meetings were held in various localities and communities, with invitations to all groups to join the discussions. The members of the MP and its chairperson and deputies were elected through a democratic process. It was an exercise in community democracy, with women taking the leading role. The chief campaigners of the MP asserted two principles: first, the need to guarantee the broadest possible participation of groups from various localities and political backgrounds; and second, while maintaining plurality, to prevent stronger political groups from manipulating the campaign and thus diverting it from its objectives. The stronger political groups in question, of course, were the PA's leading political party (Fatah) and its Islamist rival (Hamas).

On 25 April 1998, the final session of the MP began in Gaza. Hundreds of guests representing political parties, the Legislative Council, regional and international guests, international news agencies and socially recognized figures attended. As Welchman *et al.* (2002) point out, almost all the speakers affirmed the important role of women in the national struggle, as well as the right of free speech as fundamental to the nationalist project. Typically, women's rights were linked to the modernist and nationalist project of state building. Nationalism was also evoked as a justification for legal reform, including personal status laws: the laws in force were repeatedly described as 'foreign' and imposed by occupying powers. When it came to the specifics of reform, however, most of the political leaders were either vague or somewhat conservative in their focus and recommendations (Welchman *et al.* 2002: 26).

During the final session, the MP members debated the measures that had been drafted by the committee and discussed in different localities and communities. At one point, while discussing a man's right to marry more than one wife, the parliament's members split into two camps. The first one advocated the man's right to marry more than one wife, not with reference to the Shari'a but to the politics of Islamic family law: '[If we opposed the right to marry more than one wife] tomorrow we would appear in the newspapers as opponents of Islam and the Shari'a, and this would be an excellent weapon in the hands of the Islamists. We have to avoid that.' The second camp advocated a ban on polygyny, arguing for radical social change: 'If we keep compromising, we will never win.' The man's right to marry more than one wife was not at issue. Nor is polygyny a symbol of adherence to or divergence from Islam. The political and social price paid by those labelled as religiously or culturally 'inauthentic' was in fact the real issue. The first camp's proposal was won narrowly, with 42 for, 32 against, and 5 abstentions.

The assembly members also disagreed over the issue of a *wali*'s rights. The MP's draft document proposed that no marriage contracts should be initiated for persons under 18 and that the consent and signature of both spouses should be required. This proposal implied abolishing the *wali*'s prerogatives, which entitle the male guardian not only to sign the contract but, on some occasions, to decide who should marry whom. Here, the divisions were more complex. Astonishingly, some female members argued against the proposal, fearing the heavy social price the family would pay if its right to consent was not acknowledged in law: 'How could we face our community if our children married without our blessing? That would not only be embarrassing, it would be disastrous,' a communist female member protested. Another member agreed: 'Our children's marriage is the occasion on which we display our pride and dignity. What would remain to us if the law robbed us of it?' One of the deputy chairpersons, a 65-year-old imam (leader of the congregation prayer), who had maintained a dignified silence in the proceedings until then, could not hold his tongue any more. 'You will all pay for that; I swear in the name of God that I am against the fathers who take advantage of their rights as *wali* to coerce their daughters to marry or not to marry, but the proposal will inflict major harm on all of us including myself. Be smart and do not force the issue because this is a red line in our society.' The proposal was not adopted.

Two discourses emerged during the year that led up to the opening of the MP. The first – expressed mostly by NGO members, for the most part funded by Western NGOs, who adopted the mainstream discourse of human rights and democracy – argued for termination of the existing power structure of marriage and its replacement with a relationship based on equality. The second insisted that any reform should preserve the Islamic quality of Palestinian legislation. Reform should be derived from the Shari'a, as it was feared that overlooking the cultural, political, and social connotations of Palestine's Islamic identity would injure perceptions of the women's movement in the wider society and give additional ammunition to its opponents. This view was by and large adopted by the activists of the General Union of Palestinian Women (GUPW). Most of them were members of the ruling party, who on the one hand stressed the need for reform, and on the other hesitated to antagonize the Islamists. The profound change in the political atmosphere symbolized by the establishment of the PA brought intense and vibrant debate over what are defined by some as 'inherited laws'. Novel appeals to various conceptions of citizenship intertwined with ambivalent statements of identity and various visions of state building.

In the Palestinian public sphere, the family law debate was both open and controlled. It was characterized by the inclusion of new participants and public elements, yet various control mechanisms were imposed by powerful actors to silence certain identities, prohibit given subjects, or impose chosen methods of deliberation (Moors 2003). Actors often shifted the debate from one domain to another. At certain moments, religious leaders, for example, asserted the right of *ahl al-ikhtisas* (religious specialists) to exclude specific participants from the process of deliberation. At others, they transferred the debate from the social and political domain to a more morally charged and religiously sensitive sphere. At yet others, they stirred the public up by stressing the danger of any reform of the family institution. The articulation of arguments and the processes of exclusion or inclusion of subjects and identities were just indicators of how the power structure can compromise the course of deliberation, even in the absence of formal acts of exclusion (see Fraser 1993).

The religious establishment influenced the debate through speeches in mosques, at public meetings, on television programmes, and in newspaper articles. Some judges kept their distance from Islamists, perhaps fearing that their attitude would be interpreted as a form of opposition to the newly established PA, while others were explicit in their association with the Islamists. The above illustration is derived from my personal involvement in the campaign for family law reform in the Gaza Strip. The following characteristics of the debate on family law reform, however, apply to both the Gaza Strip and the West Bank.

First, the question of who is allowed to speak about family law (in the public sphere) authoritatively, and depict other voices as irrelevant, was posed clearly: for example, the foremost religious figure in the counter-campaign was Shaykh Bitawi, head of the Shari'a court of appeal, who was well known in the West

Bank for his vocal opposition to the women's movement. His intervention was sparked off at an MP meeting conducted by a human rights specialist in Nablus in early March 1998. During the session, Shaykh Bitawi objected to her discussion of family law on the grounds that she was a 'Christian' interfering in 'issues that concern Muslims'. 'We do not interfere in your religion and you should not interfere in our legislation,' he told her (*Al-Ayyam* newspaper, 19 March 1998).

Second, the issue of who is allowed to speak was intertwined with the question of representation. In an article from 26 March 1998, Shaykh Jarrar denounced the MP activists as misrepresenting Palestinian women's needs and aspirations: 'There are a number of figures who claim that they represent Palestinian women. They should let the Palestinian nation decide who should talk in its name' (*Al-Ayyam*, 26 March 1998). In the same issue of the *Al-Ayyam* newspaper, Shaykh Jarrar wrote a reply to a communiqué by the GUPW, which had denounced the campaign launched in the mosques against Palestinian women 'who participated in the struggle and made every sacrifice for liberation and independence' (GUPW communiqué, *Al-Ayyam*, 25 March 1998). He wrote, 'We request the GUPW not to talk in the name of Palestinian women and not to use Palestinian women's struggle to impose the opinions of some figures. The GUPW is allowed to sign in the name of its members only when all members sign its communiqués' (*Al-Ayyam*, 26 March 1998).

The above example is better analysed if it is linked with the religious leaders' discourse regarding the issue of the special competence of *ahl al-ikhtisas*. The claim that only the religious leaders have the required competence aimed at excluding women activists from the debate. In an interview published on 5 March 1998, Shaykh Bitawi launched a fierce attack on the MP, denouncing its attempts to exclude religious jurists from the debate: 'The MP is administered by culturally alienated women who have no connection with our Islamic Shari'a. *Ahl al-ikhtisas* like judges and professors of Shari'a … and *rijal al-ifta*' [religious jurists], who have worked for decades, are kept away' (*Al-Risala*,

5 March 1998). In another interview, Shaykh Bitawi asked: 'If they claim that they want to work from within the Shari'a, why did they not consult us? We are the specialists, not they!' (*Al-Hayat al-jadida*, 19 March 1998).

Third, various religious leaders felt that their hold on the Shari'a courts, and thus their interests, were threatened by the MP proposal to replace the Shari'a with *nizamiyya* (civil) courts. It is in such incidents that the struggle over authority and institutional power is noticeably revealed. A striking element in the religious establishment's response was the accusation that Shari'a courts were being treated as an administrative rather than a religious institution. In an interview, Shaykh Bitawi said: 'The MP activists are working against the Shari'a since they propose that *nizamiyya* courts should replace the Shari'a court in issues related to marriage, custody and divorce. This implies a cancellation and elimination of the Shari'a court' (*Al-Ayyam*, 19 March 1998). Other religious leaders also expressed anger over the proposal to transfer the mandate of the Shari'a courts to civil courts. On 26 March 1998, Shaykh Mahmud Salameh, a judge in the Gaza City Shari'a courts who later became the Deputy Chief Justice and has close ties with Fatah and the Palestinian Authority, told a meeting at the Islamic University of Gaza: 'The most dangerous issue in the MP is its proposal to rule on personal status issues in the *nizamiyya* instead of the Shari'a courts' (*Al-Hayat al-jadida*, 26 March 1998).

Fourth, in addressing the public, the style of arguments was indicative: not only did religious leaders count on physical intimidation, they also labelled the MP proposals anti-Islamic. Their discourse of family ethos based on love and compassion was charged with nationalist sentiment and appeals to Palestinian masculinity. The following extract from a newspaper interview with Shaykh Jarrar (cited in Hamdan 1998: 4) is an example of how Palestinian masculinity is invoked:

> The MP wants to humiliate men; the problem is not political, but religious. The MP proposals pertain to our lives and families.... The MP proposals start from 'equality', a notion of Western origin. We

accept the 'equality' notion, but it should be clear that its definition and conceptualization have to be given in the framework of Islam, which grants women better rights than the West. What the MP presents is against the Shari'a and the Qur'an as well as the will of the *ulama* [religious scholars].

Shaykh Jarrar then employed the Islamists' favourite tactic against the MP, linking it with Western enemies of Islam: 'They are supported by Western funds; they want to enforce the Western concepts and Western lifestyle over our lives and civilization.' Commenting on the women's struggle against occupation, he said, 'All the Palestinian people participated in the struggle against Israel, not only women's groups … their participation does not give them the right to rebel against Shari'a' (cited in Hamdan 1998: 4). A few days later, Shaykh 'Ammar Badawi, the mufti of Nablus, declared that the MP's suggestions were intended to destroy the Palestinian family, an objective that even the Israelis had not achieved (*Al-Quds*, 18 March 1998).

Fifth, the competing camps were not unified. Even within the religious establishment, some voices appeared less convinced by the above discourse. For example, Shaykh Zuhayr al-Dib'i, an imam at the largest mosque in Nablus and a member of the MP, told *Al-Ayyam*:

> The personal status code is not the monopoly of *ahl al-ikhtisas*. Every citizen is affected by it and consequently all of us should discuss it. As a citizen, I have four daughters and I am concerned about their future. As a preacher, the law concerns me. They [those who attack the MP] depicted the MP campaign as if it were an attempt to assassinate the Shari'a. This is not true. This is a dangerous charge against our sisters and against us as MP members. The Shari'a is the same everywhere, but each country has to codify it according to its circumstances. What we wanted to do is to protect Islam from the abuses perpetrated in its name. Some men marry a second wife the same way they buy another car, which is not Islamic. (*Al-Ayyam*, 21 March 1998)

The need for reform was also addressed by Dr Hasan al-Juju, a practising judge, in an article on 16 March 1998 that offered a careful examination of family law, its origin, and the reasons motivating its reform (for a thorough analysis of al-Juju's position, see Welchman 2003). He is possibly the only judge who provided a balanced account of what could be done and how. In his view, family law should be reformed to meet the needs of contemporary life. He quoted Judge Ibn 'Abdin and Caliph 'Umar bin 'Abd al-'Aziz to justify the legitimacy of reform:

> It has become very important to reform the personal status laws in all the Palestinian territories and to unify them by eliciting the proper measures from the four *fiqh* schools and selecting from among them the ones that meet people's interests (*masalih*) and correspond to the spirit of the time. This could be done within the flexible and fertile framework of Islamic legislation. We should follow the methodology of selection (*takhayyur*) because confining ourselves to one *madhhab* [Islamic jurisprudence] has shown that there are dispositions that do not meet the requirements of contemporary life. If *ijtihad* does not rely on *nass* [holy text] it is often derived from '*urf* [custom]. And in this case, *ijtihad* should be treated as an opinion which might be wrong or right. (*Al-Ayyam*, 16 March 1998)

However, Judge al-Juju was firm about his rejection of certain changes suggested by the MP: 'The voices that demand equality in inheritance and the cancellation of men's *qiwama* [precedence] over women should be denied and denounced because they cause *fitna* [discord] and they declare an aggression against our religion and civilization,' he concluded (*Al-Ayyam*, 16 March 1998).

These differences in viewpoint show that the religious establishment is not a monolithic institution. There are those who construct their discourse on mere ideology, motivated by their politico-economic interests, and those who take a practical stance due to their daily contact with the problems and dilemmas of people in matters of personal status. These differences demonstrate the importance of taking into consideration the attitudes of practitioners: when they become involved in the debate, they often express more balanced and concrete views. This stance, as Masud argues, indicates that the normative basis of law lies not in the debate but elsewhere; it is in the social reality that has been disregarded by both camps. Masud (2001: 5) points out that the current debate in the Muslim world regarding the role of Islamic law indicates the existence and persistence of three levels of contradiction: (1) the political conceptualization of the Shari'a is based on a moral stance, while law is likely to be more pragmatic; (2) on the social level, women suffer from the contradictions between the ideals of the Shari'a and the social norms; (3) on the religious level, a contradiction between legal norms and Islamic ethical values still exists. While practitioners throughout Islamic history have tried to reconcile social norms and Islamic law by invoking principles of necessity, convenience, preventive measures, state of emergency, and so forth, contradictions persist because these measures have not been incorporated as 'norms' in legal theory.

The women's movement and its supporters structured their arguments in the framework of nation building, democracy, and freedom of speech. The Christian human rights specialist who was attacked by Shaykh Bitawi even claimed her right to *ijtihad* on the basis of being a Palestinian activist at the national as well as community levels: 'No one should say that I am not from *ahl al-ikhtisas* (specialists). I have the right, just as any other Palestinian, to debate the law and propose alternatives. We have a right to exercise *ijtihad* because we work with women, live in Palestinian society, and struggle to build our Palestinian society. We have the right to speak because we are legal specialists.'

The campaign continued and more actors joined the debate. Academics from Birzeit University wrote articles and produced programmes on Palestinian television in favour of the MP. The majority of Legislative Council members expressed their sympathy with the MP campaign in newspaper interviews and by attending MP sessions. Several lawyers expressed diverse attitudes and arguments. Almost every day, articles appeared in the newspapers dedicated to the issue of personal status. Arguments and counter-arguments were put forward from various quarters. Some groups in the Gaza Strip (and the West Bank) used other means of publicity. The walls, which had been freshly painted after the arrival of the PA, were taken over by some groups as a legitimate public space to convey their agreement or disagreement with the MP. Some MP posters were replaced by handwritten statements denouncing what they termed an attack on Islam and the Shari'a and threatening MP members. In this sense, laypeople were actively engaged in the debate not only through the usual forums, such as active discussion in seminars or workshops, but also by voicing their opinions through all available avenues. The Palestinian public sphere hosted conflicting and competing publics (see Fraser 1993; Eley 1993) as it witnessed one of its most intense debates ever. Family law had sharply divided Palestinians into at least two camps: those who supported pluralism and freedom of expression, and those who aimed at monopolizing Shari'a and Islam.

A survey conducted by the women's study programme of Birzeit University showed that the question of reform responds to highly conflicting interests and values. The analysts demonstrated that while respondents were committed to equality and justice, these sentiments coexisted with their desire to preserve gender hierarchy within the family (Welchman *et al.* 2002). In a similar vein, contradictory attitudes existed with regard to legal reform. People believed that they had the right to determine what religious law should be, but, simultaneously, they favoured expanding the role of religious authorities. The study concluded that these contradictions may obtain within each individual. Legal reform should thus take into consideration not only notions of equality, but also other controversial values and interests.

Before concluding, I would like to mention that the strong opposition led the women's movement to decide (after the Model Parliament completed its activities) to work on the question of family law reform by following a different strategy. In particular, activists opted for 'low-key' lobbying instead of a loud popular campaign. This meant that the focus was on activities such as meeting with politicians, lobbying decision makers, influencing Legislative Council members, and so forth, in order to muster wide political support for its new family law draft.

This strategy was meant to counteract Islamists and religious leaders, who have better access to the public thanks to better means of communication and a discourse that invokes people's religious and cultural heritage. The women's movement lacked this capacity to communicate with the public.

Conclusion

This chapter has investigated the identity and positions of the participants in the debates, the way they conceptualized family law and the idioms they used to communicate their positions. The main factor affecting any activity in Palestine is the Israeli occupation. Checkpoints on Palestinian territory prevent the free movement of goods and people. Settlements, in conjunction with these barricades, fragment the population and land. With Israel controlling Palestinian internal revenue, the PA has limited power and resources at its disposal – and thus the need for independence and self-determination overshadows everything else. These conditions explain why Palestinian public discussion on family law differs from that conducted in other Arab countries. Whereas debate in the latter reflects tension between the state and civil society, the Palestinian debate has developed in the context of the national struggle for liberation and state building. Thus, in Palestine, not only is the question of who may claim the right to interpret the sources of law central, but so is the clash between appeals for reinforcing equal citizenship rights as opposed to cultural and religious specificities in the framework of the national struggle for independence. This aspect has influenced participants' discourse and shaped their arguments. They often refer to the substance of family law, yet frequently argue with reference to nationalism and state building.

With this in mind, the chapter analysed the MP, which was the climactic focus of the debate on reforming family law in Palestine. The MP was a popular exercise to analyse and recommend changes to the law. Four main features were observed. First, the question of who is allowed to speak about family law authoritatively while depicting other voices as irrelevant was posed clearly. Second, neither the women's movement nor the religious establishment were unified. While the Gaza MP based its discourse on Shari'a by stretching the principle of *takhayyur* to its utmost limits, the West Bank MP referred to the principles of human rights. The religious establishment, for its part, did not emerge as a monolithic bloc; some of its members did realize the need to remedy certain gender-based injustices of family law. Third, analogously to the debate in other Arab countries, the Palestinian discussion appeared both open and controlled: open in that it included new participants and publics, yet controlled in that powerful actors silenced certain identities, prohibited given subjects, or imposed chosen methods of deliberation (see Moors 2003). Fourth, significant among the controlling mechanisms was the strategy of both opponents and supporters of reform in shifting the domains of debate from one sphere to another. Religious leaders in some instances asserted the right of *ahl al-ikhtisas* (religious specialists) to exclude particular actors from the process of deliberation; in other instances, they transferred the debate from the social domain to the political, or entered a more morally charged and religiously sensitive sphere. Still, they always stressed the danger that reform would pose for the institution of the family. The women's movement (in both Gaza and the West Bank), in contrast, was less successful in shifting course. The main thrust of its discourse was to articulate gender needs and interests in idioms related to nationalism, state building, and democracy. This strategy was generated from the movement's conscious attempt to locate its arguments around issues less related to sexuality and sexual rights (see Peteet 1999), which family law regulates.

The year-long discussions and deliberations were a marathon social exercise not only for the women's movement but also for other social actors. Family law reform was a political project in which diverging assumptions about the role of the Shari'a, Islam, and gender were put forward as an expression of the 'social will' (Hammami 2004: 126) that each group claimed to represent. The chapter showed the extent to which such debates can be divisive.

Notes

1 See Moors (1999), which compares the text of family law with social practice in the Arab world, and Moors (2003), which explores various positions, styles, and modes of argumentation that appeared in the 1990s. Welchman's contribution to Moors (2003) reviews the debate in Palestine, whereas her previous work (Welchman *et al.* 2002) assesses the legislative and lobbying initiatives related to Islamic law. Welchman (2000) further examines both the debate and application of family law in the West Bank from a legal perspective. Buskens (2003) links the debate on family law with the emergence of a public sphere in Morocco and the struggle of various political actors for legitimacy and power. Shaham (1999) examines Islamic marriage contracts in Egypt. Mir-Hosseini (2000) compares the application of family law in Iran and Morocco. Moghadam (2001) studies the emergence of Islamist feminists and their engagement in the reform debate. Würth (2003) deals with Yemen and shows how perspectives emerge from the different positionalities of women. Hammami and Johnson (1999) and Sh'hada (1999) analyse the Model Parliament for Women and Legislation in Palestine.

2 Women's involvement in the national struggle has been extensively researched in the last two decades. Researchers have focused on investigating whether the national struggle provides sufficient room for women's emancipation or presents an obstacle to it. Most feminist scholars have confirmed that national movements are predominantly patriarchal and that women are often co-opted during national struggles. Palestinian nationalism, as Peteet (1999: 71) observes, is characterized by 'contradictory potential'. On the one hand, it acknowledges the multiplicity of women's positionalities; on the other, it has 'denied them the status of … independent agency [and has not] accept[ed] them as a basis from which to launch political organizing'. For reasons related to the scope and focus of this chapter, I will not review the history of the women's movement in Palestine. There is, however, a vast amount of literature concerning particular sections of Palestinian women's activism, often linked with the secular national movement. See, for example, Abdo 1999; Abdulhadi 1998; Ameri 1999; Dajani 1994; Gluck 1997; Hammami 1990; Hammami and Kuttab 1999; Hiltermann 1991; Jad 1995; Kuttab 1993; Peteet 1991, 1999; Sayigh 1993; and Sharoni 1998. For literature related to the question of women and nationalism in the Third World, see, for example, Badran 1993; Chatterjee 1993; Hatem 1993; Jayawardena 1989; Joseph 1986, 1991; Kandiyoti 1991, 1997; Mohanty *et al.* 1991; and Molyneux 1998, 2001. For a more general theorization of women and nationalism, see, for example, Pettman 1996; Walby 1996; and Yuval-Davis 1992, 1997.

3 The *intifada* (uprising) was a mass protest against the Israeli occupation of the West Bank and Gaza. It started in December 1987 and continued until the beginning of the so-called peace process initiated by the US after the

Iraqi defeat in the Gulf War of 1991. It shifted from mass-based actions to prolonged, institutionalized actions. The main objective of the uprising was to exhaust rather than evict the occupying power through a combination of local and international pressure. The most remarkable features of the *intifada* were not only the participation of Palestinians from all sectors and classes, but also the ease with which mobilization was carried out and a support structure built within a few months of its eruption (Hiltermann 1991).

4 The members were selected on the basis of 'democratic' election among the activists of civil society organizations. More than three months of preparations were spent in deliberations and discussion to find the proper form on the basis of which the committee should be 'elected', its mandate, responsibilities, and representation.

5 Gazans often feel that West Bankers treat them with a certain arrogance. There are historical reasons for this, but it is beyond the scope of this study to go into them.

6 *The Book of Personal Status Rulings According to the School of Abu Hanifa* compiled by Qadri Pasha of 1875 specified that the *baligh* (mature woman) does not need the permission of a *wali* to initiate her marriage contract. This article is derived from the Hanafi school of thought. Article 34 states that 'the *wali* is a condition for the legitimacy of under-age men and women' (*al- wali shart li-sihhat nikah al-saghir wa al-saghira*) and 'the *wali* is not a condition for the legitimacy of the marriage of free, mature and *baligh* [men and women]' (*wa laysa al- wali shartan li nikah al-hur wa al-hurra al-'aqilayn al-balighayn*); their marriage is valid without a *wali* (*bal yanfuth nikahahuma bila wali*).

References

Abdo, N. (1999) 'Gender and Politics under the Palestinian Authority', *Journal of Palestinian Studies*, Vol. 28, No. 2, p. 38.

Abdulhadi, R. (1998) 'The Palestinian Women's Autonomous Movement: Emergence, Dynamics, and Challenges', *Gender and Society*, Vol. 12, No. 6, pp. 649–73.

Ameri, A. (1999) 'Conflict in Peace: Challenges Confronting the Palestinian Women's Movement', in A. Afsaruddin (ed.), *Hermeneutics and Honor: Negotiating Female 'Public' Space in Islamic/Ate Societies,* Harvard University Press, Cambridge, MA.

Badran, M. (1993) 'Independent Women', in J. Tucker (ed.), *Arab Women: Old Boundaries, New Frontiers*, Indiana University Press, Bloomington and Indianapolis, IN.

Bishara, A. (1998) 'Reflections on the Reality of the Oslo Process', in G. Giacaman and D. J. Lonning (eds), *After Oslo: New Realities, Old Problems*, Pluto Press, London.

Buskens, L. (2003) 'Recent Debates on Family Law Reform in Morocco:

Islamic Law as Politics in an Emerging Public Sphere', *Islamic Law and Society*, Vol. 10, No. 1, pp. 70–132.

Chatterjee, P. (1993) 'The Nationalist Resolution of the Women's Question', in K. Sangari and S. Vaid (eds), *Recasting Women*, Gayatri Press, New Delhi.

Dajani, S. (1994) 'Between National and Social Liberation: The Palestinian Women's Movement in the West Bank and Gaza Strip', in T. Mayer (ed.), *Women and the Israeli Occupation: The Politics of Change*, Routledge, London.

Eley, G. (1993) 'Nations, Publics, and Political Cultures: Placing Habermas in the Nineteenth Century', in C. Calhoun (ed.), *Habermas and the Public Sphere*, MIT Press, Cambridge, MA and London.

Fraser. N. (1993) 'Rethinking the Public Sphere: A Contribution to the Critique of Actually Existing Democracy', in C. Calhoun (ed.), *Habermas and the Public Sphere*, MIT Press, Cambridge, MA and London.

Gluck, S. (1997) 'Palestine: Shifting Sands: The Feminist-Nationalist Connection in the Palestinian Movement', in L. West (ed.), *Feminist Nationalist*, Routledge, London.

Hamdan, M. (1998) 'Sheik Jarrar Responds to MP proposals', *Al-Hayat Al-Jadida*, 13 March.

Hammami, R. (1990) 'Women, the Hijab and the Intifada', *Middle East Report*, Vol. 20, Nos 3 and 4, pp. 24–8.

—— (2004) 'Attitudes Towards Legal Reform of Personal Status Law in Palestine', in L. Welchman (ed.), *Women's Rights and Islamic Family Law: Perspectives on Reform*, Zed Books, London and New York, NY.

Hammami, R. and J. Hilal (2001) 'An Uprising at a Crossroad', *Middle East Research and Information Project*, Vol. 31, No. 219, pp. 2–8.

Hammami, R. and P. Johnson (1999) 'Equality with a Difference: Gender and Citizenship in Transitional Palestine', *Social Politics*, Vol. 6, No. 3, pp. 314–43.

Hammami, R. and E. Kuttab (1999) 'The Palestinian Feminist Movement: Strategies Towards Freedom and Democracy', *The Alternative Information Center*, Vol. XV, No. 4, http://aic.netgate.net/nfw/April99/9904po3-09.html, accessed 11 March 2000.

Hatem, M. (1993) 'Toward the Development of Post-Islamist and Post-Nationalist Feminist Discourses in the Middle East', in J. Tucker (ed.), *Arab Women: Old Boundaries, New Frontiers*, Indiana University Press, Bloomington and Indianapolis, IN.

Hiltermann, J. (1991) *Behind the Intifada*, Princeton University Press, Princeton, NJ.

Jad, I. (1995) 'Claiming Feminism, Claiming Nationalism: Women's Activism in the Occupied Territories', in A. Basu (ed.), *The Challenge of Local Feminisms*, Westview Press, Boulder, CO.

Jayawardena, K. (1989) *Feminism and Nationalism in the Third World*, Zed Books, London.

Joseph, S. (1986) 'Women and Politics in the Middle East', *Middle East Report*, Vol. 16, No. 1, pp. 3–8.

—— (1991) 'Elite Strategies: Iraq and Lebanon', in D. Kandiyoti (ed.), *Women, Islam and the State*, Macmillan, London.

Kandiyoti, D. (1991) 'Introduction', in D. Kandiyoti (ed.), *Women, Islam and the State*, Macmillan, London.

—— (1997) 'Identity and Its Discontents: Women and the Nation', *Dossier, Women Living Under Muslim Laws Series*, No. 20, pp. 7–23, International Solidarity Network of Women Living Under Muslim Laws, Grabels, France.

Khadr, A. (1998) 'Al-qanun wa mustaqbal al-mar'a al-filastiniyya' [Law and the Future of Palestinian Women], Women's Centre for Legal Aid and Counselling and United Nations Development Programme, Jerusalem.

Kuttab, E. (1993) 'Palestinian Women and the Intifada: Fighting on Two Fronts', *Arab Studies Journal*, Vol. 15, pp. 69–85.

Masud, M. K. (2001) *Muslim Jurists' Quest for the Normative Basis of Shari'a*, International Institute for the Study of Islam in the Modern World, Leiden.

Mir-Hosseini, Z. (2000) *Marriage on Trial: A Study of Islamic Family Law, Iran and Morocco Compared*, I. B. Tauris, London.

Moghadam, V. (2001) 'Feminism and Islamic Fundamentalism: A Secularist Interpretation', *Journal of Women's History*, Vol. 13, No. 1, pp. 42–5.

Mohanty, C., A. Rosso, and L. Torres (1991) *Third World Women and the Politics of Feminism*, Indiana University Press, Bloomington, IN.

Molyneux, M. (1998) 'Analysing Women's Movements', *Development and Change*, Vol. 29, No. 2, pp. 219–47.

—— (2001) *Women's Movement in International Perspective: Latin America and Beyond*, Palgrave, New York, NY.

Moors, A. (1999) 'Debating Islamic Family Law: Legal Texts and Social Practices', in M. L. Meiwether and J. Tucker (eds), *A Social History of Women and Gender in the Modern Middle East*, Westview Press, Boulder, CO and Oxford.

—— (2003) 'Introduction: Public Debates on Family Law Reform: Participants, Positions, and Styles of Argumentation in the 1990s', *Islamic Law and Society*, Vol. 10, No. 1, pp. 1–12.

Nashwan, K. (1998) 'Miswaddat Muqtadayat Li-Qanun Ahwal Al-Shakhsiyya Filastini Muwahhad' [Draft Requirements for a Unified Palestinian Law of Personal Status], Discussion Paper from the Model Parliament for Women and Legislation, Gaza.

Peteet, J. (1991) *Gender in Crisis: Women and the Palestinian Resistance Movement*, Columbia University Press, New York, NY.

—— (1999) 'Gender and Sexuality: Belonging to the National and Moral Order', in A. Afsaruddin (ed.), *Hermeneutics and Honor: Negotiating Female 'Public' Space in Islamic/Ate Societies*, Harvard University Press, Cambridge, MA.

Pettman, J. J. (1996) 'Boundary Politics: Women, Nationalism and Danger', in M. Maynard and J. Purvic (eds), *New Frontiers in Women's Studies: Knowledge, Identity and Nationalism*, Taylor and Francis, London.

Sayigh, R. (1993) 'Palestinian Women and Politics in Lebanon', in J. Tucker (ed.), *Arab Women: Old Boundaries, New Frontiers*, Indiana University Press, Bloomington and Indianapolis, IN.

Shaham, R. (1999) 'State, Feminists and Islamists: The Debate over Stipulations in Marriage Contracts in Egypt', *Bulletin of the School of Oriental and African Studies*, Vol. 62, No. 3, pp. 462–83.

Sharoni, S. (1998) 'Gendering Conflict and Peace in Israel/Palestine and the North of Ireland', *Millennium – Journal of International Studies*, Vol. 27, No. 4, pp. 1061–89.

Sh'hada, N. (1999) 'Gender and Politics in Palestine: Discourse Analysis of the Palestinian Authority and Islamists', ISS Working Paper No. 307, Institute of Social Studies, The Hague.

Usher, G. (1995) 'Bantustanisation or Bi-nationalism? An Interview with Azmi Bishara', *Race and Class*, Vol. 37, No. 2, pp. 43–50.

Walby, S. (1996) 'Women and Nation', in G. Balakriohman (ed.), *Mapping the Nation*, Verso in association with New Left Review, London.

Welchman, L. (2000) *Beyond the Code: Muslim Family Law and the Shar'i Judiciary in the Palestinian West Bank*, Kluwer Law International, The Hague.

—— (2003) 'In the Interim: Civil Society, the Shar'ī Judiciary and Palestinian Personal Status Law in the Transitional Period', *Islamic Law and Society*, Vol. 10, No. 1, pp. 34–70.

Welchman, L., F. Labadi, P. Johnson, and R. Hammami (2002) 'Islamic Family Law and the Transition to Palestinian Statehood: Constraints and Opportunities for Legal Reform', http://www.law.emory.edu/IFL/cases/Palestine.htm, accessed 26 February 2009.

Würth, A. (2003) 'Stalled Reform: Family Law in Post-Unification Yemen', *Islamic Law and Society*, Vol. 10, No. 1, pp. 12–34.

Yuval-Davis, N. (1992) 'Nationalism, Racism and Gender Relations', ISS Working Paper No. 130, Institute of Social Studies, The Hague.

—— (1997) *Gender and Nation*, Sage, London.

2

Readjusting Women's Too Many Rights

The State, the Public Voice, and Women's Rights in South Yemen

• •

Susanne Dahlgren

In 1974, with the promulgation of the first statutory law on family affairs, women's rights were inscribed in law for the first time in the Arabian Peninsula. *Code no. 1 of 1974 in Connection with the Family*, the family law of the People's Democratic Republic of Yemen (PDRY), came to be known, alongside the Tunisian Family Code of 1956, as the most progressive family law in the entire Arab world. Enacted after a wide popular debate throughout the country, this legislation was called the Women's Law as it was widely believed throughout South Yemen that it enabled women to gain their rights for the first time in their history. But this success story did not last long. Once the PDRY joined with the Yemen Arab Republic (YAR) to form the Republic of Yemen in 1990, the former country's progressive law was soon replaced by a Personal Status Code based on women's impaired legal capacity, the way it was in the more traditionalist North Yemen. The case of reversing women's rights is interesting from the perspective of today, too, as the Southern Movement – the political movement aimed at regaining independence for South Yemen – has adopted women's rights as one of its key demands. Women's rights activists have now gained a powerful partner in promoting women's rights after many years of marginalization following Yemeni unification.

During the past fifty years, family law reforms in the Muslim world have shown a progressive trend allowing women more rights either step by step (as in Egypt: see Al-Sharmani in this volume) or through a comprehensive reform as in Morocco (see Carlisle in this volume). South Yemen stands alone as a case of development gone badly wrong. In this chapter, I examine the two Yemeni family law reforms, the short-lived 'success story' of the early 1970s and that of the 1990s, and analyse the public debates that surrounded both laws. I take a look at the two states, the PDRY and the unified Yemen Republic, and identify differences between them that might explain such contradictory developments. Further, I examine the promulgation processes of the two codes and argue that the democratic nature of the very law-enacting process, or the lack of it, indexes the role of the state in each case. I collected this material through participant observation in different women's activities through the years since the late 1980s, and by studying newspaper material and other texts from relevant years. My ethnographic fieldwork in the southern Yemeni city of Aden spans the late 1980s–2013; in this period I spent a total of three years in Yemen. In developing my argument, I test what the late Louise Halper has suggested in the case of women's rights in Turkey and Iran. According to her, women's rights are more dependent on the explicit gender ideology of the state than on a history of women's mobilization. In secular Turkey, as in Iran after the Islamic revolution, women have played an active role in the nationalist project, and thus their rights have remained on the state political agenda (Halper 2007). But in the Yemeni case, women have taken part in the nationalist project only in one part of the unified state – the South. So it is vital to see how such participation has evolved after the unification of North and South Yemen.

I also draw on the ideas of Mounira Charrad, who has suggested that gender issues ultimately speak about the role of the state as power centre. In the Middle East, gender debates tend to hide the crucial question of political power behind discourses of 'traditions' and 'modernity'. Thus we need to look at whose interests such discourses play to, and what these tell about the stakes in play. And as Charrad also argues, states in the Middle

East represent particular kin-based alliances (2007). By shedding light on such alliances and the power structures they embody, and how from the very outset they exclude women and other non-empowered sectors of society, we can proceed to a truly political analysis of the mechanisms behind particular law reforms and relapses. By calling for a political analysis of the process, I want to argue against a simplistic explanatory approach that relies on false binaries such as 'modernist versus Islamic' or 'religious versus secular'.

In looking at Yemen, where alongside the statutory law other normative ordering systems exist, it is vital to take into account a normative pluralistic approach. While the state law on family affairs attempts to include a statutory perspective on intimate relations between men and women, framed in terms of 'the family', it has to compete with other non-legal forms of normative ordering (Merry 1988) that frame these relations differently, such as customary practices understood as a particular 'system of tradition' (in Yemen called 'customary law', *'urf*)[1] and Islam as a moral system. These normative orders provide temporally parallel, but spatially exclusive frameworks to organize male–female relations on a community basis.[2] On the state level, these orders compete over hegemony in law debates.

Accordingly I look at these two law-enacting processes from a larger societal perspective and focus on the actors who pushed forward the law reforms and the kinds of public debates that were encouraged or allowed. In particular, I discuss the theoretical implications of undoing the reforms and cancelling the advancement women made during the leftist regime in South Yemen: to what kind of rhetoric does a state turn when it takes away women's rights that have gained popular approval?

Setting the parameters of the new Yemeni woman

When it emerged to independence in 1967, South Yemen consisted of smaller and bigger sultanates and emirates, along with the British Crown Colony of Aden. Following a popular uprising, the new regime sought reforms that reflected both Arab nationalist and European and Asian socialist inspirations. Echoing similar nationalist calls for women to participate in building society as had been earlier heard in Egypt, the policies of 'the new Yemeni woman' (*al-mar'a al-jadīda*) and 'women's emancipation' (*tahrīr al-mar'a*) were drawn up as part of the state-building process. These were outlined by severely criticizing the state of gender relations before independence. As the constitution enacted in 1970 put it, the new state was built upon the ideas of economic, social, and educational equality, and equal treatment of citizens irrespective of race, ethnic origin, religion, social status, or gender. Accordingly, the new official discourse considered women 'half the society', thus making them welcome partners in nation building. Along these lines, women were invited to participate 'alongside her brother' in acquiring education, participating in all sectors of the national economy, and taking up political roles. Women had joined the anti-colonial struggle during the 1950s when their charity organizations radicalized during the course of fighting for independence. These associations were started by colonial wives and their local elite partners. The leaders of these associations, who were women from prominent business and intellectual families, invited women to step 'out from purdah' to join societal activities. By the time of independence in 1967, the two biggest women's associations, each with 300 members, joined together to form the General Union of Yemeni Women (GUYW).[3]

All these measures were in sharp contrast with what happened during the same period in the 'Northern part of the homeland', the Yemen Arab Republic, where the modernist anti–Imamate revolution left women's issues to patriarchal kin alliances to handle. In the YAR women were discouraged from assuming roles that required 'rational judgement', such as being members of legislative bodies or the judiciary. Thus, while in the South the one-party system relied on partnership with the GUYW to call women to participate in all fields of life, in the non-party system[4] in the North the Women's Union concentrated on running women's literacy classes in bigger cities without official recognition.

In the South, the Women's Union was one of the first civil society organizations to emerge following independence, and was soon to be integrated into government policies. The early years of independence saw demands to introduce legislation to regulate family affairs, and guarantee women protection from ill treatment in marriage. The first attempt to achieve these goals was the Zingibar Circular in 1971, unofficially issued by local authorities in a countryside area some 50 kilometres east of Aden. The circular was drafted by local people together with the governor and some *qadhi*s (scholars of Islamic jurisprudence who act as judges) such as *qadhi* 'Abdullah Qahtan. He commented on the radical provisions of the circular that included, among other issues, limitations on polygamy:

> At the beginning there were always difficulties, but we found a general awareness which enabled us to apply the clauses of this Circular which need to be further established to convince the people. The Circular is not inconsistent with Islamic Shari'a, and the Qur'an ordained that 'if you fear that you shall be unjust, then one (wife only)'. (*Al-'Arabi* magazine, No. 162 (May 1972), p. 127, as quoted in Ghanem 1972: 100–1)

The circular also set 15 as the legal age for marriage, made a bride's consent a requirement to marriage, limited dower (*mahr*) to an affordable 200 Yemeni dinars, granted women the right to apply for a dissolution of marriage in the case of a husband's prolonged absence, and proclaimed out-of-court repudiation void (*Al-'Arabi*, p. 127, as quoted in Ghanem 1972: 101). In this manner, the circular paved the way to drafting national legislation.

Promulgating 'women's law' in South Yemen

The 1974 Family Code represents a reformist interpretation of the Shari'a.[5] Like most laws at that time, it was widely discussed in popular meetings and the media (government-controlled newspapers, radio, and TV). Several of the provisions such as the dower (*mahr*) had already been discussed in civil society gatherings during the colonial period.[6] As with the land reform law that was promulgated after popular uprisings, sometimes the need for new legislation came from popular demand, reflecting the post-independence turmoil. The drafting process involved, alongside some prominent *qadhi*s, people such as women's activists, intellectuals, and ordinary men and women who had never been consulted on matters of Shari'a and legal reasoning.

To start with, the draft and its provisions were discussed by the ruling party[7] and by mass organizations such as the Women's Union, as well as by the Ministry of Justice, the *Waqf* (religious endowments), and the People's Supreme Council, the formal legislative body. As part of the drafting process, the provisions were also discussed over a period of four months in public meetings in main towns and throughout the countryside – as women's activists who participated in these meetings recalled (*The Middle East* 1983: 47). The entire process of amending the draft lasted for three years. One of the matters debated in these meetings involved the legal question of how long a woman had to wait to divorce a husband who migrated and left her.[8] Some of the notaries and women's rights activists in the drafting committee later recalled that, in public discussions, women were in favour of more radical reform than men (Molyneux 1982: 9, note 14). In particular, women were eager to render polygamy illegal, as one of the Women's Union activists who participated in these meetings told me (Interview with Khawla Sharif, leader of Adeni Women's Union, Aden, April 1989).

During these meetings, members of the drafting committee were at pains to defend the new law from an Islamic perspective. This was a new interpretation of Shari'a and different from legal practices that used to prevail during the colonial era in Aden when British judges implemented Anglo-Muhammedan law.[9] As one member of the committee was reported to have said: 'We researched the old books of *hadith* (tradition) to show that we had not created anything; everything is in Islam. We only gave vitamins to old ideas, to have them triumph' (*The Middle East* 1983: 46–7). Women's Union activists in hindsight recalled that one of the main achievements of the 1974 law was that it did not form a part of a collection of laws 'on women', a kind of *mudawwana* (collection of laws) with provisions that place women under male authority. This, a women's rights activist explained to me, would have given the false signal that women were not legal persons in their own right, but were under male *'isma* (authority) in the family domain, and furthermore were represented by a man in society at large (interview conducted in November 1998 with Radhia Shamsir, longstanding functionary of the General Union of Yemeni Women and, after unification, of the Yemeni Women's League).

The main provisions that benefited women in the 1974 law were: a bride's consent to her own marriage (Article 3); age limits to all marriages (men 18 and women 16, Article 7); the prohibition of an age gap of more than 20 years between spouses unless the woman had reached 35 years of age (Article 9); a woman's right to apply for court separation (Article 29); *khul*, or divorce in exchange of reasonable compensation not exceeding the dower (*mahr*) (Article 30b); rendering out-of-court repudiation void (Article 25a, 25b); limitations to bigamy subject to a court's decision (Article 11); a woman's right to keep her children (boy until 10 and girl until 15 years) even if she remarries (Article 46); and the stipulation that a woman can act as a witness for marriage (Article 8). While *talāq* (man's unconditional right to repudiation) was allowed in the law, it was made subject to court decision and pertinent to financial compensation to the wife (Article 30a) (Law No. 1 of 1974 (PDRY 1976)). In contrast to today's practice, the court was entitled to make maintenance and custody settlements in connection with the divorce ruling in one hearing, while under the present law the wife has to file a separate application to obtain maintenance (*nafaqa*) or custody (*hadhāna*) of her children.

Women with too many rights

Despite many pro-women policies in South Yemen, by the time of unification in 1990 the situation for women was still full of challenges. They had answered the state call to join education, politics, and the labour market, but their problems were no longer addressed as a priority within the state agenda. Following unity, state executive and legislative structures were formed with the principle of one-plus-one (merging the two parliaments, form-ing a government that represented both sides, and setting up a presidential council with three members from the more populous North and two from the South). Political parties were formed and the previous ruling coalition partners, the Socialist Party in the South and the People's General Congress in the North, were transformed to suit the new circumstances. A coalition of influential Northern tribal *shaykhs* and religious leaders formed the third influential party nationwide, the Islah Party ('Reform' Party). In the beginning, unity was greeted with enthusiasm. When debating whose way to follow, northerners tended to refer to their major share of the population (about 11 million in the North and 2.5 million in the South) (Dresch 2000: 186), while the southerners claimed a higher level of education. Four years after unification, girls' school enrolment in the northern capital city Sana'a was as low as 25.8 per cent, while in the southern former capital of Aden it was 76.6 per cent. For boys, the figures were 73.7 and 80.5 per cent respectively (Central Statistical Organization 2008: Table 4).

By 1993 things started to go wrong once it became evident to many southerners that unification was a mere Trojan horse for the northern elite to get access to their land, properties, and drinking water. Mineral resources located in the South were accumulated by the new political elites while basic infrastructure in southern governorates was left to decay. During the 1990s and 2000s, most accomplishments in the South, including its education system, national health care and women's rights became discursively 'forgotten', as if they had not existed. A new state discourse emerged promoting the idea that only unification brought progress to the South. This discourse was based on the false notion that the central government had succeeded in securing welfare services in the North in the same way as had been achieved in the South before union. Following the marginalization policies in the southern governorates, girls' school attendance dropped in ten years from 76.6 to 74.8 per cent, while in the capital Sana'a there had been a miraculous upswing from 25.8 to 46.2 per cent (Central Statistical Organization 2008, estimates for the years 2005/2006).

Following unification, both parts of the new state kept their family codes in force until the spring of 1992, when a new Personal Status Law was issued. With this reform, southern women lost the rights they had gained in the 1974 law. There has been a lot of speculation about why the southern leaders abandoned the 1974 Family Law and failed to fight for women's earlier accomplishments.

Already before unification, the 1974 law seems to have divided male members of the power elite, with a majority standing on the side of women's rights. As a leading member of the PDRY judiciary told me in November 1989, six months before unification, 'Women have too many rights, and I will personally take care that the situation will be corrected' (discussion, Little Aden, November 1989). While among the ordinary men I interviewed in Aden during 1988 and 1989 support for women's rights was strong, the perspective of some male members of the elite was different. By the late 1980s, the Women's Union already had difficulty gaining support from the ruling party, the Yemeni Socialist Party, for reforms that would improve women's situation, as a former member of the secretariat of the Women's Union recalled (discussion with Radhia Shamsir, November 1998).

Unification provided a perfect framework to serve those who took issue with what they thought to be 'women's too many rights'. Still, this naturally is only one side of the new Yemeni state. The changed political setting, where northern and southern male elites were busy securing positions in the new unified state hierarchy, placed women's concerns at the margins. Women were no longer 'partners in building up the nation' the way they had been in the early years of the PDRY. Instead, women were now treated as part of the *harīm*, the sacred 'private' domain where the state had no role to play, as had been the case in the North.

Accordingly, women in the South were expected to relinquish their rights, since those legal gains were thought to be alien to the majority of the population living under tribal rule in the vast countryside of the North. Radhia Ihsanullah, one of the early 'suffragettes' and leaders of the pre-independence women's activism in the 1950s, explained this changed atmosphere in a newspaper interview she gave after returning to Aden in 1990 from years of voluntary exile:

> There are conservative forces who want to return Yemen to the times of the Imamate. They see a threat in the liberated, educated and self-confident woman to those women who still live subordinated in some parts of the country. None of those women can gain anything if she does not belong to some powerful family or tribe. After unification, those conservative tendencies have felt that their reign [*dawlataha*] is disappearing. Their methods of rule, such as terrorism, threatening with violence and brainwashing are no longer effective on young people. They can no longer fight back development that is about to enter to the 'Bride of the Arabian Peninsula' and the 'Pearl of the Red Sea'. (*14 uktubr*, 20 April 1992)

Here Radhia Ihsanullah highlighted some of the most vital issues that emerged as political facts after unification. She contrasted the situation of the 'liberated, educated and self-confident' southern woman to that of the North, where no woman could advance in society unless she was the relative of a prominent man. The method of rule she describes, terrorism, became violently manifest in the South after unification. Secret assassinations that were never solved by the police saw Socialist party activists eliminated one by one, until the numbers finally reached more than 150 people. Places of saint worshipping, restaurants, hotels, and the beer factory were declared by Islamic radicals as 'un-Islamic' and became the targets of terrorist bombs. Earlier a safe haven void of any crimes, the streets of Aden became places where young women were kidnapped and rumours of rapes spread. Women's covering costume, *aba'a* and a headscarf, which was presented as the 'Islamic requirement', became the norm in the public space. Branding saint worshipping as un-Islamic was promoted by Salafism,[10] which became openly active in the South where previously it had been suppressed by the state. The message delivered from mosques headed by the Salafists was that women's proper Islamic place is at home raising a happy family.[11]

A discourse of 'othering' played a role in how southern women's rights were perceived after union, too. While the southerners tended to call the northerners 'uncivilized *badu*' or '*dahbāsh*',[12] northerners called southerners 'unbelievers' and their women 'morally loose'. In anti-PDRY propaganda, broadcast before unity from North Yemen and Saudi Arabia, women's rights in South Yemen were considered as evidence of how 'un-Islamic' the country was.[13] Women who did not wear the covering costume following union risked being harassed in the street. Why did all this suddenly emerge? Evidently the transfer of the government to the new capital Sana'a contributed to it. While the regime was no longer present, a moral anomaly spread, as Radhia Ihsanullah explained in her interview.[14]

At the same time, a leading member of the Islah party, Shaykh Abd ul-Majid al-Zindani, was building a network of religious schools (*al-ma'had al-'ilmiyya*, sing.) in the North that, among other controversial issues, promoted hostile attitudes towards women's public roles.[15] The mere risk that such tendencies would spread among young people paved the way for an atmosphere in which the southern women's rights activists were left to decide what would be their priority in the legal reforms that were soon to be passed by the unified state.

More rights to the woman – no to selling her rights![16]

As a southern Women's Union activist later recalled, various political threats narrowed the marginal zone where women's demands for rights could be discussed in the new republic to a minimum. Women's Union activists were now part of the Yemeni Women's Union, which was formed after unification by northern and southern women's unions. Without official support, these activists were struggling to establish a national voice in a situation in which they encountered only hostility.

About a year after unification, preparations started for drafting a new family code for the two parts of the country. A draft was distributed in 1991 among selected people in Sana'a and a lively debate began in southern newspapers. Ever since unification there had been discussion in newspapers both in favour of and against the 1974 law. Debates on the future of the Yemeni state seemed to crystallize around the family code: the country's future was depicted as depending either on a 'modern' family code that grants women their rights or a 'code that is based on Shari'a'. The latter categorization was a camouflage for not allowing women any rights, in accordance with what had been customary in the North. In retrospect this polarization marked how unification was to develop during the next twenty years. What is still under debate is what exactly in these two codes is derived from Islamic *fiqh* (jurisprudence) and what derives from misinterpretation and the blurring of customs within Islam.

Even those who had not seen the draft feared the worst and started well in advance to defend southern women's rights. A woman named Bilqis al-Rubi'iyy wrote in the readers' column in the government-run *14 uktubr* (14th October) newspaper in August 1990, some months after unification, about the fears southern women have regarding unrestricted polygamy. She expressed her view under the title 'The woman has her dignity' (*wa lil-mar'at karāmah*). According to her, there are two types of men, depending on their perceptions of a woman. One respects her as a human being and treats her in the same way as a man, while the other sees her as a piece of furniture in his house, making her serve him like a slave. According to al-Rubi'iyy, in the new environment (following union) the talk of allowing men unrestricted access to more than one wife sends the signal to society at large that the man is the master of the family (*14 uktubr*, 16 August 1990).

Reflecting similar thinking, typical of many men in the South at that time, a man called Muhammad 'Abdallah Aburas wrote a piece in the same newspaper some months prior to unification with the title 'Women's cause is as important as democracy and the union'. According to him, the unified nation's constitution (approved in a referendum held in 1991) does not guarantee women's rights, unlike the situation in the South before unification. He asked, 'Can a modern Yemeni state be built if half of its society is paralysed?' (*14 uktubr*, 6 March 1990).

After the enactment of the Personal Status Law, a man called Ahmad Nasir Salih wrote a column in the Adeni newspaper *al-Ayyam* where he reflected on what he had learned in a men's *qat* gathering about the new law.[17] A man had criticized the new law on the basis that it did not obligate the man to keep a wife who had fallen ill and thus was of no sexual use to him. The writer was shocked. He had not himself read the law but he had heard that the law was based on Islamic Shari'a, and thus assumed it would not include any provisions that would be harmful to women – as it is not God's will, the writer explained, to limit women's role in society (*Al-Ayyam*, 22 April 1992).

Girls' education or women's rights in the family?

Concerned about what they read in the draft law, the Women's Union started to discuss their own standpoints. A group of female lawyers and Women's Union activists from both North and South presented their suggestions to the Speaker of Parliament in September 1991. According to a member of this group, the Union tried to push forward changes to women's rights in marriage on the premise that the advancement that had been made in the South was too progressive for the northern part of the country. The proposed changes included the principles of equivalence (*takāfu*) in marriage, respect between the spouses, and equal care for the children. In a meeting with the Speaker Yasin Sa'id Nu'man, a southern politician sympathetic to the women's cause, and his northern deputy Abdulla al-Hakimi, the activists also pointed out that Yemen had signed the Convention to Eliminate All Forms of Violence against Women (CEDAW) without reservations,[18] 'but now you are asking us to go backward' (talk with Radhia Shamsir, 2008).

At the next meeting with the Speaker, the Women's Union representatives were told that women could not expect to keep the rights attained in the South prior to unification. That is, the South had to make compromises to the much larger northern population. This same point came up in all the unification discussions at that time: northerners insisted that while Parliament in the beginning had been formed by merging together the two former legislative bodies, in the future southerners could not expect as large a share. The Speaker explained to the women's activists that they had to consider the conditions in society after unification; there were problems with the Islah Party and terrorism throughout the South. According to the Speaker, an urgent issue would be to reform the Education Bill so that girls would be guaranteed an education, and Zindani's schools, where boys were encouraged to take a hostile attitude towards women's rights, would be separated from the official syllabus, thus rendering them an unattractive option for boys' education. A Women's Union activist who participated in the talks recalled how the Union's decision to support the Education Bill rather than insist on a balanced family law was a hard one, but seemed more urgent at that time (talk with Adeni women's rights veterans, 2008).

A draft for the new family code, called the Personal Status Law (Law No. 20 of 1992) included provisions not only on marriage, divorce, and custody of children but also on foster relationships, inheritance, and different Islamic donations. It was merely a minor improvement to the northern Yemeni Family Law from 1978. In other words, it was not new legislation, unlike the new constitution prepared by a joint North–South body years before unification. The draft personal status law was prepared by the North Yemeni justice ministry and the parliamentary committee, and it mostly codified norms and Shari'a doctrines that prevailed in the North prior to unification. Furthermore, instead of being discussed and passed by Parliament, the draft law was enacted by a presidential decree during Ramadan when Parliament was in recess.[19]

It is evident that the Women's Union was unhappy with this law, but its criticism was constrained on the one hand by the discrepancy in the situations of women in the North and the South, and, on the other, by the discourse that framed the new law as complying with Shari'a, while the 1974 law was depicted as 'void of Shari'a'.[20] While at the beginning the new law and its precedent, the 1978 northern family law, were presented as reflecting prevailing 'traditions', in later debates the tone changed and the new law was framed as being derived 'from the Shari'a'. As the Women National Committee, a government body representing women in official frameworks, explained in its document 'Status of Woman in Yemen' (1996: 19), 'the present Law of personal status has considered the rights and obligations of the wife and the husband as well as the rights of the child from an Islamic perspective'. In presenting the three family codes, the text discusses the 1978 law together with that of 1992, but deals with the 1974 law separately – thus indicating that the 1978 and 1992 laws come from the same root. This new framing reflected the atmosphere that had emerged, where all kinds of rights claims, be they from a human rights or from a women's rights perspective, were juxtaposed with Shari'a as the final and only criteria for all laws.[21] In those debates, there did not seem to be a middle ground, where women's rights could be viewed as corresponding with Islam, a discourse that Adeni women's activists developed only at the end of the 1990s.

The 1994 civil war led to the demise of the southern political opposition. Also, women's activism was thrown into disarray. Some of the leading activists withdrew from politics, and disappointment and frustration spread among the population at large in the South. An insightful southern politician, 'Umar al-Gawi, leader of the small leftist party al-Tagammu', told the President that he was inviting trouble by not addressing the concerns of the southern people, and that one day the steam would burst out. It took some years but the geyser of steam finally broke through in the spring of 2007 as Al-harak al-janubi (Southern Movement). This movement emerged throughout the southern governorates, reflecting wide popular dissent towards northern ways of ruling, which was marked by clientelism, corruption, and disregard for rule of law. By 2013 the movement had spread to every corner of the South, with wide popular support.

As a reward for backing the northern army's invasion and victory over the South in the 1994 civil war, the ruling People's General Congress (PGC) Party gave its ally the Islah Party – a coalition of northern tribal shaykhs, members of the Ikhwan (Muslim Brothers), technocrats, and others who take Islam as the focal point of politics – the chance to rule over Aden. As a result, Islah appointed activists from the North to leading positions within the city administration. These cadres, however, met resistance to their view of Islamic politics, which Adenis perceived as alien to the South. By 1998, Islah had failed to impose its rule on Aden and was replaced by the PGC. By the turn of the millennium, Adeni public space had become homosocial: women were no longer seen about, and when they were seen, they were clad in overcoats (*aba'a* or *balto*), headscarves, and face veils, hurrying to their 'women only' activities.

Putting woman in her place

The Personal Status Law that replaced the 1974 law was a readjustment of male–female rights in the family to the benefit of the man. The law was later amended in 1998 and 1999, making it even worse from the perspective of women's rights. It seeks to impose a conservative and customs-oriented reading of *fiqh* (Islamic jurisprudence), as compared to the 1974 law which manifests a modernist, women's-rights-based reading of the *fiqh*.

A disparity between women's and men's duties and rights in

marriage is evident in many of its provisions. The legal age for marriage was originally set at 15 in 1992 (Article 15), but the age limit was later dropped and the ruling changed to allow the guardian of a minor of any age to arrange her wedding (*zaffa*)[22] on the condition that she is fit for sexual intercourse (Article 15 as amended in 1999 [Law No. 20 of 1992 as amended, no date]). Only the bride's guardian can sign her marriage contract, though her consent is required; however her silence suffices as a sign of consent (Article 23). Two women, as opposed to one man, are required for bearing witness to the officiating of a marriage contract. A man has the unconditional right to repudiation of marriage (*talāq*), and the wife cannot reverse such a divorce. In the 1992 version of the law a wife had the right to compensation if the court found the divorce unjust (Article 71). The compensation could amount to one year's maintenance (as it was in the 1974 law), but this stipulation was abolished in 1998.

Some of the most controversial parts of the law from the perspective of southern women have to do with the rights and duties of the spouses. While the 1974 law did not separate men's and women's duties in marriage, the 1992 law applies a clear gender division. The wife's duties are written under the legal notion of *al-tā'a* (obedience), elaborated in the following aspects: she has to allow her husband free sexual access whenever he requires it; she has to carry out the household work in the matrimonial home; she has to obey him in all matters and to ask for his permission whenever leaving the house (Article 40). In the original 1992 version of the law, the provision on a husband's free access to sexual intercourse included the specification: free sexual access *without the presence of anyone else* (Article 40, 2). This provision might be linked to the housing arrangements of newly wed couples, but it can also refer to an old custom that used to be prevalent in some parts of the country. During the wedding night (*laylat al-dukhula*), it was the custom that a female marriage helper, an older married woman called *mukaddia* or *haria*, was present while the couple performed first intercourse. Her task was to show the blood-stained sheet to female relatives as proof of bridal virginity (Serjeant 1991). The provision was dropped in the 1998 amendments.

The husband's duties in the law include maintaining his wife/ wives and children. He also has to honour the living standard she was accustomed to prior to marriage and to treat all his wives equally. These provisions simply repeat Article 27 of the northern law (Yemen Arab Republic 1987). The law constructs the man as the provider and the woman as the one being provided for, a legal fact difficult to sustain in southern cities where many women earn salaries from work outside the home or in the countryside at large, where women perform a considerable share of the agricultural work. The law treats the wife as a person with diminished legal capacity, who needs her husband's permission even when going out on a simple errand. From the perspective of the women's rights activists in the South, the law relegates all Yemeni women to the position of women in the most backward areas of the countryside.

Still, not all legal developments after Yemeni unity have been negative. Women's rights activists gained a considerable victory in 2000–1 when they succeeded in killing a draft law that was going to expand the provisions regarding *bayt al-tā ʿa*. The law, initiated by MPs from the Islah Party, was secretly prepared in Parliament. The new formulation of this legal principle included provisions granting a husband the right to send the police to bring a renegade wife back to the marital home. Women's activists who participated in appealing against this provision labelled it as violence against women, a popular slogan that had reached Yemeni civil society from international NGO platforms during the 1990s. The activists' appeal to the President and their publicizing of the matter to some of the leading foreign donor countries' embassies persuaded the President not to sign the proposed law, and thus it was dropped.

Another example of civil society lobbying to bring forward legal reform has to do with marital age. In spring 2009, Parliament was debating a bill to increase the marital age to 17 for both men and women. The issue had emerged some months earlier when the case of Nugum, an 8-year-old girl from the northern town of Hajja, became known. She was awarded a divorce from a 30-year-old husband she had been forced to marry by her father (*Yemen Times* 2008). The case was widely reported in the international media and pressure was placed on the Yemeni government to reform the marital age, which was no longer defined after the 1999 amendments were introduced. The issue divided MPs from the Islah Party, with the more pragmatic members of Parliament favouring the amendment while others opposed it (both basing their rationalizations on the Shari'a). At the time of writing, the question is still to be decided.

Women's rights, politics, and ground for bargaining

It has been suggested that the Personal Status Law is there to support the most vulnerable sector of society, namely, women of modest means who have to go to court to gain some rights (Würth 2003: 18).[23] Still, the threat of being thrown out of one's own home or losing one's children as a result of divorce, or being forced to share a husband with another woman, are vulnerabilities that upper-class women also face. It is clear that the deterioration of women's rights in the most intimate relations, those of her family, affects all women in Yemen irrespective of social standing. Still, as Radhia Ihsanullah pointed out, in today's Yemen the destiny of a woman depends on how well situated she is socially – that is, through her connection to a significant man. Family law reforms in Yemen during the 1990s have thus contributed directly to putting women at the mercy of patriarchal kin, thus narrowing the space women's activism succeeded in carving out between the state and the kin alliances in the South prior to unification.

The advances women in the South made during the PDRY have not become a part of the process of building a 'modern new Yemen'. It is evident that the 1992 Personal Status Law, together with the collapse of resistance to such policies that resulted from the 1994 civil war, led to a situation where political forces that favour patriarchal alliances as the foundation of all social relations have been given what amounts to free rein to implement their national ideals. Still, as the Southern Movement that emerged in 2007 clearly demonstrates, people in the South are no longer willing to live under such rule. As dissent spread throughout the country – reaching the northern governorates in the Arab Spring of 2011 – and women took a visible role in the mass demonstrations, youth activists remained optimistic about the possibility of a new era for Yemeni women. Since then, this optimism has found a new base within the ranks of the Southern cause, that is, within the framework of re-establishing an independent southern state. The Southern Movement advocates women's rights as a vital part of the future state. Thus, at last, the women's movement has an ally in its fight for rights.

Conclusion

The case of reversing women's rights in Yemen is unique in the entire Arab world. As I have attempted to show in this chapter, the process of unifying Yemen entailed placing women in a subordinate position in relation to men. The marginalization of women was sealed by the 1992 Personal Status Law. This was made possible as a result of three factors that typify the Yemen case. First, following unification women's voices were marginalized and the legacy of strong women fighting alongside pro-women's rights men – a characteristic of the southern nationalist project – no longer had a hegemonic standing.[24] Second, unification of North and South Yemen turned from the genuine enthusiasm and mutual respect of the early years into a forced unity after the 1994 civil war, a process in which the northern political system based on clientelist alliances was introduced to the South. Third, the transformation into a system that, from the southern perspective, has been perceived as a return to the past, was made possible by camouflaging traditionalist thinking in legal debates with a discourse presented as Islamic. Cancelling southern women's rights was thus facilitated by applying a language that presented the negative changes as inevitable and coming from God, a discourse that is hard to resist without risk of being labelled as un-Islamic or pagan (*kāfir*), that is, outside the scope of all legitimate social deliberations. These three factors formed great obstacles for those promoting women's issues in society at large.

To challenge this negative development, the southern women's activists have adopted a discourse that links women's rights to Islamic Shari'a. However, to transform this discourse into a powerful voice in the national fight for women's rights, the women's activists have to gain a more central role in state structures. Women's struggle for their rights also has to address the question of the state as a domain where power relations are articulated and contested. As Leila Ahmed has suggested, during the independence struggle in Aden in the 1950s and 1960s women participated in the political fight, and were able to transform their own aims as part of that fight – instead of the fight tapping women to achieve its nationalist goals, as was the case in Algeria (Ahmed 1983: 169–70). Today the women's movement has a powerful partner in the Southern Movement, which has declared women's rights an important part of its political agenda. Still, as history has proved in Yemen, it is always up to women to keep their agenda alive.

Notes

1   On different perspectives of *'urf* in Yemen, see Maktari 1971; Chelhod 1975; Adra 1985; and Weir 2007.
2   I have developed the idea of temporally parallel but spatially exclusive moral orders in Dahlgren (2010).
3   On women's organizations and the independence struggle, see Dahlgren (2010).
4   The People's General Congress, formed in 1982, was the legitimate playground for politics while political parties were banned in the North. The PGC had been transformed into a political party by the time of unification.
5   See for example Mir-Hosseini 2003, according to whom Islamic legal

commentary of the modern age can be divided into traditionalist, neo-traditionalist, and reformist tendencies.

6   Among other issues, the dower was critically reviewed in a meeting that gathered Adeni young men to the premises of the Aden Tennis Club, where a public meeting on the 'dearness of marriage' was held in 1961. See Dahlgren 2010: 144–6.

7   During the years 1971–4 the ruling party was called National Front. It collaborated with two smaller parties, the Popular Democratic Union (Communists) and the Vanguard Party (Baathists). See Ismael and Ismael 1986: 20–41.

8   In the Zingibar circular the waiting time was set at two years.

9   I have characterized colonial-era legal practice in Aden as Anglo-Muhammedan law; see Dahlgren (2010).

10 Salafism is an Islamic reform movement initiated by Jamal al-din al-Afghani and Muhammad Abduh in Egypt in the nineteenth century. Their original idea of reconciling the original teachings of the 'elders' of Islam with contemporary science and thought, however, has changed among present-day Salafists into a dictum of following norms identified in the traditions.

11 This message was also delivered on audio cassettes, distributed in all the main markets in Aden. These cassettes also instruct women in how to dress the proper Islamic way and on women's rights in marriage. The preachers included Shaykh Sa'id Masfar, Shaykh Muhammad al-Muhayisni, Abu Bakr al-Mashtud and Abu Bakr al-Haddad.

12 A pejorative name for northerners; for its meaning see Dahlgren (2010: 269).

13 Such propaganda was disseminated through radio before unification, and afterwards in booklets and books available in bookshops and from street peddlers. See Al-Wadi'iy (no date).

14 I have discussed this phenomenon in Dahlgren (2006).

15 Interpol has issued a global warrant for al-Zindani, who is charged with supporting global terrorism.

16 Title of a newspaper article by Amira Muhammad Sa'id in *'Adn* (Aden), 21 May 1991.

17 *Qat* is a mild narcotic shrub that is chewed in societal gatherings during afternoons. The habit is more popular among men than women and prior to union, it was more widespread in the North than in the South, where its consumption was limited to weekends.

18 South Yemen signed CEDAW in 1984 without reservations. All international commitments were kept in the union.

19 During the first two years (from May 1990 to May 1992) the interim Parliament had problems in agreeing on laws. Consequently some fifty

laws were enacted by presidential decree (Sharif 1996: 24).

20 YWU leader 'Aida 'Ali Sa'id wrote a critical column in the trade union newspaper *Sawt al-'ummal* where she did not directly criticize the new law but aimed her arguments at the 'negative customs' that family practices in Yemen manifest (*Sawt al-'ummal*, 30 April 1992). A northern intellectual and academic, 'Abu Bakr al-Saqqaf, wrote about the new law in the *al-Ayyam* newspaper, where he criticized those who claimed that the 1974 Family Law had foreign elements in its provisions (*al-Ayyam*, 25 March 1992, *mashrū' qānūn al-ahwāl al-shakhsiyya wa mustaqbal al-tatwir al-ijtimā'iyy*).

21 The constitution had originally been accepted in a referendum held in 1991, with the provision that Islam is the 'main source' of all laws. Some of the religious parties boycotted the referendum over that particular notion. The formulation was changed after 1994 to 'the sole source'.

22 In Yemen, *zaffa* means to organize a wedding party which will accompany the bridal couple at the end of the party to the marital home to spend a night together, culminating in the bride's penetration and the consummation of the marriage.

23 Danya C. Wright has studied mid-nineteenth-century English family law reforms and tells how a similar understanding prevailed in the early English law reform movement, a discourse of protection of the weak (Wright 2007: 39–40).

24 Leila Ahmed, who has analysed the development of women's rights in some Middle Eastern countries against the background of larger historical developments, suggests that the policy of women's emancipation in South Yemen was a result of a living tradition in the Arabian Peninsula of strong independent women and a history of women's agency (Ahmed 1983: 169–70).

References

14 uktubr (1992) 'After Twenty Years, Radhia Ihsanullah Has Woken Up and Spoken', interview by Safa' 'Ali Ibrahim, *14 uktubr* newspaper, 20 April.

Adra, N. (1985) 'The Tribal Concept in the Central Highlands of the Yemen Arab Republic', in N. S. Hopkins and S. E. Ibrahim (eds), *Arab Society*, The American University of Cairo Press, Cairo.

Ahmed, L. (1983) 'Feminism and Feminist Movements in the Middle East, a Preliminary Exploration: Turkey, Egypt, Algeria, People's Democratic Republic of Yemen', in R. Bidwell and G. Rex Smith (eds), *Arabian and Islamic Studies*, Longman, London.

Al-Wadi'iy, M. B. H. (no date) *al-suyūf al-bātirah li-lhādi al-shuyū'īyah al-kāfirah.*

Central Statistical Organization (2008) 'Education, Table 4 "Population Enrolment Rate in Basic Schooling (6–15 years) by Sex and Governorate, According to 1994 Census"', in *Statistical Yearbook 2008*, Central Statistical Organization, Sana'a.

Charrad, M. M. (2007) 'Contexts, Concepts and Contentions: Gender Legislation as Politics in the Middle East', *Hawwa: Journal of Women of the Middle East and the Islamic World*, Vol. 5, No. 1, pp. 55–72.

Chelhod, J. (1975) 'La Societé Yéménite et le Droit', *L'Homme*, Vol. 15, No. 2, pp. 67–86.

Dahlgren, S. (2006) 'Segregation, Illegitimate Encounters and Contextual Moralities: Sexualities in the Changing Public Sphere in Aden', *Hawwa: Journal of Women of the Middle East and the Islamic World*, Vol. 4, Nos 2–3, pp. 214–36.

—— (2010) *Contesting Realities: The Public Sphere and Morality in Southern Yemen*, Syracuse University Press, Syracuse, NY.

Dresch, P. (2000) *A History of Modern Yemen*, Cambridge University Press, Cambridge.

Ghanem, I. (1972) 'Social Aspects of the Legal Systems in South-West Arabia with Special Reference to the Application of Islamic Family Law in the Aden Courts', unpublished Master's thesis, University of London, School of Oriental and African Studies.

Halper, L. (2007) 'Disrupted Societies, Transformative States: Politics of Law and Gender in Republican Turkey and Iran', *Hawwa: Journal of Women of the Middle East and the Islamic World*, Vol. 5, No. 1, pp. 90–110.

Ismael, T. Y. and J. S. Ismael (1986) *PDR Yemen: Politics, Economics and Society – the Politics of Socialist Transformation*, Frances Pinter Publishers, London.

Maktari, A. M. A. (1971) *Water Rights and Irrigation Practices in Lahj: A Study of the Application of Customary and Sharī'ah Law in South-West Arabia*, Cambridge University Press, Cambridge.

Merry, S. E. (1988) 'Legal Pluralism', *Law and Society Review*, Vol. 22, pp. 867–96.

The Middle East (1983) 'Freedom Takes Time', February, pp. 46–8.

Mir-Hosseini, Z. (2003) 'The Construction of Gender in Islamic Legal Thought and Strategies for Reform', *Hawwa: Journal of Women of the Middle East and the Islamic World*, Vol. 1, No. 1, pp. 1–28.

Molyneux, M. (1982) *State Politics and the Position of Women Workers in the People's Democratic Republic of Yemen 1967–77*, Women, Work, and

Development No. 3, International Labour Office, Geneva.

People's Democratic Republic of Yemen (1976) *Family Law. Law No. 1 of 1974 in Connection with the Family*, official English translation by the Information Department of Ministry of Information, 14th October Corporation, Aden.

Republic of Yemen, Women National Committee (1996) *Status of Woman in Yemen*, Sana'a.

Republic of Yemen, Law No. 20 of 1992 (no date) *qarār al-jumhūrī bi'l-qānūn raqm 20 li-sanat 1992 bisha'n al-ahwāl al-shakhsiyyat*, 'mu'assasat 14 uktūbr, Aden.

Republic of Yemen, Law no. 20 of 1992 (as amended) (no date) *qānūn raqim (20) li-sanat 1992m bisha'n al-ahwāl al-shakhsiyyat wa taʿdiyylāthu*, tauzīʿ maktabat Khālid bin al-Walīd, Sana'a.

Serjeant, R. B. (1991) *Customary and Shariah Law in Arabian Society*, Ashgate Variorum, Surrey.

Sharif, A. H. (1996) 'The Post-Unification Yemeni Parliament and Democratization in Comparative Perspective', paper presented at the Annual Meeting of the Middle East Studies Association, 21–24 November, Providence, Rhode Island.

Weir, S. (2007) *A Tribal Order: Politics and Law in the Mountains of Yemen*, University of Texas Press: Austin TX.

Wright, D. C. (2007) 'Legal Rights and Women's Autonomy: Can Family Law Reform in Muslim Countries Avoid the Contradictions of Victorian Domesticity?', *Hawwa: Journal of Women of the Middle East and the Islamic World*, Vol. 5, No. 1, pp. 33–54.

Würth, A. (2003) 'Stalled Reform: Family Law in Post-Unification Yemen', *Islamic Law and Society*, Vol. 10, No. 1, pp. 12–33.

Yemen Arab Republic (1987) *Law No. 3 of 1978 (Family Code)*, 8 January 1978, summarized in Y. Hakim, *Yemen Arab Republic: A Country Law Study Prepared for the Department of the Navy*, Office of the Judge Advocate General, Washington, DC, Library of Congress, 1985, pp. 33–39, as reprinted in 14 *Annual Review of Population Law*, 425, 1987.

Yemen Times (2008) 'For the First Time in Yemen: An 8-year-old Girl Asks for Divorce in Court', 10 April, http://www.yementimes.com/article.shtml?i=1145&p=front&a=2 (accessed 4 June 2009).

3

Reforming Egyptian Family Laws
The Debate about a New Substantive Code

Mulki Al-Sharmani

In its annual convention in early November 2008, the now dissolved National Democratic Party (NDP), the ruling party of the Egyptian government in the former regime of President Mubarak, announced an initiative to reform the substantive personal status laws.[1] This announcement was the culmination of a year-long effort undertaken by the Women's Committee in the party to review current personal status laws and propose changes to address gaps and problematic articles that discriminate against women. Shortly after the convention, the party presented its proposed changes to the Ministry of Justice. The Legislative Committee at the National Council for Women (NCW)[2] also presented a set of proposed changes.

In addition, women's rights groups had been very active in advocating for comprehensive legal reforms and had undertaken a number of initiatives to contribute to the process of drafting a new law. For instance, twelve of these organizations formed the Network for Women's Rights Organizations in 2005 (NWRO). The NWRO began a five-year multidimensional project whose overall aim was to contribute to the introduction of comprehensive legal reforms and to help create an enabling societal environment, which would facilitate the effective implementation of proposed changes to the personal status laws. The activities of the NWRO project combined legal advocacy, research, building constituencies among different sectors of society, and providing a forum for public debates about the proposed reforms through a series of workshops with public thinkers, religious scholars, lawyers, judges, women's rights activists, journalists, and representatives of government agencies.

The Department of Legislation at the Ministry of Justice reviewed the proposals submitted by the different governmental and non-governmental entities, and worked on drafting a comprehensive family code. It was widely expected by women's rights groups and the media that the Ministry would present a new draft code to Parliament in 2009 or 2010. But this did not happen because the draft code, according to the Ministry, was not yet ready. On 25 January 2011, the Egyptian Revolution took place and Mubarak's regime was overthrown. The proposed draft code was never submitted to the new post-revolution Parliament that was elected in January 2012, and which was dissolved by the country's Supreme Constitutional Court a few months later in June of the same year.[3]

These initiatives to reform the substantive personal status laws[4] came after – or perhaps because of – a decade in which a series of new procedural laws were passed. Many reformers felt that the lack of comprehensive changes in the substantive laws not only undermined the newly passed procedural laws, but also maintained a legal system that legitimized hierarchal gender roles and relations. But the different reform initiatives being put forward at the time were accompanied by a heated public debate in different venues such as printed and TV media; workshops organized by women's rights activists; and scholarship produced by a number of religious scholars and public thinkers.

In this chapter, I shed light on this debate. I identify the main interlocutors and analyse their arguments, highlighting the ideological frameworks and socio-political context shaping their positions. I seek to highlight the multiplicity and diversity among the 'religious' arguments and positions that were adopted by the interlocutors, whether they were supportive of the proposed reforms or opposed to them. Further, I seek to show that there are a number of issues that were driving this debate, and which went beyond the question of whether the proposed reforms were compatible with the doctrines of Islamic Shari'a. These issues are as follows: the struggle among different religious discourses for public legitimacy; the contradictions of seeking gender justice through state institutions such as the law in a context where citizens were suffering from state oppression and its failure to ensure their citizenship rights; and disagreements among different actors who sought (or endorsed) gender justice in the family domain, about the suitability of global feminism (inspired by international conventions) as a credible framework for advocacy and action.

The analysis in this chapter is based on: (1) semi-structured interviews conducted with nine informants, namely, seven religious scholars and public intellectuals,[5] one religious functionary (Secretary General of the Jurists' Department and the Director of the E-learning and Training Programme for mosque imams and jurists at the Azhar University), and one prominent legal figure (Judge Tahany El Gibaly of the Supreme Constitutional Court);[6] (2) a background paper written by Marwa Sharafeldin (2008) on Egyptian women's rights organizations' use of religious discourses in their advocacy work to reform family laws;[7] (3) a review of the coverage of the proposed reforms in government-owned and independent daily and weekly printed (and television) media during the period January 2007 to May 2010; and (4) participant observation by the author in five workshops that were organized by the NWRO, Alliance for Arab Women, the Centre for Egyptian Women's Legal Assistance, and the Forum for the Development of Women in 2008.

Proposed changes in personal status laws

Neither the Women's Committee at the NDP nor the Legislative Committee at the NCW made public the draft laws that they submitted to the Ministry of Justice. Some members of both committees gave the explanation for this as a strategy to work quietly without attracting unwanted attention from conservative religious scholars, which might then lead to their premature objections, thus undermining the work of the two committees.[8] This meant that there was not much societal involvement in the drafting of the proposals for a new law by these two committees. However, although the draft laws were not made public in their entirety, some of the proposed changes were disclosed and discussed in the media.

Women's rights organizations, however, were quite vocal about their propositions for the content of a new substantive family law. For instance, the NWRO penned a concept paper about the organization's vision and suggestions for legal reforms. This concept paper was circulated to other women's rights organizations and concerned policy makers. The paper was also the subject of discussion in a workshop held by the NWRO in June 2008. The Centre for Egyptian Women's Legal Assistance, a member of the NWRO, had also been working on a comprehensive unified draft law for both Muslim and Christian Egyptians.

The key proposals in the various drafts that were being put together by the NDP, NCW, and the NWRO can be summarized as follows:[9]

- Change the minimum marriage age for women from 16 to 18. This proposal was particularly high on the government's agenda since the newly passed Child Law in June 2008 changed the marriage age for females from 16 to 18.
- Restrict a husband's unconditional right to polygyny by obligating him to apply for court approval before entering into a new marriage. This was mainly a goal sought by the NWRO, as stated in their concept paper and public work-shops. The Women's Committee at the NDP and the NCW, however, did not endorse this proposal, particularly in the wake of fierce opposition from religious scholars. The most notable of these scholars was Dr Soad Saleh, Professor of Comparative Jurisprudence at Azhar University. In a religious talk show entitled *Ama Yata Sa'aluun* (What Are They Asking About) aired on the Egyptian satellite channel *Dream 2*, on 20 June 2009, Saleh argued that the Islamic juristic law which

sanctioned men's right to polygamy was based on a Qur'anic verse that was definitive in its meaning and hence could not be subject to new interpretations. When asked by the presenter and other guest speakers about current social problems that had risen from men's exercise of polygamy (such as leaving their multiple wives without support, or failing to provide adequate care and education for their children), Saleh answered that men's failure to live by the Islamic values of justice and moral responsibility did not justify changing divine laws.

- Restrict a husband's right to unilateral repudiation. There were various propositions for the legal modality through which this goal was to be achieved. For instance, some of the women's rights organizations favoured making husband's right to exercise repudiation contingent on court approval. Other reform groups (among them the Women's Committee at the NDP), however, did not go as far as restricting a husband's right to exercise repudiation. Instead, they were pushing for abolishing repudiations taking place in the absence of wives, and proposed obligating husbands to repudiate in the presence of their wives and a government notary.
- Abolish male guardianship over women and the wife's duty to obey her husband.
- Abolish existing law which makes a wife's right to spousal economic support contingent on her physical and sexual availability to her husband, and instead construct a new legal definition of marital roles which stresses equal partnership between spouses.
- Extend full parental guardianship over children to mothers (particularly in the light of the new Child Law of June 2008, which gives custodial mothers guardianship over their children in affairs pertaining to their education).
- Give childless women who were divorced by their husbands after fifteen or more years of marriage the right to the conjugal home.
- Make divorced fathers' rights to visit children contingent on their payment of child alimony.

- Restrict judges' discretionary power in allocating spousal maintenance and child alimony by setting a minimum amount.
- Extend the non-custodial father's visiting rights with their children from three hours per week to weekends and summer holidays.

Women's rights organizations and reforming family law: multiple terms of reference

Women's rights organizations (such as the NWRO) made use of four terms of reference when making the case for the proposed legal changes: (1) Egyptian women's daily realities of marriage; (2) objectives of Islamic Shari'a and the diversity in the doctrines of Islamic jurisprudence; (3) women's constitutional right to equal citizenship alongside men; and (4) Egypt's obligation to honour its commitment to international conventions such as the Convention for the Elimination of All Forms of Discrimination against Women (CEDAW), and the Universal Declaration of Human Rights. However, in the framing of their arguments and positions in the public debate about the proposed reforms, women's rights activists did not give equal weight to all four terms of reference. Perhaps this is due to the fact that these frameworks vary greatly in their effectiveness as a persuasive impetus for reform, as far as other interlocutors and the general public are concerned.

For instance, in engagement with the media, religious scholars, and the general public, women's rights activists rarely appealed to the country's obligation to uphold its commitment to the CEDAW principles. Neither was the principle of human rights highlighted in their arguments. This is understandable given a prevalent public view in the country that links CEDAW and the notion of human rights to a Western agenda that is perceived to pose a threat to Egyptian society and family values. Such a view, for instance, is espoused by groups such as the International Islamic Committee for Women and Children, which I will discuss in a subsequent section.

Invoking women's constitutional right to equal citizenship escaped this taint of association with a Western agenda. Still, appealing to the notion of equal citizenship rights was not a very effective strategy. This is because although the Egyptian constitution of 1971, which was still the law of the country at the time, affirms equal citizenship rights to all Egyptian nationals regardless of their religion and gender (Article 40), it also privileges women's gendered and dependent roles within the family over their public roles as equal members of the society and polity (Article 11).[10]

Highlighting the suffering and injustice encountered by women in their marriages and divorces because of the existing personal status law was the strategy most extensively used by women's rights activists in making the case for legal reforms. For instance, almost all the workshops organized by women's rights groups included testimonials by women from different walks of life who were embroiled in marital conflicts and law suits. In addition, women's rights organizations commissioned studies and drew on the research of various academic institutions to highlight the shortcomings of existing laws (the negative impact of polygamy on children's welfare, for example, or the discrepancy between women's legal dependence on their husbands and their real-life role as co-provider or in some cases sole provider for their conjugal families). Although advocacy through real-life testimonials had been effective in driving home the shortcomings of the existing laws, it had not necessarily persuaded opponents of the proposed legal changes.

The main challenge for women's rights activists was claiming religious legitimacy for their proposed reforms. It was not surprising, then, that religion took the central place in the arguments made by women's rights organizations in order to justify the changes for which they were campaigning. Marwa Sharafeldin (2008) reported that the informants she interviewed from the women's rights organizations justified their use of a religious-based framework on the following grounds: (1) such an approach enabled them to build larger constituencies;

(2) religious beliefs and doctrines were part and parcel of the dominant cultural identity of the society; and (3) some of the members of these organizations themselves believed in the principles and doctrines of Islamic Shari'a as a guiding framework for their reform agenda.

According to Sharafeldin, women's rights organizations used a number of religion-centred approaches to promote their specific reform proposals. One approach was the use of a historically situated interpretation of the specific rules stated in the Qur'an pertaining to marriage and marital rights in order to arrive at interpretations that would either suspend these rules or propose new ones. One such example was historicizing the Qur'anic verse 34, chapter 4, concerning Muslim men's duty to support women, which early jurists interpreted as the basis for male guardianship over women. The verse says, 'Men shall take full care of women with the bounties which God has bestowed more abundantly on the former than on the latter, and with what they may spend out of their possessions' (translation by Asad 1980). Sharafeldin's informants, for example, argued that since nowadays many men and women share financial obligations and other qualifications (such as education and life experience), man's guardianship over women is no longer justified.

Another approach employed by these activists was to emphasize the primacy of upholding Shari'a objectives over the implementation of specific religious doctrines. The informants broadly defined Shari'a objectives as justice (entailing equality) and serving the public good.[11] Other approaches used by the activists were: distinguishing between *fiqh* (early jurists' human understanding of the doctrines of the sacred texts) and Shari'a (the divine path of sacred truth); taking into account the questionable credibility of the sources of some *hadith* sayings that may condone gender inequality or ill treatment of women; and drawing on examples from the Prophet's actions and decisions that reflect a preference for an alternative rule to the one that may be drawn from certain Qur'anic verses. For instance, the Prophet's objection to his son-in-law Ali Ibn Abi Taleb's desire to take a new wife while he was married to the Prophet's daughter, Fatima, was often cited by women's rights activists as an argument against sanctioning polygny.

Most of all, women's rights activists were successful in incorporating into their advocacy work the production and dissemination of new scholarship in religious knowledge, which called for gender-sensitive family laws. This scholarship was being produced by well-known and knowledgeable religious scholars such as Amna Nosseir, the late Abdel Moty Bayoumy, and Zeinab Radwan. The significance of the work of these three scholars, in particular, is that they highlight the human and historical dimension of Islamic jurisprudence, and hence the need for interpretations that are based on a sound understanding of the social contexts of the targeted people, and which meet the objectives of Shari'a. In the subsequent section, I will analyse some of their arguments and positions.

Contemporary religious scholarship and Egyptian feminist legal activism

Abdel Moty Bayoumy, former Professor of Islamic Jurisprudence at Azhar University and a member of the Islamic Research Academy,[12] who died in 2012, had been very active in augmenting the work of feminist and government reformers with his scholarship and public talks. As a member of the Islamic Research Academy, Bayoumy was instrumental in securing its approval of the draft *khul* law before it was presented to the Parliament in 2000.[13] At the time, Bayoumy published five articles in the Egyptian magazine *Al Musawir*, refuting the opposition of religious scholars with carefully formulated religious arguments. The main point of disagreement between the proponents and critics of the *khul* law was whether the consent of the husband to a wife's decision to initiate *khul* was a necessary religious requirement or not. Religious scholars who were opposed to the law argued that the consensus among the jurists of the four schools of Sunni jurisprudence was that the husband's consent was essential. On the other hand, proponents of the law, such as Abdel Moty, argued that a close interpretation of the Qur'anic verse on *khul* as well as the precedent case which took place during the Prophet's life negated the jurists' requirement of the husband's consent.

In May 2008, in a workshop organized by NWRO, Bayoumy gave a talk in which he presented religious arguments that supported many of the proposals that were put forward in the NWRO concept paper. On 25 November 2008 he participated in a workshop organized by the Centre for Egyptian Women's Legal Assistance (CEWLA) as part of a regional initiative to reform family laws in Egypt, Lebanon, Jordan, and Palestine. In the workshop, Bayoumy presented the summary of an eighty-page paper which he wrote for CEWLA. The paper presented religious arguments for a contextual understanding of the rules of Islamic jurisprudence.

According to Bayoumy, the challenges of reforming Egyptian family laws arose from three main factors: (1) the religious establishment in the country (the Islamic Research Academy, for example) was dominated by religious scholars who were either too rigid or uncommitted professionally to engage scientifically and dynamically with the religious tradition; (2) the wide-scale production and consumption of religious knowledge through satellite channels, which contributed to the emergence of religious arguments and injunctions that were flawed and discriminatory against women; and (3) the rising hegemony of an international Western-based secular agenda that was threatening what he called the harmony of Egyptian heterosexual families.[14]

Bayoumy's work interpreted the concept of *qiwama*, traditionally understood as a husband's financial obligation and guardianship over his wife, as a spousal obligation that entailed multidimensional support and was conditioned on the caretaker's possession of a number of assets such as financial means, education, and life experience. Thus, whichever spouse was best equipped to be the caretaker would assume some leadership in the marital relations, not as an absolute right, but as a necessary aspect of providing care and support. According to him, it was a flawed understanding of the religious sources to obligate a wife to be obedient to her husband in exchange for the latter's role as a financial provider. Rather, he saw that both spouses should defer to one another in a marital relationship based on love, compassion, and consultation.

Amna Nosseir, Professor of Islamic Philosophy at Ain-Shams University, also defined *qiwama* as an Islamic obligation to provide financial support for one's spouse. She argued that this obligation was originally placed on the shoulders of the husband. However, it was not an absolute obligation and could be reinterpreted in the context of the realities of today's world where husbands and wives shared responsibility. Like Bayoumy, she disassociated wifely obedience from the husband's financial role and did not see the former as an obligation that solely fell on the wife. Instead, she defined it as the mutual obligation of both spouses to respect and defer to one another.[15] However, Nosseir did not agree with restricting polygyny for all men – but only for those who were unable to provide for multiple wives. Nosseir attributed the challenges of reforming Egyptian personal status laws to: (1) the rising dominance of what she called 'Bedouin jurisprudence' that was being exported from Gulf countries since the widespread Egyptian migration to these countries; and (2) the absence of an understanding of Islamic philosophy in the religious knowledge that was being produced and consumed in the country at the time. Nosseir saw that a philosophically grounded religious knowledge facilitated finding the commonalities between human rights conventions such as CEDAW and those of Islamic Shari'a. She pointed out that she herself was asked by women's rights organizations to determine and analyse the compatibility of CEDAW and the principles and doctrines of Islamic Shari'a, and her finding was that the two were '80 per cent similar'.

Zeinab Radwan, Professor of Islamic Jurisprudence at Cairo University, is another religious scholar who had been pushing for the proposed reforms through her scholarship. In her book *Woman Between Heritage and Modernity* (2003), she defined Islamic marriage as one in which both spouses found comfort with one another, and in which a wife had the right to freely choose her partner, to receive dower, to be financially supported by her husband, to be sexually fulfilled and pleasured by her partner, to be well treated, and to have the right to claim divorce through *khul* or to insert stipulations in marriage contracts. Radwan saw a husband's unilateral right to repudiation as a flawed understanding of the Qur'anic injunctions on divorce. In fact, according to Radwan, the Qur'an restricted the right of husbands to initiate divorce by obligating them to resort to familial arbitration before they decided upon divorce, and if husbands decided to initiate divorce, they were obligated by the sacred text to make known (to the wife and others) their pronouncement of divorce so that the post-divorce waiting period (*idda*) could be calculated and accordingly the wife's financial rights could be secured.[16] Moreover, Radwan saw the Qur'anic injunction that prohibited men from divorcing their wives during their menstruation or when they had sexual intercourse with them as a means to put checks on men's rash resort to divorce. Radwan also argued that *qiwama* was an obligation rather than a right and was not a male prerogative. She interpreted the Qur'anic verse 34, chapter 4 to mean that both males and females could be equally obligated to take care of and provide for their spouses. This obligation was to be assigned to any of the spouses who possessed the necessary human and material assets such as good health, physical strength, intelligence, piety, and financial means.

Radwan faulted the methodologies used by current religious scholars for lacking critical engagement with the religious tradition.[17] Since 2000, she has written a number of papers that were presented in workshops organized by women's rights groups and published in the print media. In her writing, she has called for a new religious interpretation that equates the court testimony of a female witness to that of a male; equates the court testimony of the non-Muslim with a Muslim, and gives the non-Muslim wife the right to inherit from her Muslim husband. Although Radwan's work was based on careful religious scholarship, her recent arguments have run into concerted opposition from a number of scholars in the religious establishment. For example, in an article published by the daily newspaper *Akhbar Al Youm* on 28 March 2008, six of the members of the Islamic Research Academy, in addition to Farid Abd il Wasil, former Grand Mufti of Egypt, opposed Radwan's arguments. These scholars argued that Radwan's interpretations were contradicting the consensus reached by early jurists on these matters. Another significant reason for their opposition was their rejection of individual scholars (such as Radwan) taking part in the interpretive process, a task which they think should only be carried out by the religious establishment.

Perhaps part of the opposition to Radwan's interpretive project was also related to her being the Speaker of the now-dissolved Parliament and a member of the Women's Committee at the NDP. That is, Radwan's scholarly and interpretive contribution to reform efforts were undermined by her role as a political actor in a regime that was increasingly losing credibility and legitimacy in the eyes of the Egyptian public amidst widespread practices of corruption and oppression. A few months after the 25th January Revolution in 2011, a strong backlash against the post-2000 reforms was initiated by the Society for the Rescue of the Egyptian Family, a newly formed organization of divorced non-custodial fathers and their supporters, and the Men of Revolution, a new organization established by Islamist lawyers. Both organizations viciously attacked Zeinab Radwan and Farkhounda Hassan, the Secretary General of the NCW, and accused them of aiding the wife of the former President in introducing 'un-Islamic' family laws that, according to them, destroyed the Egyptian family and increased divorce rates.

Gamal El Banna, who died in 2013, was another religious voice heard not only in support of many of the reforms proposed by the government and women's rights organizations, but also in outlining the challenge of changes he thought were necessary in order to have a just model of marriage. El Banna, the brother of the former leader of the Muslim Brotherhood, adopted a historical method by which he traced many of the rules of early jurists (who discriminate against women) in shaping the trajectory of the establishment of a political Islamic system. He traced this system to the period of Islamic empire in which rulers were concerned with consolidating their political powers, and he argued that Islamic jurisprudence was deified because it was part of a political process of controlling different societal sectors and maintaining asymmetrical power relations (between male and female, Arab and non-Arab, Muslim and non-Muslim, slave master and slave).

El Banna saw Shari'a as a historically conditioned understanding of the Qur'an; considered all Qur'anic verses pertaining to human life and relations as open to interpretation; and filtered his understanding of the sayings of Prophet Mohamed through the standards of credibility of transmission sources and the compatibility of the content of the prophetic saying with what is perceived and accepted as the common good nowadays. This methodology enabled El Banna to arrive at very bold proposals for marital relations and roles. He argued that Islamic marriage should not be based on the necessity of giving a dower to the wife, and that men and women should have equal rights to initiate marriage and divorce.[18]

El Banna faulted the religious establishment for its inability to break free from a long tradition of deifying the teachings of early jurists. Despite his position, which seemed to go further than most religious scholars in pushing for a model of marriage based on complete equality between the spouses, El Banna was seen as a controversial figure, and during his lifetime he was avoided by both government and some feminist reformers. This may be related to some of his controversial religious opinions – for instance, he argued that a smoker's fasting was still admissible if he or she smoked during fasting hours. He also argued that veiling was not a required religious practice; moreover, he considered it unhelpful for present-day Muslim women. But another important reason, in my view, is that El Banna was not an Azhar-trained scholar, and hence was not perceived by many public intellectuals and religious scholars as being part of the mainstream community of religious scholars.[19]

My goal in presenting and analysing some of the arguments of the above-mentioned religious scholars is to unpack the religion-based frameworks of reform. These scholars supported most of the proposed changes in the substantive laws. Some of the scholars were actively working with women's rights organizations or government agencies, while others, such as El Banna, were pushing for an even more radical reform agenda. Yet they varied in their views of the challenges encountered in reforming family laws; in the ways in which they interrogated and reinterpreted the imparted tradition of juristic knowledge; as well as in their impact on the efforts undertaken by governmental and non-governmental reformers.

Dissenting voices: culturalist or religious purists?

Some religious groups, however, voiced their opposition to some or most of the proposed legal reforms. I will focus on one group named the International Islamic Committee for Woman and Child (IICWC). IICWC was founded in 1995 under the auspices of the International Islamic Council for Religious Call and Rescue. IICWC sees itself as an international movement whose aims, as stated on their website, are 'to preserve the Islamic identity of Muslim women and children; to face all plans aiming at stripping them of it; to present the prestigious value of women in Islamic Shari'a; to improve and promote Muslim women in all areas through symposia and training programmes; to unify exerted efforts of Muslim women organizations and entities that represent women and children'.[20] The IICWC is headquartered in Egypt and headed by the Egyptian Camilia Helmy, who previously worked as an engineer before she assumed her work in the committee more than a decade ago.

In an interview conducted for this research, Helmy defined

the mission of IICWC as shielding Muslim families from the threat of the West, presented in UN organizations and international conventions such as CEDAW.[21] Helmy argued that such conventions sought to erase the 'Islamic identity' of Muslim societies by changing their personal status laws. Thus, one of IICWC's main tasks had been to review and critique existing and newly proposed personal status laws, which were found by the committee to be espousing the principles and values of international conventions. Helmy, for instance, saw male *qiwama* and wifely obedience as central to Islamic marriage. Pamphlets produced by the IICWC define *qiwama* as a husband's protection and guardianship over his wife. Moreover, *qiwama* is not simply based on a husband's religious duty as the provider for the family, but also on his role as the moral authority and guide for his wife and children. Helmy dismissed the model of marriage proposed by the NWRO, which emphasized equal partnership and cooperation between spouses, as un-Islamic and unjust to women because it deprived them of the right to the protection of their husbands. Helmy also objected to changing the minimum legal marriage age of women from 16 to 18, and giving women the right to obtain *khul* divorce without the approval of their husband.

To counter the model of family and marital roles constructed by CEDAW, the IICWC spearheaded an initiative to compile a Charter for Muslim Families. The charter was published in 2007, after seven years of work by a group of well-known religious scholars from the region, including Mohamed Imara, the Qatar-based Egyptian religious scholar, Youssef El Qardawi, the President of the International Union for Muslims, and Ali Gomaa, the Grand Mufti of Egypt. The idea of the charter is to provide a legal model for the drafting of family laws in Muslim countries. The charter consists of 164 articles which are grouped in five chapters. It is mixed in the rights it grants women and the restrictions it imposes on them. For instance, Article 59 in the charter dictates that the husband is to be the provider, the caregiver, and the guardian of the family. Article 68 affirms a wife's right to work provided that this work is religiously permissible and serves the interest of the woman, her children, and the community, but the same article also dictates that both husband and wife must be in agreement about her work. Article 72 dictates that a husband should help his working wife with the housework. Article 73 dictates that a wife obeys her husband in all that is 'permissible and good', and Article 75 gives the husband the right to forbid his wife from going to entertainment places where 'immodest and immoral acts are committed'. However, Article 54 gives the wife the right to enter stipulations into her marriage contract and dictates that these stipulations should be upheld by the court.

Perhaps the Family Charter is mixed in the rights it grants and denies women because it was drafted by a diverse group of religious scholars, some of whom do not espouse the mission and perspective of the IICWC. However, the *modus vivendi* of the IICWC's discourse and advocacy work remains resistant to what it sees as a Western secular onslaught on the Muslim identity and on the values of Muslim families. The 'other' to be resisted is defined as international conventions and global agendas that promote gender equality, and the site of this struggle and resistance becomes the family laws. Yet this obsession with self-preservation and resistance against a 'Western' other, I believe, led to the failure of IICWC to: (1) address the real problems existing on the ground for women who were living the kind of gendered model of marriage which the IICWC was promoting; and (2) engage substantively with the arguments of religious scholars calling for reforms in family laws.

An example of the first failure is when the IICWC rejected the proposal to increase the legal marriage age for Egyptian women from 16 to 18 on the grounds that there was no defined marriage age for either women or men in Islamic jurisprudence. But what was overlooked by IICWC members like Helmy is the abuses that Egyptian female minors suffer from when married off at a young age; this is a particularly serious problem for under-age girls who are married off to older men from Gulf countries. An example of the second failure was the IICWC's rejection of the recently introduced *khul* law despite the undisputed existence of a Muslim woman's right to this kind of divorce in classical Islamic law, as well as its prevalence in pre-codification eras in Egypt and elsewhere in the region.

Western feminism and alternative religion-based models of reform

In what follows, I wish to shed light on a distinct kind of religion-based reform discourse in Egypt. This discourse is not merely concerned with whether the proposed new laws were compatible with the principles and doctrines of Shari'a; it also engages with issues such as re-examining the role of the Muslim family, female subjectivity, and the role of the state in regulating family relations and roles. Moreover, this discourse questions the role of law in bringing about social transformation.

Mohamed Imara, the Egyptian religious scholar and author of *The Islamic Emancipation of Women* (2001), rejects what he sees as two dominant but highly problematic models for shaping gender roles and rights within marriage. The first is what he calls a secularist Western model premised on an adversarial relationship between the male and female and able to envision the empowerment of women only through an individualistic subjectivity emancipated from religious norms. Imara argues that the weakness of this model is that it inhibits the wholeness and the real enjoyment of individual freedom, which – he believes – cannot be shaped through reaction or resistance, but only through a monotheistic religious tradition and its underlying normative system. On the other hand, Imara is highly critical of what he calls a fundamentalist religion-based model of gender relations in which the role of women, particularly in marriage, is reduced to their being sexual beings created for the pleasure of men, who are denied autonomy and the right to active and empowering public life.

He proposes a third model that grounds the emancipation and the empowerment of women in what he sees as the foundational essence of Islam, namely the equal obligation entrusted to both men and women to be God's vicar on this earth and to lead a life of activity and remembrance. In my interview with him, Imara agreed that existing family laws did not uphold this model and were discriminatory against women. For instance, he pointed out that the Islamic concept of *qiwama* was misunderstood and abused. Imara saw *qiwama* as a spousal obligation to provide for, care for, and guide one's family. He argued that both husbands and wives undertake responsibilities under their role as *qaiim*, or care provider for the family. These responsibilities may or may not be the same for males and females in all cases. In some cases, the husband holds a job and provides for the family, while the wife takes care of the children. In other cases, the wife might be working and both spouses share the housework and child care. Therefore, Imara does not see *qiwama* as a role that is exclusive to a husband. However, he added that it is the husband that is assigned (by sacred texts) the role of leading the family, yet this authority is always kept in check because husbands have a religious obligation to consult wives in all family affairs.[22]

Imara also argued that the legal notion of 'wifely obedience' (*ta'a*), is incongruent with the Islamic model of marriage in which both husbands and wives are expected to defer to one another. He added that the Qur'an put many checks on the man's right to repudiation, so that it does not end up being exercised unilaterally and irresponsibly. However, he acknowledged that these Qur'anic injunctions were not incorporated into state family laws. He is, furthermore, in favour of restricting polygny, which he believes is not intended, in the sacred texts, to be an unconditional right of the husband.

Imara sees the Family Charter as an Islamic guiding framework for reforming family laws. However, he believes that law making is a limited tool for social transformation. To him, what really needs to change are the prevalent cultural norms that trap women in inferior, disempowered, and sexualized roles, but he has pointed out that the difficulty of bringing about a cultural and normative transformation in the society arose from the practice of cloaking gendered cultural norms that discriminate against women in religious arguments and language. This discourse, according to Imara, is partly rooted in some stigmatizing ideas about women's status and roles that are found in the work of early jurists, and partly in the new forms of gendered religious knowledge that continue to marginalize women and erase their multidimensional contributions to their families and societies.

I think Imara's arguments raise two important points. First, they highlight the need to ground religion-based reform agendas in a coherent Islamic philosophy of a Muslim self and its relation to others in society. It is precisely the lack of this distinct notion of a Muslim subjectivity in the discourse of international conventions of human rights that Imara finds problematic and inhibiting to empowering and positive gender relations and roles. Second, Imara raises the issue of the adequacy of law as a tool for social transformation because, according to him, law shapes and operates the daily lives of people in much less powerful and more diluted ways than other institutions (such as mosques, schools, family) do.

Heba Raouf, Professor of Political Science at Cairo University and a well-known female public thinker and Islamic scholar, also voiced misgivings about the role of law in reforming gender relations and rights.[23] However, Raouf's concerns about the law are somewhat different from Imara's. She cautions against the problems of seeking equal gender rights primarily through legal reforms because, according to her, it allowed a corrupt state which lacked credibility among its citizens to assume an even more intrusive role in their daily lives, by regulating their family lives and marital relations. In addition, Raouf believes that by focusing on changing laws, reforming other influential societal institutions was relegated to second or third place. Yet it is precisely by institutions such as mosques, schools, and the family that cultural and religious norms are shaped, distorted, or changed.

Raouf's call for a multidimensional reform project is connected to her goal of creating the space that enables the emergence of new male and female Muslim subjectivities and modalities for Muslim families. In her numerous articles in *Islam Online*, she talks about the need for new societal norms that equally value men and women for their personal achievements; consider self-confidence and speaking one's mind to be just as much female qualities as they are male; do not perceive modesty as a female virtue and a male weakness; and equally value the sexual rights of both wives and husbands. In addition, Raouf argues against the prevalent notion of family in current Egyptian society. This notion depicts the Egyptian family as sacred, untouchable, and to be privileged at all times over the interests of its individual members. Raouf instead calls for a model in which the family's stability and cohesiveness are still important, yet the family does not take precedence over the well-being of its individual members. Accordingly, Raouf does not see divorce as intrinsically the disintegration of a family, but more like a new ordering of familial relations and roles, which is sometimes necessary for the happiness of individual members.

Raouf rejects Western feminism. Like Imara, she sees that such a project is an unsuitable framework for reform in Muslim countries because, according to her, it is historically premised on the rejection of religious traditions (Christianity in the first place) that are thought to favour men above women. This historical trajectory of the Western feminist project, according to Raouf, results in an inherent tension between the ideational framework and goals of this project and that of religion as a normative system. Islam, on the other hand, Raouf argues, provides an adequate model for emancipating Muslim women because the starting point and the end result under this framework are not the woman's relation to man, but her role as God's vicar on this earth.

Nonetheless, Raouf acknowledges the challenges of distorted religious knowledge and interpretations of the past and present, which hinder the emancipation of Egyptian women. She critiqued the gendered and discriminatory legal opinions of early jurists as well as modern-day forms of gendered religious arguments, *fatwas*, and interpretations. It is important to add, though, that Raouf's interest in and work on gender rights and Islamic law are part and parcel of her larger concern with the issue of social justice in Egypt, and the inhibiting role of the state on the one hand, and the potentially enabling role of civil society on the other.

Supreme Constitutional Court: alternative engagement with religious tradition

While both Imara and Raouf are sceptical of the role of law in reforming gender rights and relations, Supreme Constitutional Court (SCC) Judge Tahany El Gibaly sees her court as playing a significant role in (1) protecting the legal rights gained by women, and (2) providing an enlightened understanding of Shari'a through critical engagement with Islamic jurisprudence.[24]

In the past two decades, a number of significant cases have been brought before the court in which the constitutionality of certain personal status laws were challenged on the basis of their violating Islamic Shari'a, the main source of legislation in the country as stated in Article 2 of the constitution. Some of the disputed laws were those that gave women the right to file for *khul* and prejudicial divorce on the grounds of polygny. The court upheld the constitutionality of these laws, basing its judgement on a significant religious/legal principle, which is the distinction between definitive uncontested Shari'a doctrines and contested flexible interpretations (Brown and Sherif 2004; Hirschl 2008). In addition, the court adopted the principle of upholding Article 2 of the constitution only as part of an organic entity consisting of all the articles in the constitution, rather than as autonomous law standing on its own.

Judge Gibaly argued that the SCC established a new methodology in engaging with sacred texts and Islamic jurisprudence. She believed that this would be helpful to religious scholars, legislators, and other actors who were interested in developing a religious framework for their reform agendas. But the more immediate impact was that the court's interpretive role was likely to protect the hard-earned and the now sought-after legal reforms. Judge Gibaly added that the crucial factor in the success of the interpretive process was to have a clear understanding of the distinction between the guiding objectives of the Shari'a and its directives. According to her, it is the former that should always guide law making, and in her opinion the most important of these are to serve the public good and to do no harm. Thus, she argued that it was religiously sanctioned to suspend the rules of the Qur'anic verses in some cases if those did not serve the good of the community. Furthermore, Judge Gibaly saw that there was a lot of open space for critical engagement and reinterpretation of the rules of the Islamic schools of jurisprudence She took issue with contemporary religious scholars who rejected new interpretations if they went against the consensus of early jurists; in this respect she wondered what the point of an interpretive process was if it was shackled by the weight of preponderant opinions among early jurists.

Thus, while the SCC was not directly taking a part in the debate, the reform efforts of women's rights activists had been strengthened by the SCC's rulings on cases that were directly concerned with women's rights as well as the public position of some of its notable judges (such as Judge Gibaly) on gender rights and the need for an enlightened dynamic interpretation of sacred texts and juristic knowledge in the process of law-making. It is perhaps also the reputation that the SCC enjoys for juristic independence and integrity in much of the mainstream media that also made the court a valuable source of support for women's rights activists.

Conclusion

In this chapter, I have sought to shed light on a public debate that was taking place in Egypt in the period from 2007 to 2010 as initiatives were being proposed by the government and women's rights organizations to draft a comprehensive family code. It was a debate that was taking place on TV talk shows and in printed media as well as through the production and consumption of new religious scholarship.

It is common and temptingly easy in the public discourse in Egypt (and elsewhere) to reduce contestations about reforming Muslim family laws solely to the question of religion. But I have argued here that the debate and the disagreement among different interlocutors were about multiple issues that went beyond the question of religion. These issues could be summarized as follows: struggles among different religious discourses for legitimacy; the contradictions of seeking gender justice through state institutions such as the law in a context where citizens were suffering from state oppression and its failure to ensure their citizenship rights; and disagreements among different actors who sought (or endorsed) gender justice in the family domain, about the suitability of global feminism (inspired by international conventions) as a credible framework for advocacy and action.

Notes

1   The existing substantive personal status laws are PSL No. 25 of 1920 and PSL No. 25 of 1929, amended by PSL No. 100 of 1985.

2   The National Council for Women was established by the government in 2000. Its goals were (1) to promote policies to strengthen women's rights and enhance their development; and (2) to monitor the implementation and impact of government policies that pertain to women.

3   The first elected Parliament after the revolution was dissolved in June 2012 by the Supreme Constitutional Court. While the dissolved Parliament was in seat, a draft law to abolish or make substantive amendments to the *khul* law was proposed to Parliament by one of its members, Mohamed El Oumda, backed by several groups and factions in the society opposing the reforms that were introduced in the personal status laws in Mubarak's era. The most vocal of these groups were the Society for the Rescue of Egyptian Family, a newly formed organization of divorced non-custodial fathers and their supporters, and the Men of Revolution, a new organization established by Islamist

lawyers. Also, Montaser Zayad, a well-known lawyer and member of the Muslim Brotherhood, published two articles in the daily newspaper *Masry el Youm* on 19 and 20 April 2011 in which he described the *khul* law as incompatible with the Islamic Shari'a, and as the mere product of the personal agenda of key figures in the previous regime such as Suzanne Mubarak, the wife of the former President.

4   Family laws in Egypt, which are known as personal status laws, are divided into two types, procedural and substantive. Procedural personal status laws regulate the legal processes and court proceedings in family dispute cases, while the substantive laws define and determine legal rights, roles, and relations concerning different aspects of familial life such as marriage, divorce, parenting, child guardianship and custody, and inheritance.

5   The choice of these interviewees was based on their active involvement in either the reform efforts or debates. Their participation was variously in the form of publishing books on the matter, taking part in workshops organized by different advocates for the proposed reforms, reviewing and commenting on drafts of personal status laws through their work in the Islamic Research Academy, and contributing to the debate about the issue in the printed media as well as on TV shows. Eight of the interviews were conducted by the author, and one by Sawsan El Sherif, the author's research assistant.

6   El Gibaly is the first female to assume the judicial bench. She was appointed by former President Mubarak to the Supreme Consitutional Court in 2003.

7   Marwa Sharafeldin is an Egyptian researcher and doctoral candidate at Oxford University. The paper was based on interviews conducted by Sharafeldin with key figures in six women's rights organizations: the Association for Enhancement and Development of Women (ADEW); New Women's Foundation; Women and Memory Group; Egyptian Centre for Women's Rights; Forum for Women in Development; and Centre for Egyptian Women's Legal Assistance (CEWLA). The background paper was commissioned by the Social Research Center, the American University in Cairo, as part of the activities of a four-year study at the centre, led by Mulki Al-Sharmani, on reforms in Egyptian personal status laws since 2000 and women's empowerment.

8   Personal communication with three members of the Women's Committee at the NDP and of the Legislative Committee at the NCW, June 2008 and September 2008 respectively.

9   The author had the opportunity to review earlier versions of the draft put together by the Women's Committee at the NDP during the first phase of this research project. In addition, the author reviewed the

concept paper drafted by NWRO and attended the workshop they organized for the purpose of discussing it.

10 The first post-revolution constitution of 2012, which has been suspended since the deposing of President Morsi on 3 July 2013, also has a number of contradictions regarding women's citizenship rights. It affirms the state's responsibility to ensure the equality of all Egyptian citizens in opportunities, duties, and rights (Preamble, Principle 4, Article 9, Article 33). However, Article 33, which specifically addresses the equality of all citizens before the law, does not explicitly spell out prohibition of gender-based inequality. In Article 10, the new constitution also affirms the state's responsibility to enable women to reconcile their familial and public roles, and does not make this contingent on compatibility with Islamic Shari'a as was the case in Article 11 of the 1971 constitution. In an earlier draft of the new constitution, this condition was maintained in the article but it was dropped after a lot of opposition from civil society, women's rights organizations, and some of the new liberal political parties. Article 10 of the new constitution also states that the state will provide care and protection to female heads of households, divorced women, and widows. Yet this same article grants the state the responsibility to ensure the preservation of the 'genuine' character of the Egyptian family and its cohesion and stability. Women's rights activists pointed out that this latter part of the article can be used as a loophole through which gender inequality and discrimination against women can be justified. Furthermore, Article 219 defines the principles of Islamic Shari'a, which is, according to the constitution, the source of legislation in the country, in a way that conflates them with majority opinions in classical Sunni Islamic jurisprudence. In other words, this article grants majority opinions in classical Sunni jurisprudence a 'sacred' status and thus makes it difficult to problematize particular doctrines in classical Islamic jurisprudence that condone certain forms of inequality and discrimination against women (for example, minor marriage, or the husband's unfettered right to unilateral repudiation).

11 The activists' frequent use of the term 'objectives of the Shari'a' (*maqaasid al-Shari'a*) denoted an appeal to the notion of the spirit of Islamic law rather than its letter. But the term *maqaasid al-Shari'a* itself historically refers to a theory of interpretation developed by a number of classical jurists, the most notable of whom are al-Ghazali and al-Shatbi.

12 This academy is part of Al-Azhar, the main religious establishment in the country. The academy consists of 40 religious scholars, who are nominated by senior members in the academy and appointed by the

Grand Sheikh of Al-Azhar. One of the main tasks of the academy is to review draft laws before they are presented to Parliament to ascertain whether these proposed laws are in agreement with doctrines of Islamic Shari'a.

13   Article 20 in this law granted women the right to obtain divorce through *khul* in exchange for forfeiting their post-divorce financial rights. In 2004, Law No. 10 was passed, which introduced new mediation-based family courts.

14   Personal interview with the author, June 2008. In his opposition to what he termed the agenda of international organizations, he referred to the International Conference for Population Development (ICPD), which was held in Cairo, Egypt, in 1994.

15   Personal interview with the author, June 2008.

16   During the first three menstrual cycles after the pronouncement of divorce, the wife is entitled to stay in the conjugal home and to receive financial support from the husband. After the end of this waiting period, the divorce becomes final and the wife is entitled to indemnity (if the divorce was caused by no fault of hers).

17   Personal interview with the author, August 2008.

18   Personal interview with the author, July 2008.

19   In an interview with the author, Heba Raouf said that despite his good intentions El Banna was not connected to the religious tradition whether through his methodology or his religious training, and thus was not equipped to interrogate this tradition.

20   See www.un.org/africa/osaa/ngodirectory/dest/countries/Egypt.htm.

21   Personal interview conducted by the author's research assistant, Sawsan Sharif, July 2008.

22   Personal interview with the author, June 2008.

23   Personal interview with the author, August 2008.

24   Personal interview with the author, May 2008.

References

Asad, M. (1980) (translation) *Message of the Qur'an*, Dar Al-Andalus, Gibraltar.

Brown, N. and A. Sherif (2004) 'Inscribing the Islamic Sharia in Arab Constitutional Law', in Y. Haddad and B. Stowasser (eds), *Islamic Law and the Challenges of Modernity*, AltaMira Press, Walnut Creek, CA.

Hirschl, R. (2008) 'The Judicialization of Mega Politics and the Rise of Political Courts', *Annual Review of Political Science*, 11, pp. 93–118.

Imara, M. (2001) *Islamic Emancipation of Women*, Dar El Shorouk (Arabic Publication), Cairo.

Radwan, Z. (2003) *Women between Heritage and Modernity*, Dar El Shorouk (Arabic Publication), Cairo.

Sharafeldin, M. (2008) 'NGOs' Use of Religious Discourse in Personal Status Law Reform in Egypt', September, Social Research Center, American University in Cairo.

4

Men Aboard?

Movement for a Uniform Family Code in Bangladesh
• •

Sohela Nazneen

> This is not a movement for legal reform but a political movement.
> How will you make this a part of the larger political agenda? How
> would you convince us (men)?
> (male participant, Uniform Family Code workshop; BMP 1993:
> 251)

In the late 1980s and early 1990s, Bangladeshi feminists and their
allies mobilized for a Uniform Family Code. In what has come
to be perceived as the golden period of the feminist movement in
Bangladesh, feminist groups were able to create broader alliances
with other civil society organizations and human rights groups
participating in an anti-authoritarian movement that emerged at
this time. This made their presence visible within civil society
and also drew attention to the issues they were promoting.
During the early 1990s, the period of democratic transition, there
was a greater willingness among feminists to engage with the
state on various reform issues. The state was also willing to open
up policy spaces to various women's groups, particularly since it
needed help in preparing for the United Nation's Fourth World
Women's Conference in Beijing. The chapter focuses on a time
of hope, when these factors encouraged women's organizations
and feminist groups to promote the agenda of a Uniform Family
Code.

The women's organizations,[1] along with feminist lawyers'
networks and other civil society organizations, drafted the
required legal changes, engaged in discussions with different

sections of society, and extensively lobbied the state for legal reforms to create a Uniform Family Code. Despite the wide-scale mobilization among women's organizations and their allies, especially the discussion this generated in the media and at the state level, the movement failed to attain its goal. This chapter aims to explore the strategies used by feminist organizations, the reasons for employing these strategies, and why they failed to produce the desired result.

The movement for a Uniform Family Code occupies a prominent part in the history of the feminist movement in Bangladesh. It pushed different women's groups to form alliances and challenged feminists to reassess their strategies and positions. There are very few studies that analyse the strategies employed and their impact. Most of the studies describe the different events (BMP 1993), or focus on how the problem of cultural relativism should be addressed, or discuss the nature of legal changes required to ensure equity for women in matters such as divorce, inheritance, or guardianship (Pereira 2002). This chapter aims to address this gap. By analysing the reform strategies they used, it investigates the difficulties feminists had to negotiate and the pitfalls they experienced in demanding a Uniform Family Code. This analysis has a wider relevance, since feminists in many other countries may have experienced similar difficulties.

The chapter makes the following argument. The demand for a uniform code in Bangladesh challenges the male privileges based on Anglo-Mohammedan law and other religious laws of the minority communities. The feminists in Bangladesh were aware that their demand would be portrayed as a majoritarian imposition on the religious freedom of the minority communities. Thus, the feminist demand for a uniform code which is based on a 'right to equality' would be pitted against the 'right to religion' of minority communities. 'Right to equality' in this context implies women belonging to different religious communities possessing the same rights in matters related to divorce, guardianship, maintenance, and inheritance. It also implies possessing the same rights as men in these matters. The 'right to religion' in Bangladesh translates as different religious communities being free to practise their religion and live according to its dictates – in a word, non-interference by the state in personal matters.

In order to demonstrate that these two rights are not mutually exclusive, the feminists focused on changing their discursive framework of advocacy. This was done by 'framing and packaging' (Tarrow 1998) the demand for a Uniform Family Code as a social justice issue and drawing on constitutional sanctions and the international conventions on women's rights. Women's organizations also created alliances with feminist and human rights lawyers to work on the necessary legal changes to establish legitimacy for the proposed reforms. They also tried to use the 'media as transmitters' (Gaventa and McGee 2010) of how proposed changes lead to equitable outcomes for women. These efforts to introduce a Uniform Family Code strengthened the feminist debate, and the lobbying of state officials gave the issue a higher profile. But these endeavours did not create support for the code at the grassroots. Feminist failure to tackle male fear and incorporate men in the movement, particularly men belonging to the minority communities, left the space open for a backlash against the movement.

The data used in this chapter were collected as a part of a larger project exploring how feminist organizations built constituencies for demanding gender justice in 2008–9. The larger study focused on three national-level women's organizations: Bangladesh Mohila Parishad (BMP), a mass-level women's organization; Naripokkho, a feminist activist organization; and Women for Women (WFW), a feminist research and policy advocacy organization. These organizations are the pioneers in advocating for women's rights in Bangladesh. Open-ended interviews,[2] participatory workshops with members of these organizations, and organizational document analysis were used to collect data on the strategies employed by the organizations to mobilize support for various gender equity causes among their own members and their allies within civil society, political parties, and the state bureaucracy. To supplement the findings on the strategies, interviews were conducted with feminist and human rights activists of other organizations, particularly with members of the Bangladesh National Women Lawyers' Association (BNWLA) and Ain O Salish Kendra (Law and Mediation Centre), which emerged as key actors in the movement for a Uniform Family Code.

The political and social context in Bangladesh

An analysis of the strategies used by the feminist organizations needs to take into account the nature of the Bangladeshi state and its relationship with society, the history of the feminist movement, and the changes in the wider social and political systems.

Bangladesh gained independence in 1971 through a war against Pakistan. It is relatively homogeneous in cultural and linguistic terms. A cultural interpretation of Bengali national identity was a key factor in countering the religious national identity, based on Islam, which led to the creation of the eastern (now Bangladesh) and western wings of Pakistan by the British. The state is built on a social structure that is hierarchical by gender and class (Goetz 2001). Patron–client relationships remain the dominant form of social organization for structuring relationships between classes (Hassan 2002). Weak state capacity is due to: (1) continuous aid dependence, though this dependence has decreased significantly in the current decade; and (2) the politicization of the bureaucracy.

Bangladesh went through alternating periods of democratic (1971–5, 1979–82, 1991–2006, 2009–present) and military rule (1975–9, 1982–90, 2006–8).[3] This alternation between different forms of political system created a repressive and confrontational form of political contestation that discouraged women's organizations from engaging in formal party politics. Despite the 30 per cent quota for women in Parliament and local government bodies, and the fact that both centrist parties are led by women, women's rights issues do not command attention in formal politics. All of these factors influenced why the BMP and its allies, in spite of their links with the political left, were reluctant to raise the matter of the formulation of a Uniform Family Code in the wider political discourse.

Another reason why feminist organizations do not engage in the formal political arena when it comes to issues that are linked to religion, is the role religion plays in national politics and the risks associated with being branded as anti-religion. After independence, the party that led the liberation struggle, the Awami League, espoused secularism and incorporated it as a fundamental principle within the constitution, but later it moved away from its secularist position. The other dominant centrist party, the Bangladesh Nationalist Party (BNP) formed by General Zia, removed secularism from the constitution as a fundamental principle through a constitutional amendment in 1976. In 1988, the military dictator, General Ershad, who took over after BNP rule, introduced Islam as a state religion through another amendment. Both of these regimes suspended the ban on Jamaat-e-Islami, the main Islamist party. The key reason behind state sponsorship of Islam by both generals was to legitimize their regimes and ensure friendly relations with the Middle Eastern countries, particularly Saudi Arabia (Hossain 2005).

The anti-authoritarian movement in 1990 was spearheaded by the Awami League and the BNP, and they have dominated the political scene in the post-authoritarian period. The power struggle between the left and the Awami League led to the left's weakening in the 1970s. This created a *de facto* two-party system. In the parliamentary system of government, both centrist parties have entered into tacit and overt alliances with Jamaat-e-Islami in order to win elections and form governments (Nazneen 2008). Both parties highlighted the role of Islam and emphasized the construction of a Bengali Muslim identity (Nazneen 2008). This emphasis on Islam and the tacit or overt alliances with Jamaat have affected both the space and the way in which issues linked to religion are raised in the public sphere, and this is also relevant to the issue of the Uniform Family Code.

In addition, the Awami League and the BNP have managed to penetrate all significant civil society organizations, from professional groups to non-governmental organizations or local associations (Nazneen 2008). This has significantly undermined the ability of civil society organizations to counter the state and promote their interests. The interactions between political parties and civil society organizations are dominated by concerns the latter have about how the relationship would affect their own legitimacy and autonomy. The state has emerged as the key actor with whom the civil society organizations negotiate directly, rather than pursuing their agendas within the formal political sphere. It is within this context that feminist organizations operate and mobilize around different issues.

The women's empowerment agenda is promoted by different actors in Bangladesh: the women's organizations, local and international non-governmental organizations (NGOs), the government, and the donor community. In the 1970s and 1980s, the availability of donor funding for gender-related projects created an incentive for the Bangladeshi state to promote a gender and development agenda (Goetz 2001). This has led to the development of a particular type of women's empowerment discourse that promotes women's productive role, economic empowerment, and family welfare. The state has a contradictory attitude towards women's rights, at times enacting progressive laws and at other times taking measures to sustain patriarchal values and norms (Jahan 1995).

Despite the overwhelming emphasis in the official discourse on women's economic empowerment, feminists have succeeded in advocating for issues that do not fit this agenda. In fact, Bangladesh has a long history of feminist mobilization, going back to the anti-colonial nationalist movements, first against the British and then against the Pakistanis (*ibid.*). In the post-liberation period feminists have mobilized around issues such as women's political participation, economic equality, legal reform of gender-biased laws, and violence against women (*ibid.*).

Personal laws and special laws concerning women in Bangladesh

About 88 per cent of Bangladeshis are Muslims, around 10 per cent are Hindus and the other 2 per cent, including ethnic minorities, belong to other faiths (Nazneen 2008). In Bangladesh, as in other South Asian states, personal status laws as modified by religion, custom, case law, or legislation determine an individual's rights in matters relating to marriage, divorce, maintenance, guardianship, inheritance, and custody. These laws, as they exist, perpetuate women's subordinate position within the family and also 'constitute discrimination between the religious and ethnic groups' (Hossain 1994: 473). For example, Muslim women have the right to divorce if it has been delegated or if it falls under the categories specified by the Shari'a; Hindu women are not entitled to seek a divorce; and Roman Catholic women in Bangladesh cannot divorce. The constitution recognizes the right to equality and stipulates in Article 28 that the state shall not discriminate against citizens on the grounds of sex. It also guarantees equal rights for women in the state and public spheres (Constitution of the Republic of Bangladesh 1972). Article 29 adds that the state can make special provisions in favour of women. Despite these expansive provisions, traditionally the principle of the right to equality has not been applied to the personal laws.

On the whole, the colonial state had left women's position within the family to be governed by personal laws (Hossain 1994). Under British colonial rule, the state was governed through statutes, and case laws codified the Hindu and Muslim personal laws (Anglo-Mohammedan Laws; Mansoor 1999). The 1772 Regulation stated that both Hindus and Muslims would be allowed to be governed by their own laws. These laws were inherited by Bangladesh. The Muslim Personal Law Application Act (Shariat) of 1937, Child Marriage Restraint Act of 1929, and Dissolution of Muslim Marriage Act of 1939 all apply to Muslim women. The Personal Law Application Act of 1937 ensured that Shari'a prevailed over customary law and practices in different parts of British India. The areas that fall under the purview of this act are: marriage (all forms), divorce (all forms), maintenance, inheritance, guardianship, and intestate succession. The Dissolution of Muslim Marriage Act of 1939 grants Muslim women the right to file for judicial divorce, and the Child Marriage Restraint Act of 1929 raised the age of marriage for girls to 14.

The personal status laws underwent piecemeal reforms in countries in South Asia, including Bangladesh, after they gained independence from Britain. The only major family law reform during the Pakistan period was the Muslim Family Laws Ordinance of 1961. This was the result of demands raised by the All Pakistan Women's Association (APWA). APWA members mobilized to change laws regarding polygamy, divorce, and maintenance. The pressure from the women's movement led to the establishment of a Commission on Marriage and Family Law in 1955. The Commission's recommendations were the basis for the Ordinance of 1961. The Ordinance curtailed a husband's right to unilateral divorce (*talaq al bidah*) and required divorce and maintenance claims to be settled through an Arbitration Council. It also required registration of marriage, and provided a standard *kabin nama* (marriage contract) with certain clauses, which allowed the wife to seek enforcement by the court in case of contravention. The Ordinance also provided the option to the husband to delegate the right of divorce to the wife, and required men desiring to marry a second or subsequent times to seek permission from the Arbitration Council (up to four wives only). The Bangladeshi state supplemented these reforms through the Muslim Marriage and Divorce Registration Act of 1974 and the Family Courts Act of 1985. Family Courts have exclusive jurisdiction over five areas: divorce, restitution of conjugal rights, maintenance, custody, and guardianship.

The laws governing Hindus in Bangladesh date back to the British colonial period and have not undergone any reforms, as has happened in India. Hindu marriage is a sacrament and not a contract, and may take place without civil registration. Divorce for Hindu men and women is not permissible. Hindu men can take multiple wives. The position of a Hindu woman regarding maintenance is the same as for a Muslim woman in Bangladesh. Under the *Dayabhaga* law (a particular school of law for the Bengal region) the right to inherit parental property for Hindu women is non-existent. A Hindu widow can inherit her husband's property as life estate (Pereira 2002). The personal status laws of other religious (Christians and Buddhists) and ethnic communities have not undergone even piecemeal reforms during either the Pakistan or the Bangladesh periods.

Nonetheless, there are a number of codes that are uniformly applied to all women regardless of their ethnic or religious background. These laws are the Dowry Prohibition Act of 1980; the Cruelty to Women (deterrent punishment) Ordinance of 1983 and the Nari O Shishu Nirjaton Domon Ain (Prevention of Violence against Women and Children Act) of 2000 (amended in 2003). The Dowry Prohibition Act of 1980 forbids anyone from giving, demanding, or taking dowry. The practice of dowry is prevalent among Hindus and Muslims in Bangladesh; it became prevalent among Muslims from the late 1970s onwards. However, dowry should not be conflated with dower. Muslim brides are entitled to *meher* (dower), generally a sum promised by the husband, and in Bangladesh paid only if the couple divorce. Dowry is one of the major triggers of domestic violence against women, when the husband's and/or the in-laws' demands for material goods and cash are not fulfilled by the women's family (Mansoor 1999). The Cruelty to Women (deterrent punishment) Ordinance of 1983 seeks to deter severe forms of violence against women, such as kidnapping, abduction, trafficking, and rape. The punishment for these offences under the Ordinance is either imprisonment for life or the death penalty. The Nari O Shishu Nirjaton Domon Ain of 2000 is almost identical to the Cruelty to Women (deterrent punishment) Act of 1983, but incorporates some of the important concerns of the women's movement. It makes sexual harassment a punishable offence; addresses the issues of compensation for survivors of rape and of security of women in police custody; and prohibits the disclosure of the identity of acid attack and rape survivors. None of the above codes effectively addressed violence against women within the family, however, and this was part of the justification for the Domestic Violence Act, finally enacted in 2010 though its rules of procedure have yet to be formulated.

Notwithstanding the above-mentioned legal reforms that address the problem of violence against women, women from different religious groups are not faring well under existing personal laws. Hindu women's rights in matters such as marriage, divorce, and inheritance are severely curtailed in Bangladesh. Christian women also face restrictions in obtaining divorce, alimony, and guardianship. Muslim family law reforms during the Pakistan and Bangladesh period have fallen short of addressing women's needs. The unilateral power of the husband to divorce has remained substantially unrestricted, with the husband only being required to notify the Arbitration Council. Issues such as custody of children remain unaddressed. The punishment for men entering into polygamous marriages without obtaining the permission of the Arbitration Council is one year's imprisonment, a clearly inadequate deterrent that is rarely enforced. Very few Muslim women inherit parental property or seek redress in court. The Family Court as it stands also serves as the lowest level of civil court presided over by Assistant Judges. The judges only hear family court cases one day a week, which leads to a backlog (Mansoor 1999). The legal procedures remain difficult for women to navigate. In addition, special acts such as the Nari O Shishu Nirjaton Domon Ain of 2000 do not take cognizance of domestic violence. It is in the light of these difficulties and shortcomings faced while trying to provide legal aid to women that women's organizations demanded a Uniform Family Code.

Uniform Family Code: the proposed changes

The Uniform Family Code, proposed by the feminists, consisted of uniform and gender-sensitive articles in the following areas:

marriage, divorce, inheritance, guardianship, maintenance, and custody. It set the marriage age for women at 18 and for men at 21. The code stated that irrespective of the ritual aspects of marriage under different religious traditions, all marriages should be registered under civil law. This implies that Hindu marriage would have to be formally registered. It also stated that polygamy would be punishable for all citizens of Bangladesh, which curtails the right of Muslim and Hindu men to take multiple wives. The code proposed that both the husband and the wife have equal rights over property acquired during marriage, which is not the customary practice in Bangladesh. The code also detailed the grounds and process for filing for divorce. It allows for both men and women of any religion to file for divorce through an arbitration council. This proposed right to divorce was particularly significant for Hindus and Roman Catholic women and men because they did not have this right. Under the new code, maintenance could be claimed by women during marriage and after divorce until the husband or wife remarries, the latter not being the customary practice. Also, the wife would provide maintenance to the husband if he is physically or psychologically ill. Both parents would have equal rights to legal guardianship over their children. In the case of the death of both parents or dissolution of the marriage, the court would decide on guardianship over the children. The code also granted men and women the right to inherit an equal share of property. The proposed law designated the following family members as primary inheritors: mother, father, husband, wife, sons, daughters, and adopted children. It also recognized sisters and brothers as secondary inheritors. In short, the changes proposed by the new code were a radical departure from what is practised under current personal status laws in Bangladesh.

Strategies used for mobilization: why were they ineffective?

The BMP, the largest women's organization in Bangladesh with 150,000 members, first proposed the idea of a unified family code and incorporated it into its agenda in 1985. Later on, several women's and human rights organizations, such as Ain O Salish Kendra (ASK), BNWLA, and WFW also took up the issue.[4] The activities of these organizations in the late 1980s largely centred on organizing national-level seminars and workshops that brought together lawyers, judges, journalists, and activists. The BMP also worked closely with women lawyers to draft the Uniform Family Code. Other women's rights organizations later collaborated with the BMP to modify the code. It was presented and publicized in the media, and through workshops with civil society organizations at the divisional and district levels, as well as with the state. However, by the beginning of the 2000s the movement had reached a stagnant phase.

Why did the movement fail? On the surface it had a significant chance of success. It was taken up by the largest women's organization in Bangladesh, which had an extensive grassroots network. The organization had created coalitions and networks with allies such as other women's organizations, women lawyers, and human rights organizations. The ability to mobilize specialist knowledge led to detailed research and ensured quality in drafting the proposed reforms. The BMP also emphasized that their demand for change was based on the organization's and their allies' experience of providing legal aid at the grassroots level. This provided legitimacy to the campaign and ensured that the government could not dismiss it as 'lightweight'. The following statement by BMP highlights these issues.

> Our work on women's rights and experience of providing legal aid show that these religious personal laws are biased, discriminatory and undemocratic. Women experience discrimination and inequality since they do not have equal rights under religious personal law and these experiences are also linked to family violence. (BMP 1993: 36)

The coalition of organizations mobilizing for the new law targeted the media to promote their cause. Workshops were held in divisional and district towns, which were well attended and reported on by journalists. However, some of the activists interviewed for this study (interview with the BMP Vice-President, 30 August 2008; interview with a general member, 31 August 2008) pointed out that these strategies were not effective in reaching the grassroots. A quick scan of the participant lists of the 147 workshops held in district and divisional cities reveals that many of the participants were members of BMP's local branch offices or members of the local bar associations or journalist associations, or were students. They were mainly from the elite section of local society and this perhaps indicates that discussion on the issue remained limited within a specific class of people.

So what led to the difficulties? A key aspect in successful movement building is how issues are framed or how groups develop shared understandings of 'certain meanings and problem-definitions' as legitimate (Leach and Scoones 2007: 11). This also implies that success requires being able to define 'meanings' that are compelling to the grassroots and/or the state, and which limit the opposition's ability to disrupt the reform process. The demand for a Uniform Family Code was framed as a social justice issue and linked to the ideals of Bengali nationalism and development. The following statements issued by BMP in the different Uniform Family Code workshops highlight these points:

> Democratization and development of a country relies on women's empowerment ... and ensuring the rights of women. The constitution of 1972 placed secularism as one of the state principles ... derived from the ideals of our nationalist movement.... Currently, women are deprived of these rights and face economic and social inequality and violence.... (BMP 1993: 23–4)

This type of framing deliberately moved the issue of reform away from Western cultural values and to some extent from the wider international referents (notably the UN Convention on Elimination of Discrimination against Women, CEDAW). The reports that contained summaries of speeches and discussions of the 147 workshops organized by BMP from the period 1994 to 2000 made only three explicit references to CEDAW and the feminist movement in the West. Interestingly, there are also very few references to the family law reforms in other Muslim-majority countries in this publication, though some of these reforms, such as the Tunisian family law code, are mentioned (BMP 1993). Admittedly, CEDAW and other international conventions are evoked by Bangladeshi feminists while advocating for different sets of demands. However, the conscious efforts by BMP and their feminist allies to link the formulation of a Uniform Family Code to fulfilling the ideals of the Bangladeshi nationalist movement and of development, placed it as a home-grown issue and thus increased the potential for gaining public support.

As stated earlier, the civil society space is polarized, with one camp aligning itself to the core principles of the nationalist movement, including secularism. The framing of the issue within the secular discourse was a deliberate choice on the part of the feminists to signal their loyalty towards Bengali identity. This allowed the movement to appeal to organizations and actors who subscribe to the nationalist ideals or profess to be 'secular with liberal values'. Feminists also felt that linking their claims to constitutional obligation, development, and social justice would create a space for the state to respond to these claims and allow it to avoid being branded as anti-Islamic. The following statement by a BMP senior leader makes this clear:

> The state faces a very sensitive situation regarding the Islamists. You have to create space for the state to respond without the fear of backlash, which is why we brought in the issue of constitutional obligation and development.... We tried to claim legitimacy by highlighting how this is linked to *our* liberation struggle and Bengali identity. (Interview with BMP member, 18 July 2008)

References to ideals of the national liberation movement and an emphasis on secularism signalled that the religious organizations, many of which were politically (and ideologically) aligned with the main Islamist party Jamaat,[5] were left out of the coalitions formed for the Uniform Family Code campaign. This limited the scope for a dialogue and negotiations with other religious organizations, some of which may have been willing to engage in discussions around the proposed code, even if they might not have agreed to all the reforms suggested. There were sessions where marriage registrars (*kazi*) and imams were targeted, since a large part of the Uniform Family Code deals with marriage-related laws and requirements. However, engagements with these actors did not create space for engaging with individuals and organizations that are perceived to have legitimacy in matters of religion and personal laws, such as the Islamic Foundation, an autonomous organization that manages the mosques, conducts research, and disseminates the teachings of Islam.[6]

The reluctance on the part of BMP and its allies to engage with religion and religious establishments partly stems from how secularism was integrated within the nationalist movement and liberation struggle. The Bengali national identity stresses the cultural and linguistic (and not religious) identity of the Bengalis, particularly since the original creation of Pakistan (east and west) had been based on shared religious identity. Thus, the need to contain religion within the private sphere was a dominant perception among Bengali feminists and other civil society organizations in the pre- and post-independence period. Given that religion, particularly Islam, has been used as a political tool to challenge women's demands and weaken their claim for equality by the state and other actors, the feminist organizations avoided engagement with the religious organizations and discourse. The following observation by a feminist leader highlights these points:

> For our generation, though some of us are deeply religious, secularism is an important political ideal that led us to confine religion in private. However, for most Bengalis it plays a key role in their private lives and how they act in the wider society…. We have been reluctant to engage with that or explore how religion can be used to further our goals … whether because of political backlash or our own preconceived notions about religion…. (Interview with Naripokkho member, 2 December 2008. The Uniform Family Code was not formally a part of Naripokkho's agenda; however, individual members had joined the movement.)

But this does not imply that there was no debate among the feminists themselves about engaging with religious actors or the value of proposing reforms within a religious framework. In fact, these strategies were extensively debated (Interview with ASK member, 12 May 2009). However, the majority were not willing to engage with reinterpreting religious texts and risk being branded as anti-Islamic. Interestingly, non-engagement with religious actors or religious texts did not prevent the religious right from accusing the Uniform Family Code of being anti-Islamic. Also, the emphasis on tying the Uniform Family Code to secularism created a divide between feminist organizations/leaders and the grassroots, for whom religion played a key role in private matters.

There were also extensive discussions among activists about different religious laws and codes governing the women of minority communities and the required changes. The negotiations were protracted among the feminists about what should be included in the draft code (interview with BMP member, 12 May 2009). These debates highlighted the diversity among the different communities to which the feminists belonged, an issue that is generally under-explored within the movement. The debates within the feminist movement made them aware of the inequality that is experienced by women of different communities in matters that fall under religious personal status law. The need for reform was justified as a social justice issue since rights of women were different depending on their religion. This situation, feminists argued, violated the 'right to equality' promised in the constitution. The following statement in the draft Uniform Family Code illustrates this point.

> Given that there are differences in religious personal law of each community, the rights of women in Bangladesh are different when it comes to the matter of marriage, divorce, inheritance etc.... The constitution states that all citizens are equal before the law.... We cannot have laws that create inequality between citizens of the same country. (BMP 1993: 24)

It was hoped that the emphasis on the 'right to equality' and also the creation of a code by feminist legal experts which had its base in legal aid provision at the grassroots would create a new discursive context. So what went wrong?

Unpacking resistance

Despite feminist efforts to place the issue of reform in family laws under a 'right to equality' discourse, minority communities' 'right to religion' became a key issue that was used by mainstream religious organizations and minority groups to create a backlash against the movement. The resistance against the reform came from Islamic political parties, including Jamaat e Islami (Shehabuddin 2008) and various organizations formed by the minority communities.

For one thing, Islamic religious groups questioned the legitimacy of the BMP and their allies in representing the voice of ordinary Muslim women. They also took issue with the principle of secularism, which was the basis of the advocacy and mobilization work of the feminists. These religious groups argued that secularism as a principle had been abandoned by the state when it amended the constitution in the mid-1970s. Islam was the state religion of Bangladesh (Eighth Amendment), and the religion of about 88 per cent of the population. They thus stressed that personal status laws – which, according to them, should be dictated by Shari'a – form a key component of the Bengali Muslim identity. They also argued that under Islam women received their equitable entitlements, which did not need to be changed (Shehabuddin 2008). Men's unilateral rights to repudiation, polygamy, and guardianship over children were expected to be the key issues of disagreement between the reformers and the Islamic religious groups, but it was the proposed changes in inheritance law that drew the most hostile comments. Changes in Muslim inheritance laws in a populous country that is also strapped for land, and where the dominant practice is that women do not inherit property from their families, was seen as a challenge to the economic privilege of men.

For men belonging to the minority communities, the prospect of a uniform code implied different types of losses: loss of rights to practise their religion, loss of identity, and possible loss of property. These communities argued that the personal status laws by which both men and women of the minority groups lived were crucial to the way religion operated within their lives. The notion of a Uniform Family Code posed the fear of loss of their religious identity. These men also argued that the state's duty to uphold secularism as a constitutional principle meant that it should protect every community's right to its own religion. A Uniform Family Code would undermine this state duty. One of the BNWLA activists recalled the debates:

> It was X (an influential Hindu leader) who said: 'Why are you interfering in our lives? You are not one of us! How we treat our women is our business. These codes (Hindu codes) are ancient. They define who we are ... our relations within the home.... The state cannot change this and claim that it is secular.... Is not our ability to practise (religion) freely what secularism is?' (Interview with BNWLA member, 25 September 2009)

Some of the men of ethnic minority groups (animists) also had other grounds for opposing the code. They pointed out that the status of some ethnic minority women, particularly those belonging to matrilineal/matriarchal groups, made them better off than the Bengali women. Therefore, the introduction of the code would place these women in a disadvantageous position (*Star* magazine, 7 March 2008).

Men from minority groups also feared that if women in their communities (particularly Hindus) inherited property, Muslim men might marry them forcibly or elope with them to gain access to property (interview with BNWLA member, 25 September 2009). This fear was also influenced, perhaps, by the fact that properties belonging to minority communities are affected by various laws such as the Vested Property Act of 1974 (repealed in 2000, but its repeal has yet to take effect). This law allowed the Bangladesh government to confiscate property belonging to any individual it deemed an enemy of the state. Before the independence of Bangladesh this law was known as the Enemy Property Act, after the Indo-Pak war in 1965. The law was used by politicians and local elites to confiscate minority property and land, and led to the forced migration of Hindus and other minority communities (Barkat and Zaman 2000).

Admittedly, not all men of these minority groups opposed the code. Some of the well-established members of the Hindu and other communities worked to support it (BMP 1993). However, their numbers were few. BMP and their allies were aware that there would be opposition from men belonging to the Islamic and minority groups, but were unable to engage with them effectively to influence their way of thinking or assuage their fear partly for the following reasons. First, as discussed above, the state has remained the key target for feminist advocacy, which at times has led activists to place less emphasis on building grassroots support. BMP tried to disseminate the code widely at district levels, but their engagement remained limited to certain sections of people given their dissemination strategies. Moreover, other women's organizations working on this issue had weak links with the grassroots. Despite the best efforts of BMP and its allies to mobilize the state for their cause, the latter was unwilling to risk being branded as 'anti-Islamic'. This is understandable given the significant role played by Islam in Bangladeshi politics, making this a politically costly issue.

Second, women's organizations other than BMP try to keep a distance from the mainstream political parties. As we have seen, being linked to political parties implies a loss of credibility for civil society organizations within the civil society sphere, since this sphere is polarized between two party camps. These organizations are largely composed of middle-class, educated, urban women. As a group, they have a weak voice in formal politics. As a result the issue did not enter mainstream public debate. As for BMP, it has links with the weak political left, which again did not help feminists in campaigning for the Uniform Family Code in the political arena.

In addition, the women's groups (or even the state) could not offer the minority communities anything in return for their support. One feminist activist made the following observation:

> If one read the code and agreed with the principles of justice [one] could not have opposed it. But that is not how the real world works.... We did not sit with them (men of minority groups) properly. Sure we had x and y, but they were the elite members and not with the *amjanata* (public). We (the state) needed to be able to offer them something tangible – more seats in the Parliament or other benefits ... it is a political deal after all. (Interview with WFW member, 30 August 2008)

Consequently, support for the code among women belonging to minority groups was very low. While, some of these women publicly supported the code (BMP 1993), many of them pointed out in private that they were unwilling to appear disloyal towards the concerns of their communities, particularly since these matters were related to community identity issues and the freedom of religion. This silence on the part of minority women and their reluctance to challenge community concerns publicly are not unique to Bangladesh or to the matter of a Uniform Family Code. Black women in the US, the Palestinian feminists, and Indian Muslim women have all experienced similar dilemmas (Hasan 1998; Jad 1995). In addition, feminist activists themselves pointed out during interviews with our research team that the mainstream movement had failed to help minority women create a stronger platform within their own communities. This perhaps reduced the effectiveness of minority women's voice and partially contributed to the failure to tackle male resistance (interviews with WFW member, 30 August 2008; BNWLA member, 25 September 2009).

To sum up, there were a number of reasons why the strategies used to mobilize support for a Uniform Family Code failed. The use of a social justice and nation-building framework did not mitigate male resistance to the code among the Muslim and minority communities. Members of minority communities perceived the Uniform Family Code as a threat to their right to maintain their identity and way of life, and they felt that the changes proposed by the code did not accommodate these issues. The feminists (and also the state) were unable to offer these communities any viable political deals in exchange for the reforms. In addition, the feminists had failed to create a strong platform for minority women within their own communities. This would have allowed minority women to voice and negotiate their demands for reform without appearing disloyal. The lack of support from the women of the minority groups undermined the legitimacy of the proposed reforms. The strategic decision by the feminists not to rely on religion-based arguments and to tie the code to nationalist/secular discourse helped to garner support among civil society actors, but this did not help the feminists to avoid being branded as anti-Islamic. It did not create a scope for exploring whether there was space for engaging with some of the Islamist groups on certain reforms. Admittedly, even if the feminists had used religion-based arguments, they would have been branded as anti-Islamic or anti-religion and their eligibility to propose reforms would have been challenged. However, since they had no religious groups in their fold, it was difficult for the feminist movement to counter resistance by the Islamists and other religious groups. Meanwhile, the state was reluctant to take any measures.

Conclusion

This chapter has analysed the strategies used by feminists to demand a Uniform Family Code. It discussed why feminists focused on drafting an alternative unified code, and how they packaged the demand for the new law as a matter of social justice to fulfil the goals of addressing the inequality experienced by many women of different communities in Bangladesh, and of upholding nationalist ideals and principles of secularism as stated in the constitution. These strategies were chosen in the light of the role played by Islam in politics and the partisan nature of the civil society arena. However, these strategies failed to address the male resistance both within the dominant Muslim community and within other religious minority communities. Islamic groups challenged whether it was legitimate for the women's groups to propose reforms and played on the state's fear of being branded anti-Islamic. Men from minority communities feared the loss of identity and their right to religion, along with a possible loss of property if inheritance laws were reformed to allow women to acquire property. All of these factors led to the feminists' failure to push through reforms for a uniform code.

Despite this failure, the campaign led to some positive changes for women. The debates triggered by the campaign efforts made women from minority communities more aware of their interests and the conflict that at times arises between one's gender and ethnic/religious identities. Slowly, the demand for reform is being raised by women within these communities in different forums. The most significant of these is the demand for a Hindu Marriage Act, which would require the registration of Hindu marriages (interviews with BMP member, 15 May 2009; BNWLA member, 25 September 2009). Some recent state policy documents from the Bangladesh government, and actions on the part of some of its institutions show a partial espousal of some of the proposals in the draft Uniform Family Code. For example, the National Women's Development Policy, which was proposed under the previous caretaker regime, includes a clause which states that women have full control over the assets they acquire. The policy left the option open to apply the clause to inherited property, which is in line with the proposed uniform code. This created a furore among the Islamic political parties and groups, but the women's groups came out strongly in favour of this policy. In addition, a recent High Court judgement ruled that people can have their school completion certificates issued with only their mother's name stated as their guardian rather than their father's, which also fits in with arguments put forward by the Uniform Family Code. It remains to be seen, though, how this process of piecemeal change will evolve, and what will be its long-term impacts.

Acknowledgement

This research was conducted for the Pathways of Women's Empowerment Research Programme Consortium supported by the UK Department for International Development.

Notes

1 Debates on women's movement, organizing, and activism in the developing world, particularly Latin America, show that not all women's organizations are feminist organizations, since they may not share the goal of changing power relations through structural change. This particular understanding of the nature of feminist organizations has been highlighted by feminist scholars and activists such as Basu (1995), Molyneux (2001), and Batliwala (2008). The organizations referred to in this chapter currently identify themselves as feminist organizations, though their origins may have not have had an explicitly feminist character.

2 Twenty interviews were conducted in total with members from the following organizations: BMP, BNWLA, ASK, Naripokkho, and WFW.

3 The 2006 military intervention led to the creation of a caretaker government which was in power for two years to implement the necessary electoral reforms.

4 The organizations that are a part of the coalition – the Samajik Protirodh Committee, formed after 2001 – have taken the UFC on board as a way to address violence against women in the private sphere.

5 Jamaat collaborated with Pakistan during the war of liberation; it was vocal against Bengali nationalism and secular values, and includes in its top leadership people who are currently being tried for war crimes. Ideological and other forms of association with Jamaat by civil society actors signal anti-Bengali-nationalist and anti-secular positions.

6 www.bssrcbd.org, accessed 6 April 2010.

References

BMP (Bangladesh Mohila Parishad) (1993) *Uniform Family Code*, BMP, Dhaka.

Barkat, A. and S. U. Zaman (2000) 'Forced Outmigration of the Hindu Minority: Human Deprivation Due to Vested Property Act', in C.R. Abrar (ed.), *On the Margins: Refugees, Migrants, Minority*, Dhaka University Press, Dhaka.

Basu, A. (ed.) (1995) *The Challenges of Local Feminism: Women's Movement in a Global Perspective*, Westview Press, Boulder, CO.

Batliwala, S. (2008) 'Building Feminist Movements and Organizations:

Clarifying Our Concepts', www.awid.org, accessed 30 June 2009.

Constitution of the Republic of Bangladesh (1972), Government of Bangladesh.

Gaventa, J. and R. McGee (2010) 'Introduction', in J. Gaventa and R. McGee (eds), *Citizen Action and National Policy Reform: Making Change Happen*, Zed Books, London.

Goetz, A.-M. (2001) *Women Development Workers*, University Press Ltd, Dhaka.

Hasan, Z. 1998, 'Gender Politics, Legal Reform and Muslim Community in India', in P. Jeffery and A. Basu (eds), *Appropriating Gender: Women's Activism and Politicized Religion in South Asia*, Routledge, London.

Hassan, M. M. (2002) 'The Demand for Second Generation Reform: The Case of Bangladesh', PhD thesis, University of London.

Hossain, N. (2005) *Elite Perceptions of Poverty in Bangladesh*, University Press Ltd, Dhaka.

Hossain, S. (1994) 'Equality in the Home: Women's Rights and Personal Laws in South Asia', in R. J. Cook (ed.), *Human Rights of Women*, University of Pennsylvania Press, Philadelphia, PA.

Jad, I. (1995), 'Claiming Feminism, Claiming Nationalism: Women's Activism in the Occupied Territories', in A. Basu (ed.), *The Challenges of Local Feminism: Women's Movement in a Global Perspective*, Westview Press, Boulder, CO.

Jahan, R. (1995) 'Men in Seclusion and Women in Public: Rokeya's Dreams and Women's Struggles in Bangladesh', in A. Basu (ed.), *The Challenges of Local Feminism: Women's Movement in a Global Perspective*, Westview Press, Boulder, CO.

Leach, M. and I. Scoones (2007) 'Mobilising Citizens: Social Movements and Politics of Knowledge', IDS Working Paper 276, Institute of Development Studies, Brighton.

Mansoor, T. (1999) *From Patriarchy to Gender Equity: Family Law and Its Impact on Women in Bangladesh*, University Press Ltd, Dhaka.

Molyneux, M. (2001) *Women's Movement in International Perspective: Latin America and Beyond*, Palgrave, London.

Nazneen, S. (2008) 'Group Discrimination at Elections: Bangladesh', in D. Mendis (ed.), *Electoral Process and Governance in South Asia*, Sage, London and New Delhi.

Pereira, F. (2002) *Fractured Scales: The Search for a Uniform Personal Code*, University Press Ltd, Dhaka.

Shehabuddin, E. (2008) *Reshaping the Holy: Democracy, Development and Muslim Women in Bangladesh*, Columbia University Press, New York, NY.

Star magazine (2008) 'Equality Begins at Home', Vol. 7, Issue 10, 7 March.

Tarrow, S. (1998) *The Power in Movements: Social Movement and Contentious Politics*, Cambridge University Press, Cambridge.

5

From Status to Rights

The Shifting Dimensions of Women's Activism in Iranian Family Law Reform

Arzoo Osanloo

Introduction: socio-legal developments in Iranian family law

In August 2011 the Iranian Parliament amended Iran's Family Protection Act. The amendments to the law had been pending for several years while a parliamentary commission debated the merits of several key provisions. With the ratification of the bill, Parliament effectively revised and reinstated a law that had been suspended since the revolution. In August 2007, the executive branch introduced the bill to Iranian lawmakers, aiming to fill a legal vacuum created in 1979 when the post-revolutionary government suspended the pre-revolutionary Family Protection Act, first introduced in 1967 and revised in 1975. At the outset, Parliament sent the bill to its Legal and Judicial Commission for study and, almost a year later, the commission quietly approved the bill. That summer, July 2008, the commission sent the bill to the full Parliament for a vote.

When the details of the new bill were made public, however, scores of activists, domestic and international, mounted a campaign to defeat several provisions that they found to be at odds with women's rights in marriage and other personal status matters. Feminist activists as well as members of the Iranian Shi'i *ulama* (jurisprudential scholars) criticized key articles within the bill, saying they were against women's interests, Islamic principles, and families. This coalition effectively prevented the bill from moving to a final vote by Parliament. In response to the large-scale dissent, the Iranian Parliament sent the bill back to its Legal and Judicial Commission for further research and review.

Two of the most controversial sections of the bill were Articles 22 and 23. Article 22 proposed an end to the requirement of registering *sigheh* (temporary marriages). Removing this requirement would essentially strip away any financial or legal protections for women in temporary marriages and children born into them. Activists argued that the provision would institutionalize and facilitate prostitution. Article 23 suggested a change to the polygamy laws that required men to obtain a wife's permission to marry a second wife. This article proposed to allow a husband to marry a second wife based on a judge's finding that the husband possessed the financial means to support multiple wives and treat them equally. The article, however, did not delineate what the parameters of adequate financial resources for supporting multiple wives were, nor did it define the meaning of equal treatment of multiple wives. Thus, the article seemed to eliminate the existing requirement that a husband obtain the first wife's consent prior to entering into a second marriage. This requirement is currently a stipulation in a standard marriage contract. Several other provisions of the bill were of concern to women's rights groups, including a tax on the *mahrieh* (dower) and restrictions on women's rights to marry non-Muslims, but this chapter will deal primarily with Articles 22 and 23.[1]

The 2008 decision by the Iranian Parliament to conduct further research on the law was met with approval by women's rights activists. As I will show, the debate about the bill, with the competing visions of the family and women's roles within it, is part of a broader struggle between conservatives and reformists[2] to define the nature of the Islamic state. As stated above, after much public debate and international and domestic activism, the Iranian Parliament passed an amended version of the Family Protection Act in August 2011 – with a qualified version of Article 22 and without Article 23. Other questionable provisions were not ratified, although fears abound that they could be revived at a future date.

Through an analysis of the new family law bill, I will examine some of the activism and local understandings of the proposed laws and explore the ideological terrain through which the debates about women's rights and status are fought, providing some explanation of the stakes involved in such contests. I will trace competing discourses about women's roles − 'women's rights' and 'women's status', both of which have been central in defining and shaping women's issues *vis-à-vis* the state. As I do so, I will consider how some activists mobilize individual rights to oppose the questionable provisions of the new legislation, while groups in support of it rally behind the concept of family for protection of vulnerable members of society. I focus on the ideological underpinnings of these discursive strategies to understand the broader aims of those who lobbied for and against the bill. I will show that the discourses, far from being homogeneous, possess layered and complex meanings that are deployed by activists on both sides of the debate.

Another aim of this chapter is to highlight contestations around the codification of family law, which are animated by competing visions of gender roles, Islamic jurisprudence, and a healthy Muslim social order. The debates about the Family Protection Act derive from its multiple foundations and objectives, including its religious moorings in Islamic jurisprudence, the civil institutions and legal processes through which it is implemented, and the effects of strategically delineating and blurring the boundaries between religious interpretations and law making.

Finally, two key notions of governance animate debates around the Family Protection Act: 'Islamic government' and 'Islamic republic'. Contemporary debates about women's roles go hand-in-hand with the wider struggle to shape and define governance in post-revolutionary Iran. These debates, moreover, speak to this broader contest about the Islamic republican state, the nature of governance, and, alongside it, authority to interpret Islamic principles.

Framing discourses:
from 'women's rights to 'women's status'

The Family Protection Act of 1967, revised in 1975, was a key development in the modernization of laws pertaining to women. It gave women legal rights to obtain dissolution of marriage through a petition to a newly created family court and afforded women rights in child custody. In the late 1960s, the act was seen by progressive modernists as an important reform that offered women basic civil rights and protections. Conservative religious leaders, however, found fault with the act that seemingly moved questions of personal status, such as marriage and marriage dissolution, from the domain of Islamic jurisprudential authority to that of the civil legal apparatus.[3] From exile, Ayatollah Khomeini condemned the law as against the Shari'a and Muslim family life (Khomeini 1984: 314). He declared the law invalid and stated that women who obtained divorces under it and remarried were adulterers. Upon his return from exile, Khomeini suspended the law. The result was the lowering of the minimum age for marriage for women from 18 to 9, giving men the sole prerogative of marriage dissolution, and making men the presumed custodians of children. Despite the suspension of the law, over time a number of modifications to the post-revolutionary civil codes afforded women some strategic room for manoeuvre, especially in marriage dissolution and child custody, as well as post-dissolution financial maintenance, which did not exist in the previous era. The minimum age for marriage was also raised over time to 13 (Article 1041, Iranian Civil Code). Many, however, believe that the judicial system still leaves men legally empowered and consigns women to the goodwill of male-dominated courts and, of course, their husbands or other male kin.

After the 1979 revolution that ushered in the Islamic republic, guardians of the state made family a central focus of legislation and regulation, having deemed it to be the foundation of society, and women, as *keeyan-e khanevadeh* (crowning jewel of the family), would be regulated to preserve the family's honour and dignity. Thus, proposed changes to the family laws have not been without their supporters, who have come to see the legal modifications of the intervening years as detrimental to the family. One interlocutor I met with in the fall of 2008 told me that today women marry for financial gain, and an increasingly easy dissolution process provides easy recourse for marital troubles (personal interview, 16 September 2008).

While conducting research in 1999–2000, with annual research trips since, I have interviewed a number of women who represented more conservative positions on women's rights and roles in post-revolutionary Iran and sought to explain the logic of disputed practices such as polygamy.[4] The Director of Women's Affairs for the Ayatollah Khomeini Research Complex met with me to discuss some of the apparent inequities in the Iranian legal codes, especially as they pertained to women's rights in inheritance, marriage, and dissolution. Dr Kermani explained to me that this system 'protects women who are socially vulnerable'. For instance, in an Islamic system, she explained:

> Women are financially supported by a male relative, a husband, father, paternal uncle or perhaps brother. Women in our society are not required to work as they often are in Western societies. This way Islam envisions women as mothers and wives first. They can focus on their families and raising their children. This is how our society will improve – through the attention mothers give their sons and daughters.

And she added the oft-repeated idea that 'a woman's earnings from work are hers to keep; she does not need to share them with the family' (personal interview, 2 January 2000).

Dr Kermani's emphasis on protection was also a reference to the principles in the Shari'a of *velayat* (guardianship). In the context of female guardianship, this concept references the Qur'anic verse 34 of *Sura Al-Nisa* (Women Chapter), which states that 'men are the protectors and maintainers of women because Allah has given one more than the other and because they support them from their own means' (Ali 2004). Dr Kermani, however, was alluding to an additional source of social engineering, one that referenced what Ayatollah Khomeini famously called *Hookoomat-e Islami* (Islamic government) (Khomeini 1981). This vision of governance aimed at emulating an imagined ideal Islamic society with reference to the time of the Prophet and his followers. The problem with this vision, however, was that it carried with it few tools or infrastructural supports for governance. The focus of Islamic government, instead, was the moral restoration of society through the rehabilitation of the family. In this context, women's relational status as mothers and wives figured prominently in the appeals for a true Islamic state, and eclipsed their rights as individual citizens. Dr Kermani, among other conservatives I interviewed, suggested that the moral decline was in part spurred on by women who did not tend to their foremost duties, as mothers and wives, and instead sought individual liberties without regard for the broader social networks to which they also had responsibilities.

This conversation was in contrast with an encounter I had had just months earlier, on 1 May 1999, with a family law attorney in Tehran. I had explained my interest in learning how women in Iran were finding their 'rights' through Islam, following my readings as a student of the Islamic republic. This was an attorney whose legal career began well before the revolution; she was quite well-known, had authored many articles and books, and her representation was so highly sought after that her suite of offices was filled with clients right up to the end of the evening. She responded with dismay, telling me, 'This is a law office and I am a lawyer. In Iran we have civil codes and civil courts. I do not deal in Shari'a; I deal in the law [*qanun*]. If you want to understand how laws work, you need to go to the court to see for yourself ... how women are getting their rights.'

The lawyer's aim was not to say that Islam was absent, but rather, that there was for her a greater emphasis on *qanun* over Shari'a. This claim was quite significant if one had an understanding of the period immediately after the revolution, particularly as women's status was the issue; and it was even more significant given the unresolved debates over the nature of the state. Indeed, it was very likely that this lawyer, who by then had been practising law for almost thirty years, and whose experiences thus preceded the revolution by a decade, was well aware that the civil codes had remained relatively unchanged, despite the revolutionary discourse of returning to some sort of pure Islamic guidance.[5] In addition, the lawyer, pointing to the courts as the space for understanding women's rights, was also directing me to her own understanding of rights as belonging to the citizens and not in the domain of the religious scholars. In other words, her attitude signalled the desanctification of the concept of law, separating it out from the province of religious leaders and sacred sources (Mir-Hosseini 2006). The lawyer depicted women as citizens endowed with rights, who, as such, had rights to protection from the state as individuals. They were not duty-bound by their relational status as mothers and wives to behave in a manner that was inimical to their personal well-being.

This is where the competing visions of women and society begin to emerge. The more conservative advocate of women, Dr Kermani, saw herself supporting women's status as mothers and wives, not their rights as individuals. She saw women as part of a social fabric. Women, she found, played important roles in the family through the way they raised children and supported husbands. For her, legislation that protected families would best serve what she saw as women's biological nature, by protecting their relational status as mothers and wives.

The tensions characterized by the views above represent perhaps two extreme poles of understanding women's roles in society. While most opinions may lie somewhere in between, these divergent logics were becoming more visible in the Khatami period (1997–2005) and would grow through the Ahmadinejad presidency (2005–2013). The debates around the new Family Protection bill exemplify one expression of this tension as the controversial provisions of the new law would amount to a repeal of the modest post-revolutionary changes to the civil codes, and render them again consistent with the civil codes of 1935.[6]

The modes of discursive framing deployed by my two inter-locutors above signalled political if not ideological distinctions in how they formulated the issues about women's roles in the Islamic republic. To understand this, it is important to consider the formation and reformation of some legal and political institutions born of this contradictory state formation, the Islamic republic. Indeed, it is more than just contradictory, it was also unknown; it was not clear to anyone how this newly formed state would achieve the 'esoteric end' of administering an Islamic government (Cottam 1986: 61).

Islamic government and family protection

A persistent issue underlying many debates was the framework of the 'republic', which to some post-revolutionary leaders was a mere transitional governing phase until the realization of the final aim, the 'pure' Islamic government envisioned by Ayatollah Khomeini. The nature of the Islamic government was under a great deal of debate, more so without the ruling dictates of the first leader of the Islamic republic. For much of the first twenty years after the revolution, Iranian state institutions and the meaning of the 'republic', which emphasized the popular nature of the revolution, had remained largely the subjects of philosophical and academic inquiry, in part due to the effects of war (with Iraq) and Khomeini's charismatic leadership.

Khomeini not only abrogated the Family Protection Act but, emphasizing his aim of creating an Islamic government, argued that there was no need for 'man-made laws' (1981: 17). According to Khomeini, the Qur'an and the Sunna contained all that was needed for governance of the Islamic state. The legislative body was to become merely a planning body to carry out those laws (1981: 28). When the provisional government of the new Islamic republic attempted to purify the laws by suspending legislation and the civil codes, however, confusion over how to adjudicate the principles of the Qur'an and Sunna caused such a severe outcry that over time law had to be re-introduced. This time, however it was validated as Islamic by the governing bodies of the state. This is indeed how some of the laws from the then-suspended Family Protection Act were re-introduced in the Civil Codes of Marriage and Family.[7] Codification of Islamic principles, however, had an effect of disrupting the historical power of Islamic judges to use the wide discretion that was afforded to them in their decision making. As Zubaida has pointed out, 'codified law is the law of the state, and the judge is a functionary of the state who has to arrive at a judgment from the codes and procedures determined by it rather than by autonomous judgment through reference to sacred sources and the principle derived from them' (2005: 134). Legislative authority, too, was reinstated, though in a limited form.

Thus, despite the revolution that initially dissolved the legislative body and claimed to have abolished civil codes and civil courts, the Islamic republic re-established both.[8] These factors, which came into play after Khomeini's suspension of the Family Protection Act, re-inscribed a legal system that privileges and protects individual rights.[9] In addition, this hybrid legal system gave the Shari'a unambiguous legal force through its codification, and disrupted the earlier normative balance between the Shari'a and state-administered law (Mir-Hosseini 1993).

The combining of Shari'a and civil law was a reflection of the compromises among these disparate groups, and draws attention to an important consequence of the revolution: that the resulting state form was neither a pure version of Khomeini's 'Islamic government' nor a copy of the European state model of a republic, but something different altogether. As Islamic principles were made to accommodate the republican state form, they also reproduced and re-authenticated liberal subjects, and made the legal system justiciable through rights-based claims. Thus, if the post-revolutionary government made women the grounds on which political disputes over governance were fought, those disputes took shape through discourses and institutions that were conspicuously liberal and republican. Through this imperfect and precarious balance of

Islamic republican governance, attempts at social reform took shape with sometimes competing ideological visions of women in society: as full and equal legal persons with rights, and as mothers and wives protected by their status.

It was not until the mid-1990s, after the war had ended and Khomeini had died, that debates about the nature of the state, legal processes, and renewed discourses of rights, no longer blemished by the taint of imperialism, began to enter into newly emerging public spaces. Such rights talk and the public spaces where it was taking place were nurtured and encouraged during the Khatami presidency. Women, too, were participating in dialogue and debate, challenging the statist promulgations of their status and roles in numerous arenas, such as newspapers and magazines, but also in other venues as diverse as non-governmental organizations, scriptural reading groups, courts, their places of work, and even government ministries. These 'dialogical sites', I have argued elsewhere, have arisen as productive effects of the intersection of Islam guidelines and republican principles (Osanloo 2009).

In each of the meetings I have described above, speakers point to competing ideological spaces where political lines have been drawn around the question of women's rights and status and their relationship to questions of governance in an Islamic republic. A hardliner working in a conservative branch of the government, Dr Kermani, suggests that women's roles be defined in the context of their relational status as mothers and wives. This view sees women as vulnerable and in need of state protection. On the other side, the lawyer points to the civil laws in the rights-based province of individual citizenship, in the context of which women are to be treated as individuals on a par with male counterparts. Each in some ways creates the exaggerated mirror of its opposite.

After the election of Mohammad Khatami, whose rise to office was ushered in by the unprecedented post-revolutionary participation of women, Iranian women witnessed a shift in emphasis from their status to their individual rights. This shift was characterized by the executive's increased attention to women's participation in the civic and political spheres of life. This move emerged in tandem with Khatami's broader goals of building and strengthening the legal instruments and civil bodies of the state, giving the 'republican' organs of the Islamic republic some much-needed institutional, structural, and procedural expression. Khatami's attention to the rule of law refocused the state's (or at least the executive's) attention to women from an exclusive emphasis on women as mothers and wives, to an added focus on women as individuals, citizens, and political beings endowed with rights.

The 2005 victory of Mahmoud Ahmadinejad as President seemed to show another discursive shift taking place, and his subsequent 2009 victory, albeit contested, reconfirmed it. The trend then was to re-emphasize women's important status as mothers and wives. Ahmadinejad exemplified this discursive and substantive shift when, among his first acts as President in 2005, he changed the name and institutional focus of the executive branch office for women from 'The Women's Participation Center' to 'The Center for Women and Family Affairs'. While Iranians continued to employ discourses of rights, such discourses carried with them grave consequences amidst fraught and often volatile political situations. Indeed the effects of contemporary discourses of 'regime change' that highlight women's rights in their aims are used by Iran's conservative leaders against what are, on the one hand, domestic, internal reform movements, or, on the other, international calls for Iran to abide by treaties that it has ratified, such as the Convention on the Rights of the Child (Amani 2008). This is because, as the attacks are framed in ideological terms, the response is to further determine and restrict the field of possibility within which women may issue calls for the improvement of their lot. This field of possibility is also ideological and binary: it thus not only occludes, but even critically shifts on-the-ground possibilities for women.

Thus during the Ahmadinejad presidency we saw a backlash against rights groups (with competing calls for improvements in women's status, but not necessarily rights). Indeed, after 2009, state officials claimed that the discourse of rights was being used by reformists to foment support for a velvet-type revolution, as the indictments issued by the Islamic republic against protesters who challenged the 12 June 2009 elections demonstrated.[10] While some groups felt that the Khatami-era reforms were thwarted after the 2009 elections, there were, however, the enduring socio-legal effects of the attention to the rule of law, in particular when we return to the proposed amendments to the Family Protection Act and the developments since it was sent back to the Legal and Judicial Commission of Parliament in 2008.

Lobbying for the protection of women and family

After the provisions of the new Family Protection Bill were made public by activists in the summer of 2008, women's groups, formal and informal, began meeting to discuss them and determine their opposition or support for it. The influential and then-local One Million Signatures Campaign aimed to expose the inequities of the law by pointing out that women's legal rights in marriage and dissolution would be diminished. The campaign was created by Iranian activists to protest against discriminatory laws. It publicized the questionable articles of the bill and organized protests against it. One of the campaign's central aims was to circulate a petition signalling disapproval of Iran's discriminatory laws with the goal of receiving one million signatures. Women's groups also pointed out the obvious discriminatory practices of the bill, resulting in ever-widening gender inequality under Iranian civil law. Members of the Iranian *ulama* also spoke out against the bill, claiming it was not in keeping with Islamic principles with regard to polygamous marriage. Ayatollah Saneii wrote that Islamic principles on polygamous marriage required a husband to obtain his first wife's permission in order to marry a second wife (Payvand News 2011). Taking a less ideological approach that supported the aim of 'family protection', some activists argued that the bill, which appeared to facilitate polygamous and temporary marriages, did not support families, as it claimed.[11] Far from protecting families, such activists claimed, the Family Protection Bill was 'anti-family'. Zahra Rahnavard, an activist and wife of former presidential candidate Mir-Hossein Mousavi, said that the bill should be thrown out for the sake of family stability (Rahnavard 2010). The activists were not only reacting through the prism of individual rights, but were taking on the very terms of the conservatives' argument, family protection.

Reducing divorce and encouraging marriage were the important goals in the minds of the conservatives, who argued that the rise in divorce and increase in single women put society at risk of immoral behaviour. While the main claim of conservatives who supported the bill seemed to be its compatibility with the Shari'a and their faith (Planet Iran 2010), some tried to explain the deeper meanings behind its logic. Such commentators saw the rise in the age of marriage, even as they argued to lower the legal age, as a worrisome trend that would affect social mores (Reuters 2010). Conservative supporters of the bill claimed that it aimed to reduce divorce by making it more difficult[12] and by allowing a chance at marriage for women who possess less desirable qualities, such as being divorced, poor, or infertile. They argued that when a marriage came to an end due to a wife's illness or inability to produce a child, the wife no longer had any financial support, but with this provision, its supporters argued, the wife would now be able to enjoy the financial and social security that continued marriage provided. On the other side, a woman who was not able to marry because she was without physical or other social attributes would perhaps be satisfied by becoming the second wife of another man. She, too, they argued, would have some financial and social security. In all such cases, conservatives suggested that the aim of 'family protection' would be met by preserving marriage. At the same time, conservative commentators used rights discourse to encourage support for women in achieving their duties in the family. Dr Kermani published a statement on the 'Status and Rights of

Women in Islam and Iranian Family', in which she used the language of rights, but in a different context, one in which rights are accorded in the furtherance of their responsibilities: 'Islam defines women's rights and responsibilities in a manner that they are compatible with her feminine humanity' (Kermani no date). Dr Kermani explains those responsibilities: 'The responsibility of being a woman, being a girl, being a wife, being a mother, and being a religious human being have been defined in Iran in a manner that they are compatible with her capabilities and abilities.' Kermani then describes women's roles through their status: 'Due to her status as trainer in the family, woman is to be given free time free from any concern about the livelihood to be able to raise her children as perfect human beings.' She ends her statement with the suggestion that this respect accorded to women as mothers and wives allows them to enjoy all the positive advantages available in other societies, but blocks the social alienation they feel in 'Western and laic societies'.

While public debates carried with them an air of political machinations, local discussions proved the issue to be more complex and perhaps confusing. I had the occasion to visit with a friend who worked as a secretary at a government ministry. Her office had organized a presentation on the draft bill and she went home with a positive view of the bill. My friend, Solnaz, was not a supporter of the conservative government, nor, as a divorced woman with two children, did she feel the laws of the post-revolutionary government treated women fairly. She explained to me that, in her view, to be treated fairly meant that written laws would be gender-neutral not only at face value, but also in the way they were carried out. In fact, her views on the laws guiding marriage and dissolution of marriage were shaped by her personal experiences of going through a lengthy divorce ten years earlier and the seemingly interminable custody and child-support battles. She admitted that some laws appeared to be neutral or seemed to protect women as wives or mothers, but the particularities of the proceedings, she felt, often afforded benefits to men because the judges were more sympathetic to them and the legal process was not standardized. The only way she saw possible settlements in favour of women, she told me, was for the 'women to teach themselves the law and the legal procedures and fight every day for their rights'. She did not see any benefit for herself, in all those years of fighting for her marriage to be dissolved, in her status as a mother and wife. To the contrary, she told me, her husband's marriage to a second woman aroused so little sympathy from the (male) judges, who felt this was an inappropriate reason for a woman to leave a marriage, that they made her feel that it was her fault for being unable to satisfy her husband. Seeing her arguing her case in the courts, several judges suggested that it was her 'belligerent attitude' that compelled her husband to find another wife.

Given Solnaz's history, that I knew so well and had witnessed first-hand a decade earlier, I was surprised to learn that she came away with an optimistic assessment of this new bill. Regarding the provision on polygamy, Solnaz explained that the law would grant a hearing before a judge. This was an important legal and procedural action that would regulate a husband's ability to marry a second wife. Solnaz had been pressured, at the young age of 21, to accept her husband's second wife on the grounds that he had had an affair and that the woman had 'tricked' him into marrying her. She told the morality police that they had had sexual relations, and when he was taken into custody, his options were either jail and fines or marriage. With great reluctance, Solnaz consented to the marriage – with his promise that he would divorce the woman, but the divorce never came and it was ultimately up to Solnaz to file the petition to dissolve her marriage. Thus, Solnaz came away with a good feeling about the proposed provision because it provided a legal venue for the issue to be heard *before* the husband married the second wife, and not after, as was her situation. Moreover, Solnaz explained to me and her daughter, who had just entered the room, that the law seemed to require men to appear in court, something that the divorce process was often unable to achieve, and recognized the legal rights of women through a court proceeding – something which she experienced as lacking, as well. Given her experience, she felt it was impossible that a man could provide for two wives equally, so she was perhaps less worried about how that issue would be addressed by the courts than the activists who were campaigning against the bill. Solnaz's daughter Sara, just 19, disdained her mother's understanding of the provision and loudly proclaimed that women would have no say at all in the proceedings.

Interestingly, Sara and some of her college classmates had also discussed the provisions and found them contemptible. She said that the existing laws requiring the consent of a first wife to a husband marrying a second wife would be nullified and that women would no longer have any recourse before the courts if their husbands married without their permission. 'This makes it so that permission of the first wife is not necessary,' she said. Her mother, who had always felt her own permission was coerced, nonetheless felt that the institutionalization of the system would give more of a legal framework in which the wife's concerns could be heard and duly taken into account. Sara explained to her mother and me that there is nothing in the new bill that says that. In fact, she stated, 'the husband can go before the court, show his financial abilities, and marry a second wife without his first wife ever knowing'. To this Solnaz expressed incredulity. Sara demurred, 'That is the whole point; they say they want to encourage marriage; they don't want the first wife to say he can't.' With this explanation, Solnaz admitted that the presentation she had attended at work did not discuss the issue of the first wife's permission, which is a stipulation in the marriage contract that the new bill appeared to undermine. She now agreed with her daughter that this provision of the bill would not be good for women.

What this conversation between mother and daughter demonstrates is that the viewpoints about the law and its potential effects were somewhat nuanced, and information about their actual goals was missing and shaped through media. The overarching logic of support for the bill came from the idea that vulnerable women, such as widows and divorcees, would have a chance at financial maintenance, an opportunity to be a part of a family, and have a network of social and economic support. The logic here envisions not an existing reality, but one which could be socially engineered and could protect women by keeping them in a status in which they were financially secure – but dependent on a male relative. Some conservatives argued that this would allow them more freedom for intellectual pursuits as well (Kermani no date), while opponents argued that the conservatives privileged financial protection over mental and emotional. Thus it should come as no surprise that the issues on which the conservatives and reformists do sometimes come together are in the arenas of child care for working mothers, flexible work hours, and so on. One way in which the Family Protection Bill is in tune with this logic (and stood unopposed by reformist women) was in the provisions that were added, but which were not contested, such as arbitration for marriage dissolution proceedings and distribution of pensions to wives and unmarried daughters (including widows) (Khabaronline 2011).

Moreover, despite its questionable provisions, the bill strengthens the legal framework that recognizes claims brought forward by rights bearers – women, perhaps unintentionally, among them. As Solnaz also recognized, based on her experiences, the legal infrastructure and civil process allow women access to claims. By it requiring women to make such claims, and thus to educate themselves about both the substance of the laws and civil procedures, women are empowered to make small changes in their own lives as well as to partake in broad movements for change, such as the One Million Signatures Campaign.

From the reformist or liberal perspective, women's individual identity was to be nurtured and not subordinated to their perceived (and limited) roles as only wives and mothers. Reformists with whom I spoke about the conservative logic felt that women's lives should be understood not through an imagined sensibility, but in their specific realities. Such women were not persuaded by the logic that family would always protect them, nor did they want to be dependent on male relations for support.

Family Protection Bill: the commission's report[13]

Parliament's Legal and Judicial Commission released a statement on 29 November 2009 addressing the concerns with the bill (Iranian Students News Agency 2008, my translation). The spokesman, the MP from the town of Malayar, Amin Hossein Rahimi, stated that a special committee was formed in response to the large outcry of dissent caused by the proposed bill. The committee had completed research on the Family Protection Bill and had sent it back to the Legal and Judicial Commission with its recommendations. Rahimi explained that the committee reviewed the bill in consideration of its main aim of 'strengthening of the family'.

'Having considered this paramount aim,' Rahimi said, 'the special committee determined that the taking of another wife was not in correspondence with the expressed goal of strengthening the family and thus a second marriage would be prohibited without the consent of the first wife.' He continued:

> Because of the outcry over this article, the special committee issued new regulations for a second marriage without the consent of the first wife, which could be permissible in very limited circumstances, where special misconduct was found, such as that which would result in five years in prison or in such cases where the wife has abandoned the family.
>
> [I]f the wife does not possess any of these difficulties, and the husband marries another woman, there is a punishment of prison that has been rendered for this. In addition, he will not be permitted to register this marriage. That is to say, there are many additional legal consequences in addition to that fact that the perpetrator will have been guilty of having committed a crime.

In this passage, the parliamentary spokesman addresses the broad opposition to the bill, and acknowledges the influence activist groups had on revising these provisions, which will now make a second marriage without permission of the first wife both a criminal and a civil offence. Next the spokesman raised the issue of whether in cases like this the marriage contract is valid. He said:

> [I]n the Family Protection Bill, the debate is procedural and a debate about the substantive nature of the validity of the marriage did not take place. This issue is a matter of Islamic guidelines and jurisprudence (Shari'a and *fiqh*) in which we did not enter. However, if a man marries again without acquiring the aforementioned conditions, he will be punished and his wife has the right to make a demand for marriage dissolution.

In this, one of the most telling parts of the statement, the MP defers certain matters of validity, even in the face of illegality, to Islamic jurists. That is to say, even though the commission has proposed to criminalize a man who takes a second wife without the permission of the first, he defers to the *ulama* on the issue of whether the marriage is still considered valid, even while suggesting that the first wife would have the right to ask that her marriage be dissolved. The interesting move here is the distinction made by the MP between law and procedure, on the one hand, and jurisprudence on the other. As lawmakers, the MPs will provide procedures, even while deferring judgement on the substantive issues upon which Parliament is regulating!

The final two paragraphs of the spokesman's statement address temporary marriage, which the Family Protection Bill attempted to deregulate under Article 22. These two paragraphs will be considered together as the opinions of the commission are reiterated and expanded from one paragraph to the next:

> [T]he bill which the judiciary and the executive proposed did not make any mention of temporary marriage, except that it was stated that the registration of temporary marriage would be regulated according to memoranda to be issued by the executive's office. However, the majority of the Legal and Judicial Commission of Parliament believes, with regard to this issue, such memoranda speaking to the registration of temporary marriage can in no way be used as a basis for the regulation of temporary marriage. In reality, if necessary, laws for this must be approved; however, in the debates about the Family Protection Bill, for which we are recording law,

we understand family as permanent marriage and in Islam and our regulations, permanent marriage is foundational and it is that which creates the family. Thus, in the Family Protection Bill, with regard to permanent marriage, the type of regulations we considered were those that would offer strength to the family.

[T]emporary marriage is an issue that from the perspective of Shari'a is permissible; however, it has specific conditions which are restricted and exceptional. Thus, individuals cannot undertake temporary marriage under any conditions, unless this effort is undertaken clandestinely. Given that temporary marriage is not part of family and is not part of marriage that enters into the perspective of strengthening the family, it was not an issue of emphasis in Islam, we did not see any need to consider making laws for it in this bill. If it does exist, however, only in the face of special conditions is it possible to carry out. In conclusion, if a man would like to register his temporary marriage, he must follow the laws consistent with the laws of obtaining another wife. To better explain, temporary marriage can only be registered in the face of the consent of the first wife unless a man clandestinely carries out the temporary marriage.

Two issues are important to address here. First is the issue of the separation of powers to which the MP very subtly refers when speaking to the governmental authority for regulating temporary marriage. The MP states that the commission did not consider issuing regulations for temporary marriage through this bill because the overall aim of the bill is to strengthen the family, and not only does temporary marriage not do that, but temporary marriage does not constitute family. Moreover, the MP suggests that the commission had at least considered the executive's proviso (Article 22) that it will issue guidelines for temporary marriage and defiantly rejects that, stating that temporary marriage, while not within the purview of the bill, does need to be regulated. He adds that the opinion of the majority of the members of the commission is that those guidelines should come in the form of law from the law-making body of the government, not the executive.

The rapporteur continues to discuss temporary marriage, even after having established that it does not fall under the definition of family, let alone family protection, and thus the bill under consideration. The MP reiterates that while temporary marriage is permissible under Shari'a, it is allowable under very specific and narrow circumstances, here suggesting that even if it has some verifiable religious foundation, it is undesirable except under very strict conditions. This is interesting in that in the earlier paragraphs, the MP deferred matters of substantive Shari'a to the *ulama*, but here opines quite definitively on temporary marriage.

The final two sentences of this statement are indeed ground-breaking. Having established that the commission believes that temporary marriages should be regulated and registered by Parliament, he concludes by saying that even in the case of temporary marriage, in order for a man to register it, he must follow the laws consistent with the laws of obtaining a second wife. That is to say, he must obtain the first wife's consent, effectively making temporary marriage on a par with second marriage. Arguably, if the husband does not obtain the first wife's permission and carries it out clandestinely, which is the only way he could do it if he did not seek to register it, then she would have the right to apply for marriage dissolution were she to find out about either a clandestine temporary marriage or a temporary marriage to which she had denied consent. In the final analysis, however, the MP does not suggest any effect or consequence in cases where men do not register their temporary marriages and carry them out clandestinely. In the end, the commission created criteria through which husbands may seek a judicial ruling on obtaining a second wife without the approval of the first.

The continued public outcry shelved the bill until it was once again picked up by the Iranian Parliament in August 2010. Again the controversial bill was sent to the judicial commission for research. Finally, in August 2011 Parliament passed the amendments to the Family Protection Act. Of the two provisions discussed here, Article 22 on registration of temporary marriage passed with the qualification that the government supports permanent marriage in the aim of advancing family relations. Article 23 on a judicial ruling for a husband to marry a second wife is not in the amended version of the bill.

The words of the commission's rapporteur exemplify the complex and varied understandings of gender and family issues in Iran. The rapporteur highlights the ambiguities and the contestations about the nature and role of family law, its linkages with Islamic jurisprudence and civil legal procedures, and, finally, its broader implications for legal activism around women's rights.

Conclusion: political stakes and family protection

What lies beneath the parliamentary commission's carefully worded statement are conflicting ideological frameworks for what exactly Islamic governance is or should be. Since the 1979 Iranian revolution, images of women have become indicative of a political change. The message aimed to show that the revolution against the excesses of Western societies would recalibrate Iranian social and moral standards with some seemingly indigenous ones. Family played an important part in this debate, going back, in fact, to the introduction of the original Family Protection Act of 1967, amended in 1975.

In the post-revolutionary Islamic republic, the laws consist of a cultural production which I refer to as 'Islamico-civil' (Osanloo 2006). Understanding how these laws operate helps us to better appreciate the attention given to the status and rights of women since the revolution. Notions of women as individual citizens and women as mothers and wives within the family are in tension here. Both speak to differing cosmologies and imaginings of Islamic governance, and both are in concordance with Islamic principles as well as republican notions of protecting vulnerable members of society. The disagreements, however, lie in the meaning and execution of the notion of protection – should it be based on their rights as individual citizens or their status as mothers and wives? The tension also leave us with some spaces for manoeuvre and with results that are sometimes difficult to predict or explain. On the one hand, women are at the vanguard of reform and many observers accept that women's status in Iran is improving in some ways. Some have even pointed out that there are some legal rights today that women did not have prior to the revolution; certainly there are more female college students, more women in the workforce, and more women in higher governmental and administrative positions. Some of this, I have argued, has resulted from the discourse of improvement of the status of women as an important revolutionary aim (that is, the mobilizing image of rehabilitating society through women and the roles they play). But it also has to do with the legal reforms that women have been quite active in producing, as in the cases of marriage dissolution and child custody, and even the very public protests against the new Family Protection Bill.

Criticisms of rights discourses have again emerged, contextualized by the threat that has now been reframed – from an imperialist threat to an internal one. The deeper issue is a sharp divide and an increasingly violent battle over the nature of governance today: Islamic government or Islamic republic? Women's roles are being imagined through these two ideological paradigms, at some points complementary, at others contradictory.

Notes

1   The bill can be read in Persian at www.online-law.ir/news26.php. The other problematic provisions include Article 25 and Article 46. Article 25 imposes a tax on the dower paid to the wife. While this amount is legally owed to the wife at the time of marriage, women often do not receive it; it is frequently only paid upon marriage dissolution and constitutes a wife's leverage against her husband should she have no other grounds for dissolution. Therefore, taxation of the dower potentially reinforces a husband's financial power over his wife during marriage, and hinders a wife's financial autonomy at the time of a divorce. Article 46 would criminalize the marriage of a foreigner to an Iranian woman without proper authorization. The foreign man is subject to between ninety days' and one year's imprisonment. The woman (if she married on her own free will), her father (if he gave permission), and the marriage official would be sentenced as accomplices.

2   By conservatives, I refer to members of the *ulama* who are *usul-garan* (followers of principle), adhering to a strict textual reading of the Islamic sources of knowledge. Reformists believe in a dynamic reading

of the sources, interpreting them together with the exigencies of contemporary life.

3   This claim was questioned by some scholars, who were quick to point out the religious bases underlying the key articles on marriage and dissolution under the Act. See Vatandoust 1985.

4   I conducted research for this project during 1999–2000 and interviewed over 230 women (see, generally, Osanloo 2009). The women ranged in age from 15 to the mid-70s, with a variety of educational backgrounds. All the women I interviewed lived in Tehran, Iran's capital. I return annually to conduct follow-up research. My interviews are open-ended and semi-structured. I also conducted participant observation in Iran's family courts, in lawyers' offices, and among women in their homes and places of work. When the proposed Family Protection Act became public knowledge in September 2007, I engaged my interlocutors on this topic as well. I have 14 interviews with new interlocutors on the new Family Protection Act and 7 with former interlocutors.

5   The civil code, enacted between 1928 and 1935, was based on Islamic *fiqh*. The commission appointed to draft the codes drew on four Shi'a *fiqh* texts. Indeed it was the only piece of legislation enacted during the Reza Shah period that is entirely *fiqh*-based, and when the 1969 Family Protection laws were dismantled, they reverted back to the earlier laws.

6   With the suspension of the Family Protection Act in 1979, marriage and dissolution guidelines were relegated to the earlier civil codes enacted between 1928 and 1935. Between 1979 and the passage of the amended Family Protection Bill in 2011, revisions to marriage and dissolution laws were introduced in piecemeal fashion through changes to the civil codes.

7   Paidar (1995) details the confusion in choices of laws and courts in adjudicating divorce and Zubaida (2005) discusses the disorder that ensued in drafting penal sanctions.

8   While the civil codes remained largely intact, the penal code was replaced in 1983. In fact, while officially there was great emphasis on changes to the civil legal system, many of the pre-revolutionary legal concepts and procedures were retained. Mir-Hosseini (2010) details this process.

9   This blended legal system grew out of struggles to determine how to put into operation this unique system consisting of Islam and republic. It should be noted that not all of the Shi'i *ulama* agreed with Ayatollah Khomeini's thesis on Islamic governance. For detailed discussion, see Arjomand 1988.

10 The indictments can be read in English at www.qlineorientalist.com/
    IranRises/the-indictment/ and www.qlineorientalist.com/IranRises/
    the-complete-text-of-the-indictment-of-the-second-group-of-ac-
    cused-in-the-project-for-a-velvet-coup/ (accessed 31 January 2012).
11 Nobel-laureate Shirin Ebadi was among those making this plea (Agence
    France Presse/*The Daily Star* 2008).
12 The bill also instituted full marital arbitration with the aim of rec-
    onciliation for both spouses, regardless of which spouse initiated the
    proceedings.
13 This section is an updated version of an earlier article (Osanloo 2012).
    Reprinted with permission.

References

Agence France Presse/*The Daily Star* (2008) 'Iranian Nobel Laureate Protests
    against Polygamy Bill', 5 August, http://www.dailystar.com.lb/ArticlePrint.
    aspx?id=76055&mode=print (accessed 15 March 2012).
Ali, A. Y. trans. (2004) *Holy Qur'an*, Amana Publishers, Beltsville, MD.
Amani, E. (2008) 'Widespread Opposition to Iran's "Family Protection Bill":
    From Bad to Worse and Beyond...', 15 August, http://www.Iran-women-
    solidarity.net/spip.phP?article430 (accessed 27 November 2009).
Arjomand (1988) *The Turban for the Crown: The Islamic Revolution in Iran*, Oxford
    University Press, New York, NY.
Cottam, R. W. (1986) 'The Iranian Revolution', in J. R. I. Cole and N. R.
    Keddie (eds), *Shi'ism and Social Protest*, Yale University Press, New Haven,
    CT, pp. 55–87.
Iranian Students News Agency (2008) 'Statement by the Rapporteur for the
    Legal and Judicial Commission of Parliament', 9 August, http://www.isna.
    ir/ISNA/NewsView.aspx?ID=News-1194709&Lang=P%A0 (accessed 1
    August 2010).
Kermani, T. (no date) 'Status and Rights of Women in Islam and Iranian
    Family', http://women.gov.ir/en/pages/cprint.php?id=487 (accessed 12
    February 2012).
Khabaronline (2011) 'Chapter 6, Article 5, Iranian Family Protection Act,
    Amended 11 August 2011', http://www.khabaronline.ir/news-168927.
    aspx (accessed 12 March 2012).
Khomeini, R. (1981) *Islam and Revolution: Writings and Declarations of Imam
    Khomeini*, trans. H. Algar, Mizan, Berkeley, CA.
—— (1984) *A Clarification of Questions: An Unabridged Translation of Resaleh
    Towzih al-Masael*, trans. J. Borujerdi, Westview Press, Boulder, CO.
Mir-Hosseini, Z. (1993) *Marriage on Trial: A Study of Islamic Family Law. Iran and
    Morocco Compared*, I. B. Tauris, London.
—— (2006) 'Muslim Women's Quest for Equality: Between Islamic Law and

Feminism', *Critical Inquiry*, Vol. 32, No. 1, pp. 629–45.

—— (2010) 'Sharia and National Law in Iran', in J. Otto (ed.), *Sharia Incorporated: A Comparative Overview of the Legal Systems of Twelve Muslim Countries in Past and Present*, Leiden University Press, Leiden, pp. 319–72.

Osanloo, A. (2006) 'Islamico-Civil Rights Talk: Women, Subjectivity and Law in Iranian Family Court', *American Ethnologist*, Vol. 33, No. 2, pp. 191–209.

—— (2009) *The Politics of Women's Rights in Iran*, Princeton University Press, Princeton, NJ.

—— (2012) 'What a Focus on "Family" Means in the Islamic Republic of Iran', in M. Voorhoeve (ed.), *Family Law in Islam: Divorce, Marriage and Women in the Muslim World*, I.B. Tauris, London, pp. 51–76.

Paidar, P. (1995) *Women and the Political Process in Twentieth-Century Iran*, Cambridge University Press, Cambridge.

Payvand News (2011) 'Iranian Parliament Omits Controversial Family Law Bill', 28 July, http://www.payvand.com/news/11/jul/1279.html (accessed 12 March 2012).

Planet Iran (2010) 'Iranian Women Protest So-Called Family Protection Bill', 22 August, http://planet-iran.com/index.php/news/22202 (accessed 12 February 2012).

Rahnavard, Z. (2010) 'For the Survival of the Family, Eliminate the Family Protection Bill' (in Arabic), 21 August, http://www.kaleme.com/1389/05/30/klm-29765/ (accessed 17 November 2012).

Reuters (2010) 'Girls Should Marry Aged 16–18: Iran's Ahmadinejad', 21 November, http://www.reuters.com/article/2010/11/21/us-iran-marriage-ahmadinejad-idUSTRE6AK16K20101121 (accessed 1 March 2012).

Vatandoust, G. (1985) 'The Status of Iranian Women during the Pahlavi Regime', in A. Fathi (ed.), *Women and the Family in Iran*, E. J. Brill, Leiden, pp. 107–30.

Zubaida, S. (2005) *Law and Power in the Islamic World*, I. B. Tauris, London.

6

Moroccan Divorce Law, Family Court Judges, and Spouses' Claims
Who Pays the Cost When a Marriage is Over?

Jessica Carlisle

In 2010, a 33-year-old middle-class man told the Moroccan French-language magazine *Ousra* (Family) that 'Around ten years ago five of us from amongst my group of friends were married. Now two of us are divorced and a third is about to separate' (*Ousra* 2010: 76–8). Describing the ending of marriages as no longer unusual, the article entitled 'When Men Celebrate Their Divorce!' cited government statistics showing Moroccan divorces increasing by 14 per cent between 2006 and 2007. The magazine noted that this escalation was due to reform of the family law, which has made it easier to end a marriage.

Marriage and divorce in Morocco are regulated by the Mudawwanat al-Usra (Family Law Compilation), or Moudawana. This law was radically reformed in 2004, with changes to provisions on the age of female marital consent, polygamy, and child custody. Amongst additional reforms were far-reaching extensions of the right to request judicial divorce. Articles 94–97 of the Moudawana (2004) enable husbands or wives to request a court-pronounced divorce from a marriage that is in discord (*shiqāq*). Most of the judicial divorces recorded in government statistics since 2004 have been requested on these grounds.

This chapter explores the impact that this reform has had on divorce claims in Morocco, analysing the arguments that spouses bring to the court and judicial responses to their claims. My analysis goes beyond simply determining in what circumstances courts award divorces by also assessing the financial settlement that judges order in their rulings. Moroccan reform has undoubtedly made a judicially ordered divorce easier to obtain, both for wives and husbands, but in requesting it claimants authorize the court to investigate the reasons for the divorce and to attribute blame for the breakdown in the marriage between the spouses. This has unpredictable consequences for the financial settlement that the judge may impose in his final ruling.

I will make four observations about developing divorce trends in the initial post-reform period. The first is that claims based on allegations of *shiqāq* are rapidly increasing since the evidential requirements for the issuing of a divorce are easily met. The second remark is that as *shiqāq* claims become the most prevalent way in which both men and women initiate divorce they are less likely to use gender-determined divorce forms: other types of judicial divorce, *khul*, and repudiation. Third, I discuss the ways in which family court judges record spouses' arguments in their rulings using justifiable terms. Finally, I will note the importance of paying attention to the financial awards included in rulings on *shiqāq* divorce, since they give some indication of judges' evaluations of the claims that wives and husbands make about one another during these cases.

In conclusion I will argue that although family court judges are obliged to grant persistent, procedurally correct *shiqāq* divorce claims, they have considerable discretion in attributing blame for the marital breakdown. Their subsequent assessments of whether wives and husbands have demonstrated reasonable commitment to their marriage is twofold: based both on spouses' previous behaviours and on their involvement in court-ordered reconciliation sessions. These evaluations inform judicial rulings on the extent to which each spouse is responsible for the divorce, which can result in unpredictable financial outcomes for divorcing couples. In setting out their reasoning, judges can be seen 'thinking through' the implications of the new legislation.

Research methods: interviews, 'hanging out', and court rulings

I conducted the research for this study over seven months during 2007–8, with some follow-up during a six-week fieldwork trip in 2010. The result is largely idiographic in its description of judicial divorce cases during the first three years after reform and my analysis of judicial responses to *shiqāq* claims. I will also refer to quantitative data in the form of statistics, although these figures are unhelpful in understanding either what specific claims people make during judicial divorce cases or what the financial outcomes of these divorces might be. Most of the data presented in this chapter are qualitative and were gathered during my own fieldwork, from other socio-legal studies of court practice, or from published rulings granting *shiqāq* divorces.

Fieldwork was not conducted in family courts since I was unable to gain permission from the Moroccan Ministry of Justice to attend court sessions and to speak to judges. I subsequently concentrated on interviewing lawyers and organizations engaged in activism regarding women and social issues, discussions with Moroccan social scientists and in particular non-governmental legal advice centres, or *centres d'écoute*.

Morocco has an extensive network of *centres d'écoute*, providing a range of legal, educational, psychological, and social support to both female and male clients, often on a walk-in basis. The size of centres and the resources they command range from some that are linked to large, national NGOs to small, locally based organizations. I interviewed staff in seven *centres d'écoute* during 2007–8 about family court practices and the centres' involvement in divorce cases, in Marrakesh (two centres), Rabat, Casablanca, Beni Mellal, Tangier, and Ouarzazate. I also attended a three-day mediation training course in Casablanca for around twenty *centres d'écoute* staff from across Morocco, during which workers discussed their work.

In addition, I observed the work of staff based at Centre Hawwa in Marrakesh for a month.[1] The centre did not often permit me to sit in on sessions or to interview clients, so my understanding of their involvement in divorce cases is principally based on information provided by the staff themselves, and not on observation of their interactions with clients. Nevertheless, staff conceptualizations of legal issues and their potential remedies are informative since they are the result of repeated interaction with disputants and the family court process. The resultant assumptions held by legal advice workers regarding disputes, disputant behaviour, and judicial attitudes to cases underpin their approach to their work. Staff drew on this experience in coaching clients in strategies by which to make a legal complaint before they went to court.

Several years after legal reform it was clear that legal practices were still evolving and there was a perception amongst social scientists, lawyers, and *centres d'écoute* staff that the family courts' application of the law demonstrated considerable geographical variation.[2] My findings are therefore indebted to other studies of family court practices and social attitudes towards the Moudawana (2004). Legal reform had provoked considerable media discussion, monitoring by national NGOs, and a great deal of foreign research interest during the period of my fieldwork. In addition, several interesting studies of family courts and social attitudes towards reform have been completed by Moroccan academics. However, when considering judicial divorce, these studies tend to focus on whether divorce requests have been granted to the neglect of considering the attached financial settlements.

More detailed information regarding financial awards in *shiqāq* cases and the judges' justifications for them is available in published court rulings (Fakhury 2009). These documents record the region in which the case was heard and the date on which the case was concluded, summarize the relevant evidence, and record the judge's reasoning.[3] Those I refer to in this chapter were published in a collection of rulings that were issued in 2004–7 by courts across Morocco. Although there are an insufficient number of rulings available to support any broad conclusions about legal practices, they do demonstrate the scope of reasoning underpinning judicial evaluations of claims.

Centres d'écoute practices: making law happen for clients

Centre Hawwa is the largest and most active of Marrakesh's two *centres d'écoute*. The centre was funded and managed by the locally based Association Ennakhil, which was also involved in a variety of projects including awareness raising about HIV/AIDS, adult literacy projects, and lobbying for improvements in welfare provision for divorced or separated women. Association Ennakhil is part of a network of organizations that were involved in lobbying for reform to family law, and it was actively engaged in monitoring legal practice in the courts during 2007–8. The association holds regular round-table discussions with lawyers, has established connections with the Marrakesh family court judiciary, and has developed effective strategies towards bringing clients' claims to court and winning the resulting actions.

Centre Hawwa's core staff consisted of two full-time advice workers (*écoutants*), an administrator and a part-time social worker. The centre also employed three lawyers, each present on Monday, Wednesday, or Friday, a psychologist on Tuesdays, and a psychiatrist on Thursdays. Centre Hawwa's advice workers had received no formal training, but had developed their skills through employment in the social welfare sector and involvement in NGO networks.

The centre operated a drop-in service every weekday morning, with advice workers initially seeing clients to complete an assessment and make initial interventions that they felt were appropriate. Clients were subsequently either offered follow-up appointments with an advice worker or, if they required specialist contact, booked in to see a lawyer, social worker, psychologist, or psychiatrist. In considering potential legal claims, the centre operated a filtering system dependent on advice workers' evaluations of the mental and emotional state of clients who came in. If advice workers felt clients were vulnerable, they might resist requests to make an immediate appointment with one of the lawyers, preferring to first refer clients to a social worker, psychologist, or psychiatrist.

Although most of Centre Hawwa's clients were women, the service was also available to men. The overwhelming majority of the centre's clients were economically disadvantaged, either unemployed or working in low-paid manual work, and many were illiterate. Clients came to the centre seeking support or advice to deal with a variety of problems, including disputes involving allegations of domestic violence and non-payment of maintenance, difficulties posed by the legal status of informally adopted children or children born outside of a court-registered marriage, and requests for divorce. The centre's services were free of charge, although clients might face court costs should they decide to pursue a legal case.

Centre Hawwa staff expressed pride in the impact that they had had on family court practice in Marrakesh, for example through developing good relationships with some local judges and notaries. However, they qualified this assessment by noting that access to the legal process is problematic for some of their clients as the cost of travel to court, photocopying documentation, and court stamps may be too expensive for those litigants without an income (Kouzzi and Willem Bordat 2009). In addition, although social support from family and friends can be of vital help, it is not always guaranteed in navigating and paying for court procedures (Carlisle 2007; Kouzzi and Willem Bordat 2009).

Staff recognized the involvement of kin in many disputes by initially dealing with divorce cases as a non-legal dispute between the spouses. If they could be brought together in mediation sessions, staff might attempt to negotiate reconciliation or a mutually agreed end to the marriage. Spouses' kin were often brought into these sessions to support the process. However, if clients were determined to end their marriages, staff would encourage them and their kin to request a judicial divorce from the family court on the recently introduced grounds of *shiqāq* (discord). In giving this advice workers argued that *shiqāq* claims were always successful, privileging one divorce strategy over several alternative legal provisions and pursuing a strategy that has only been available since 2004.

The Moudawana (1957/8), divorce practices, and legal reform

Morocco's Muslim family law, which is explicitly referenced by the legislature to classical Islamic law (*fiqh*), establishes several forms of divorce. The law was first codified in the Mudawwanat al-Usra, or Moudawana (1957/8), which was a collection of provisions governing marriage, divorce, child custody and guardianship, financial maintenance, and inheritance.[4] Some minor amendments were made to the law in 1993, which included restraints on men's right to marry a co-wife and to effect divorce through unilateral repudiation (Buskens 2003; Wuerth 2005). Subsequently the Moudawana was subject to much more radical reform in 2004, including changes to provisions on the age of female marital consent, the right to contract a polygamous marriage, and ex-wives' entitlements to child custody. In addition, the reforms introduced far-reaching extensions of the right to request judicial divorce to both women and men.

Before this reform, divorce cases were largely restricted to three types: men's unilateral repudiation of their wives (*talāq*), divorce for compensation in which the husband agreed to divorce his wife in return for payment (*khul*), or judicial divorce requests largely from wives on evidence-based grounds. Spouses therefore were restricted by their gender in the types of divorce they could initiate, since repudiation is a male prerogative and only women could request most forms of judicial divorce. Moreover, the potential financial implications of each divorce type differed. These three divorce forms, all of which are retained in the reformed Moudawana (2004), therefore established both the legal criteria through which pre-reform divorce could take place and that divorce's potential financial cost.

Under the terms of the amendments in 1993, divorcing husbands had to notify the court of their intention to unilaterally repudiate their wives. This protected the wife from the husband subsequently denying that the divorce had taken place or failing to notify her of it. However, the 1993 amendments did not provide women subject to a valid repudiation the right to oppose or prevent the divorce.[5] Theoretically, ex-wives who felt that they had been repudiated without justification could request financial compensation (*mut'a*) from the court. In reality this award was often based on the judge's evaluations of the husband's ability to pay (Mir-Hosseini 2000). Nevertheless, repudiation could still be expensive for divorcing husbands, since it rendered them automatically liable to pay all of their ex-wife's financial entitlements: her unpaid dower (*sadāq*); potentially *mut'a*, if ordered by the court; and at least three months' maintenance during her observation of her *'idda*, the period during which an ex-wife cannot legally marry a new husband. A divorced father is also legally obliged to pay maintenance (*nafaqa*) to support any children from a marriage that has ended, unless excused from this payment by their mother.

The 2004 reforms further increased the potential financial cost of repudiation for men and restricted their chances of avoiding paying it. Article 83 of the Moudawana specifies that a husband who wishes to repudiate his wife must deposit the full sum of her financial entitlements with the court before the divorce will be registered. This effectively prevents him from refusing to pay his ex-wife after the divorce has been finalized. Furthermore, Article 84 adds the cost of housing for the ex-wife during her *'idda* on top of the ex-husband's obligation to pay her dower and maintenance. Both spouses must undergo mediation sessions in order to try to save the marriage before the court will register the divorce. Although husbands, therefore, retain the right to repudiate their wives, the process can be both financially costly and intrusive.

If a wife wished to initiate a divorce without her husband's consent before 2004, then her only option was to request judicial divorce from the court. Prior to the introduction of the grounds of *shiqāq*, judicial divorce could be granted on the grounds of the husband's prolonged absence from the marital home, his impotence or severe infirmity, his failure to financially support his wife, his refusal to have marital sexual relations, or behaviour resulting in harm (*darār*) to the wife.[6] All judicial divorce claims on these grounds had to be supported with evidence. If proven the divorce would entitle the divorcing wife to receive her unpaid dower and maintenance for the period of her *'idda*. In addition, the husband would be liable to pay maintenance for any children from the marriage.

Assessments of women's attempts to obtain a judicial divorce under evidence-based provisions before the reform in 2004 have stressed the limited grounds on which claims could be established, and the procedural obstacles faced by claimants. Pleas based on allegations of harm seem to have been particularly difficult to prove to a judge's satisfaction. The Moroccan court process relied heavily on documentation such as medical and police reports regarding physical injury caused to the wife by the husband. Hearings were often held in open court, which, it has been suggested, renders it difficult for wives to be frank about their marriages in support of claims of domestic abuse (Zohra Boukaissi 2007). Conducting fieldwork in courts in the 1990s, Mir-Hosseini found that procedural regulations required a wife to prove decisively the harm she had suffered, although 'the type and nature of proofs provided and accepted by the court var[ied] from one case to another' (Mir-Hosseini 2000: 107).

Although Mir-Hosseini found that in some cases establishing harm was 'straightforward', such as in a case in which the husband was imprisoned for killing his son and another in which the husband had been sentenced for sexually assaulting his stepdaughter, other pleas were based on a combination of complaints about absence, non-payment of maintenance, and maltreatment. Finding that proving harm was difficult for most claimants since there were no witnesses to what had taken place in the couple's home, Mir-Hosseini stated that '[w]hile violence appears to be a common element in most [cases], the boundaries between the grievances are hazy' (Mir-Hosseini 2000: 108). Given the difficulty of presenting sufficient evidence to secure a judicial divorce from the court, she found that women adopted a scatter-gun strategy in which they included as many grounds as they could in their petition.

Judicial divorce claims were therefore unlikely to be successful in the absence of compelling, supporting evidence. In this event, women who wished to divorce before 2004 could only try to persuade their husbands to repudiate them. This could be agreed through negotiating the terms of a *khul* contract in which the husband divorces the wife in return for payment. This contract is agreed outside of the courtroom, although the final stages of it are overseen by the judge. During her research in the courts before legal reform, Mir-Hosseini found that slightly over a third of repudiations were pronounced as a result of *khul* contracts. Under these circumstances women were in a weak bargaining position when negotiating the terms of their divorce, since they often had no alternative route by which to secure the end of their marriages. Mir-Hosseini found cases in which in addition to renouncing their own financial entitlements women agreed to give up their right to receive child maintenance in order to secure their husband's agreement to divorce.

Shiqāq: a catch-all complaint

The introduction of the grounds of *shiqāq* in Article 94 of the Moudawana (2004) considerably expanded the grounds on which both spouses can petition the court for a divorce. This provision enables both husbands and wives to request a judicial divorce stating that they are engaged in a dispute that threatens to break down their marriage. Article 95 instructs the court to appoint two arbiters to attempt to reconcile the couple and these arbiters should subsequently submit a written report to the judge. If the couple cannot be reconciled then the court, under Article 96, should investigate the causes of the difficulties and grant a divorce. This entire procedure should take no more than six months. The issuing of the divorce entitles ex-wives to potentially all of the financial entitlements that would follow repudiation. However, Article 97 instructs the judge to take into account each spouse's responsibility for the marital problems when ruling on the financial settlement. This provision, as will become clear, has been a central feature of judicial involvement in divorce.

Moroccan Ministry of Justice (MoJ) statistics record that judicial divorce claims have been increasingly preferred as a means to end marriages since 2004 and are rapidly becoming the dominant type of divorce ruled on by the courts. Table 6.1 shows MoJ figures for all divorces registered by the family courts from 2005 to 2007, detailing rapidly rising numbers of judicial divorces and a slightly decreasing incidence of non-judicial divorces, which include repudiations and divorces contracted directly between the spouses.

Table 6.1 Divorces registered by the family courts, 2006–7

Years	Non-judicial divorce	Judicial divorce	Total
2005	29,668	9,983	39,651
2006	28,239	14,791	43,030
2007	27,904	21,328	49,232
% Variation 2005–6	−4.8%	48.2%	8.5%
% Variation 2006–7	−1.2%	44.2%	14.4%

Source: http://adala.justice.gov.ma/production/statistiques/famille/FR/Activité %20des%20sections%20de%20la%20famille%20durant%20la%20période%20 (2005-2007).pdf

Furthermore, MoJ figures support anecdotal accounts I heard during my fieldwork that the majority of these judicial divorce petitions are made on the recently introduced grounds of *shiqāq* rather than on grounds requiring the submission of evidence of harm, absence, infirmity, sexual abstinence, or non-maintenance. By 2007–8, *centres d'écoute* staff were confident that *shiqāq* was becoming the standard ground for securing a judicial divorce from the family court. Although I heard reports that some Moroccan family court judges initially resisted applying the *shiqāq* provisions after 2004, the *centres d'écoute* staff I interviewed four years after legal reform stated that most court sections were processing claims without difficulty (LDDF 2006).

The reason advice workers give for the remarkable increase in *shiqāq* cases is the low evidential requirement for establishing claims. Unlike grounds for judicial divorce before reform, which required substantiation of complaints about a husband's behaviour, divorce can be granted on the grounds of *shiqāq* based solely on the claimant's refusal to reconcile. All the *centres d'écoute* advisers and lawyers I interviewed during 2007–8 confirmed that as pre-2004 judicial divorce grounds were difficult to prove they now invariably encouraged wives to base their requests to the court on the grounds of *shiqāq*. This remained their advice even if a woman has substantial evidence that she has been physically abused by her husband, amounting to a potential claim of harm.[7]

In effect, a claim based on grounds of *shiqāq* may include allegations that formerly would have supported claims for other forms of judicial divorce. An absence of an explanatory text from the legislature precisely defining *shiqāq* and a dearth of rulings from the Supreme Court allows family court judges considerable discretion in interpreting its meaning. In one evaluation of legal practice in *shiqāq* cases judges have been described as accepting a range of justifications for granting the divorce, including non-maintenance by the husband, adultery, a change in the husband's character, jealousy, drug or alcohol addiction, incompatibility, and the wife's remaining in her parental home without consummating the marriage (Zeidguy 2007).

As a result, as MoJ statistics demonstrate, there was a marked shift in the phrasing of requests for judicial divorces during the period 2006–7 from pre-reform, evidence-dependent cases towards *shiqāq* claims.

Table 6.2 Divorces by type, 2006–7

Judicial divorce claim	Cases in progress, 2006	Divorces awarded, 2006	Cases in progress, 2007	Divorces awarded, 2007	Percentage variation in ongoing cases, 2006–7	Percentage variation in rulings, 2006–7
Shiqāq	35,115	10,313	58,238	18,562	65.9%	80%
Harm	5,402	1,361	2,097	447	−61.2%	−67.2%
Non-maintenance	2,860	1,086	1,962	703	−31.4%	−35.3%
Absence	4,627	1,943	4,365	1,562	−5.7%	−19.6%
Physical defect	113	22	92	12	−18.6%	−45.5%
Sexual abstinence	165	66	204	42	23.6%	−36.7%
Total	48,282	14,791	66,958	21,328	38.7%	44.2%

Source: Statistiques Brochées du Ministère de la Justice 2008 (quoted in El-Mekkaoui 2009)

Although MoJ statistics for the total number of judicial divorce cases finalized in 2006 appear to show that judges are just as likely to reject *shiqāq* requests as other judicial divorce claims, *centres d'écoute* staff noted that claimants often abandon their cases by failing to show up at court hearings and that claims are vulnerable to being refused if the initial submission is procedurally flawed (El-Mekkaoui 2009). In addition, some couples may reconcile without informing the court of their decision. Staff at Centre Hawwa reported that they also often lose touch with clients who fail to come in for follow-up sessions, and that as a result they can only guess how these disputes may have ended.

Table 6.3 Judicial divorce claims resolved, granted or rejected on all grounds, 2007

Divorce claim	Reconciliation	Divorce	Rejected	Total
Shiqāq	3,785	10,313	4,959	19,057
'Harm'	467	1,361	846	2,674
Non-maintenance	149	1,086	461	1,696
Absence	179	1,943	501	2,623
Physical defect	13	22	17	52
Abstinence	23	66	26	115
Total	4,616	14,791	6,810	26,217

Source: *Statistiques Brochées du Ministère de la Justice* 2008 (quoted in El-Mekkaoui 2009)

While the number of complaints made to the court by women on the grounds of *shiqāq* is unsurprising, given the ease and flexibility of its procedure, MoJ figures show that the provision was also increasingly used by men in 2006–7, albeit not in the same numbers as female claimants. The main reason given for this strategy by *centres d'écoute* staff was that divorcing husbands hoped to avoid the requirement preceding the registration of repudiation that they should deposit all of their wives' financial entitlements with the court. The argument was that once the divorce was pronounced, men would simply refuse to pay the amount owing to their ex-wives. Some family court sections, notably in Casablanca, reportedly responded to this strategy in 2007 by requiring men to lodge this money with the court before they would process either repudiations or male-instigated *shiqāq* divorce petitions.

However, court rulings on *shiqāq* cases indicate a more substantial rationale for men submitting these claims. While husbands are liable to pay all of their wives' financial entitlements on repudiating them, *shiqāq* rulings may lower the cost of a divorce legitimately, given the judge's authority to award damages against either spouse. In submitting a complaint about *shiqāq*, husbands may be gambling on persuading the judge to make an award in their favour. Although men divorced by the *shiqāq* process are liable to pay their ex-wives' unpaid dower (*sadāq*) and maintenance entitlements, in practice they often successfully present the court with claims that their wives bear some responsibility for the marital breakdown, and requests that they should be financially compensated for this. Rulings may award husbands compensation equal, close to, or even in excess of the value of the financial entitlements granted to the wife. The financial costs incurred to a divorcing husband may therefore be considerably lower than those linked to repudiation. Alternatively, should the wife submit a successful counter-claim for damages, the husband may come to regret this strategy.

Table 6.4 Shiqāq claims registered with family courts, 2006–7

Year	Wives	Husbands	Total
2006	20,223	5,800	26,023
2007	26,547	14,181	40,728
% Increase 2006–7	31.3%	144.5%	56.5%

Source: El-Mekkaoui 2009

In effect, disputing spouses involved in these judicial divorce claims cede direct control over the financial outcomes on the ending of their marriage to the family court judge, and are often under pressure to make a persuasive case that they should not be given the responsibility for bearing its costs.

Rulings as records of the divorce process

The sense of uncertainty attached to the outcomes of judicial divorces is not felt only by disputing spouses. *Centres d'écoute* staff were confident by 2007 that *shiqāq* claims were a quick, easy, and effective way of bringing about divorce for both female and male claimants. However, there were differing perceptions of the financial consequences of these divorces – ranging from positive assessments that ex-wives could potentially be awarded both their financial entitlements and some compensation, to comments that medical certificates proving incidents of domestic violence did not benefit wives' cases and that judicial assessments of compensation seemed to be illogical. A lawyer I interviewed in Ouarzazate in 2007 argued that local court rulings on post-divorce financial settlements took little account of spouses' contribution to the marriage, or their post-divorce circumstances. One advice worker in Rabat was particularly pessimistic in her assessment that judges tended to have an arbitrary conceptualization of what constitutes grounds for *shiqāq*. She also noted that women were vulnerable to agreeing to contract a divorce in exchange for completely revoking their financial rights as the result of not realizing that they could apply for a *shiqāq* divorce.

Legal advice staff across Morocco argued that when women do not understand the *shiqāq* process they are particularly susceptible to poor legal advice from lawyers or relatives, who are usually appointed as arbiters to deal with their claims. They further asserted that the appointment of kin to oversee the mediation stage of these cases can be counter-productive because it may prolong the initial dispute, and exposes the wife to intimidation. *Centres d'écoute* staff, lawyers, and social scientists commented that judges spend little time directly questioning spouses about their marital discord and that their consideration of spouses' claims is subsequently often cursory (Zohra Boukaissi 2007). As a result, they stated, judges are poorly equipped to assess spouses' arguments comprehensively and to make equitable financial awards.

Court rulings on *shiqāq* petitions issued in 2004–7 suggest that, nonetheless, spouses requesting judicial divorce often do their utmost to persuade judges to admit claims that will result in financial awards in their favour. Claimants do not have to bring any evidence to court in order to secure a judicial divorce on the grounds of *shiqāq*, as their testimony that they do not wish to continue their marriage should be sufficient to support their claim. Nevertheless, it is clearly in both spouses' interests to convince the judge of their lack of culpability for the marital breakdown. Rulings issued by family courts of first instance, appeal courts, and the Supreme Court during the period 2004–7 frequently address claims made by disputing spouses for damages to be awarded in their favour in the event of the divorce being granted. *Centres d'écoute* workers emphasized this aspect of judicial divorce proceedings when coaching their clients towards lodging a *shiqāq* claim at the court, urging wives to speak out about violence, neglect, or cruelty.

The impact that such arguments have made on financial settlements related to judicial divorce does not emerge with full clarity in court rulings. Judges' justifications of their decisions are inevitably selective summaries of the testimony brought to the court and of the dynamics during the compulsory, court-ordered reconciliation sessions. Rulings on judicial divorces vary in their length and the details that they record regarding the allegations made by the spouses, the facts as accepted by the court, procedure during the hearings, and the financial entitlements owed to the wife on divorce. In addition, spouses' standards of living can usually only be surmised from the awards made by the court, as rulings rarely provide information about the spouses' professions and only sometimes include statements about husbands' incomes. As a result it is not possible to offer a fully comprehensive assessment of the content of each hearing, or the judge's reasoning in each case.

What is common to all rulings is a demonstration that the correct procedure has been followed prior to the judge's decision. Courts of first instance, in particular, record adherence to the Moudawana's provisions in that attempts have been made to bring about reconciliation (*sulh*) between the couple, which ended in failure (*fashal*) before the investigation began into each of the spouses' responsibility for (*ma'sul 'an*) the marital breakdown. Each spouse's testimony is briefly described and rulings sometimes include supporting witness testimony from family members. Courts frequently employ the same terms, including violence (*darab*), suspicion (*shakk*), failure to provide maintenance (*adam al-infāq*), a change in the husband's behaviour (*slukhu taghayr*), and lack of understanding (*adam al-tawāfiq*) in summing up the accusations that husbands and wives make about one another.

Some of these claims are determined by the Moudawana as gender-specific, such as husbands' testimony that they have previously been to court to insist (under Article 195) that their wife should either return to the marital home (*tālibat bi-l raju'a ila bayt al-zowjiyat*) or otherwise lose her right to financial maintenance (*nafaqa*). Other claims appear more pliable. Only wives are recorded in the court rulings as making accusations that their spouse has subjected them to violence, but the rulings suggest that either spouse may claim that they have been caused harm (*darar*) during the marriage. As grounds for a judicial divorce case, under Articles 99–100, the claim of harm (*darar*) can only be brought by wives. However, in these *shiqāq* rulings the term is being used in a broader descriptive sense to strengthen either spouse's arguments.

Judicial responses to divorce requests: concluding marital disputes and attributing blame

As I have already indicated, analysing judicial attributions of blame in these rulings is difficult in many cases. Rulings rarely explicitly state which of the spouses is most to blame for the divorce or to what degree, so in most cases this has to be surmised from the financial awards. Assessing each of the spouses' financial gains and losses, however, is not always possible given the frequent lack of information about the financial entitlements automatically due to wives on becoming divorced. Although rulings record what spouses receive as financial compensation (*mut'a* or *tawid*) it is not always clear what dower (*sadāq*) is also owed to wives and if they can expect to receive it. The financial compensation awarded by the court may, therefore, not fully encompass the financial repercussions of the divorce.

There are, as a result, broadly two types of identifiable financial rulings in the *shiqāq* cases I have studied in the period 2004–7: those in which one spouse was compensated, and those in which the court instructed the spouses to share the costs.[8] A ruling of the former type was issued by the Supreme Court in 2007 in upholding compensation confirmed by the Court of the Appeal in Oujda in favour of a husband who had instigated his divorce (Case 222, Supreme Court, 18 April 2007). During the case in the court of first instance the husband stated that his wife had refused to take up residence in the marital home or to begin a sexual relationship, presenting the court with bank statements in support of his claim that she owed him a debt of 330,000 dirham (29,000 euros) and requesting compensation of 50,000 dirham (4,500 euros). The wife countered with a completely different story: that the husband had always known that she lived both in France and in Morocco, to which he had expressed no objection; that he had secretly married three women and had abandoned her pregnant in Spain, paying only 40,000 dirham (3,500 euros) towards her housing and contributing nothing towards the medical treatment she needed, which had cost her 60,000 dirham (5,300 euros). She added that he was wealthy and owned several properties, stating that she did not want to divorce, but that if it was granted she should be awarded compensation in line with the degree of harm she had suffered.

The ruling from a court of first instance, which was subsequently upheld by the Court of Appeal, granted the divorce, awarded the wife 2,000 dirham (175 euros) for housing during her *'idda* and ordered her to pay 30,000 dirham (2,650 euros) compensation to her ex-husband. The Supreme Court found that there had been faults in the earlier rulings' reasoning, which should have regarded both ex-spouses as responsible for the marital breakdown, but argued that the award was justifiable given the wife's refusal to cohabit and maintain a sexual, marital relationship.

An example of a similar ruling, in which one spouse benefited financially from claiming that the marriage had not been one in which they could hope to have children, was handed down by a court of first instance in Nador in 2006 in response to a husband's request for a judicial divorce (Case 127, Court of First Instance, Nador, 1 February 2006). He stated that his wife had caused numerous problems throughout the marriage, during which time he had supported her financially while having difficulties arranging for her to join him in France. He added that during this time she had left the marital home. During the reconciliation sessions, the wife countered that for fifteen days after the wedding party the couple had lived in the marital home with the husband's family, during which time the husband had refused to consummate the marriage. The husband insisted during these sessions that he wanted a judicial divorce, while his wife claimed that she wished to continue the marriage and argued that since he had failed to consummate the relationship his request for a divorce was arbitrary. The court finally awarded the wife 2,000 dirham (175 euros) towards her housing during her *'idda* and 60,000 dirham (5,300 euros) compensation (*mut'a*), quoting Article 70 of the Moudawana, which states that marriages should only be dissolved in exceptional circumstances.

Defendants frequently argue during judicial divorce hearings that they wish to continue the marriage. It appears that spouses often benefit from insisting that they do not wish to divorce or that their spouse has been uncooperative despite attempts to resolve their dispute. Husbands in particular, possibly advised by their lawyers, often seem to anticipate this in written submissions to the courts, adding that they should be compensated if the judge grants a divorce. Used in defence against accusations of poor marital behaviour, this counter-argument can result in a ruling in which the spouses are instructed to share the costs on divorce.

This strategy was beneficial for one husband during a Marrakesh case in 2004, which was brought by his wife before consummation of their marriage (Case 1626, Court of First Instance, Marrakesh, 10 June 2004). The case began with a petition from the husband stating that his wife had failed to move into the marital home, and requesting that she be fined 250 dirham (22 euros) every day she failed to do so.[9] His wife countered that she had good reasons not to want to cohabit, since her husband was jealous, had threatened her father, had married a co-wife, and was addicted to alcohol. Her father subsequently partially confirmed this testimony during the reconciliation sessions. The wife requested a divorce, half her dower (her entitlement prior to consummation of the marriage) and for the legal costs to be awarded against the husband. The court accepted her reasons for requesting the divorce, but excused the husband from paying the dower to which she was potentially entitled. The ruling's justification for this decision was that her request for payment of dower 'did not conform to requirements'. It may be that the short length of this marriage and the fact that it had not been consummated had some influence on this ruling, but the judge's reasoning is not explained beyond the summary of the facts as accepted by the court.

Similarly, the family court in Al-Hoceima instructed an ex-wife to pay compensation to the father of her child in 2006 after he insisted that he wanted to continue the marriage (Case 419, Court of First Instance, Al-Hoceima, 9 February 2006). The wife claimed that the husband had physically abused and insulted her, and her mother stated that he had not provided financial maintenance. In addition, the wife stated that the husband had retained several items of furniture belonging to her to the value of 942 dirham, which the husband denied. The court attempted to reconcile the couple during two meetings, and investigated the dispute about the furniture by calling a witness. During proceedings, the husband also requested compensation (*tawid*) of 20,000 dirham (1,750 euros) in the event of a divorce.

This case was concluded with the granting of a judicial divorce to the wife. The court found that the husband had lied about his wife's property, and instructed him to return it to her. In addition, the wife was awarded compensation (*mut'a*) of 2,000 dirham (175 euros), 1,000 dirham (80 euros) to pay for accommodation during her '*idda*, plus 250 dirhams (22 euros) of monthly child maintenance and 50 dirham (4.5 euros) monthly 'wages for childcare'. The husband was awarded 3,000 dirham (265 euros) compensation (*tawid*). In effect the ex-wife's compensation award and the rent due to pay for her accommodation during her *'idda* was cancelled out by the award made to her ex-husband. Her financial settlement therefore consisted of any outstanding marital dower, together with child maintenance and her 'wages for childcare'. The ruling does not record whether she was due any unpaid dower.[10]

The ex-wife in this case effectively received the financial entitlements she could expect if her husband had divorced her by a repudiation to which the court had not attached compensation. My analysis of rulings has found that husbands are frequently compensated either through the awarding of direct compensation (*tawid*) or by the court ordering the wife to return any dower she has previously received. A ruling in 2007 from the Al-Hoceima Court of Appeal instructed a divorcing wife both to return her dower of 20,000 dirham and to pay her ex-husband an additional 15,000 dirham in compensation (*tawid*) (Case 358, Court of Appeal Al-Hoceima, 13 July 2007). A ruling from the Tangier Court of Appeal a year previously reduced an award made to an ex-wife who had asserted that she had been physically assaulted by her ex-husband during their marriage, from a total of 28,000 dirham (2,500 euros) for housing and compensation to 10,000 dirham (900 euros) (Case 329, Court of Appeal Tangier, 19 April 2007).

Conclusion: some reasons to celebrate, some cause for caution

As these rulings demonstrate, judicial divorce is now within easy reach of those claimants who are in a position to take their case to court. The introduction of the grounds of *shiqāq* into the reformed Moudawana (2004), as *centres d'écoute* staff confirm, has transformed access to divorce for women and has had a profound effect on the way that men bring about an end to their marriages. However, to avoid being financially penalized on the awarding of a *shiqāq* divorce, it is in the interest of both husbands and wives to demonstrate that they are not substantially at fault for the marital breakdown.

Centres d'écoute advice workers anticipate judicial evaluations of spouses' arguments and the attribution of blame when coaching their clients about what to say during the hearings. This may be as much to protect their clients from having compensation awards made against them, as it is to try to gain them an advantage in having compensation awarded in their favour. However, advice staff can offer no guarantees as to what the ruling on a claimant's case might be, beyond that the divorce will be granted.

As these rulings demonstrate, spouses often present the court with considerable evidence that they should not be made to pay for the ending of the marriage. It is difficult to analyse the reasoning behind the subsequent rulings on these claims without having observed the cases. The rulings do not include much detailed judicial argument and I have access to an insufficient number of them to draw any general conclusions about judges' attitudes towards the allegations made by spouses. Nevertheless, in their summaries of spouses' statements as justifiable claims, such as absence, suspicion, polygamy, and failure to enter into marital life, and their comments on testimonies' legal relevance, judges can be witnessed interpreting and applying the *shiqāq* provision.

Considering the rulings discussed in this chapter, it does appear that some justifications for requesting a divorce remain difficult to establish in court. In particular, it seems that allegations about physical and psychological abuse continue to be problematic for wives to prove, even after legal reform. Judges may find that claims about domestic violence are not proved during the process, or have difficulty assessing the emotional dynamic within the marriage. It is evident that the allegations discussed in some of the above cases were considered insufficient to secure the wife compensation in excess of that awarded to her husband. Judges also appear disposed to admit husbands' claims that wives have refused to fulfil their marital obligation to cohabit, or that wives have resisted attempts to save the marriage. Either spouse may hope to benefit from insisting that they do not wish their marriage to end and requesting that they be compensated in the event of a divorce.

A conclusion that can be drawn from the reading of rulings during 2004–7 is that although both men and women may have reason to celebrate their ability to end unsatisfactory marriages, this celebration may be qualified. Judicial assessments of spouses' commitments to their marriages, based on spouses' previous behaviour and their involvement in court-ordered reconciliation sessions, can result in one spouse paying significant costs on the issuing of their divorce – even in cases that *centres d'écoute* staff might feel would not justify such a ruling.

Acknowledgements

I would like to thank Professor Annelies Moors for her considerable support during this post-doctoral research, which was funded by the Centre for the Study of Islam in Leiden, the Netherlands. I am also grateful to Dr Mulki Sharmani, Dr Nahda Shehada, and an anonymous reviewer for their comments during the drafting of this chapter.

Notes

1   I did not supplement these data through interviews with divorce applicants themselves. The *centres d'écoute* are extremely busy work-places and were subject to frequent attention from journalists, researchers, and interns in 2007. Centre Hawwa's workers did not have time to assist me and did not give me permission to approach their clients directly, in addition to which my Arabic dialect is not Moroccan and I speak no Amazigh.

2   Geographic variation is particularly highlighted with regard to the granting of exceptions for the marriage of minors. See LDDF Annual Report (2006).

3   I am grateful to my former colleague Friso Kulk for providing me with a copy of this book.

4   Moudawana is something of a misnomer, since Morocco has several similarly titled compilations of laws, such as the Mudawwanat al-Shughul (Compilation of Employment Legislation) and the Mudawwanat al-Sayr ala Turuq (Compilation of Traffic Law).

5   Repudiations pronounced when intoxicated, under coercion, when angry, as a threat, by oath, or conditionally, can be overruled by the court. However, the wife must present evidence of this to the judge.

6   Husbands can also request a judicial divorce on the grounds of physical impairment, but it is rarely used.

7   This reflects findings about judicial divorce petitions in Damascus Shari'a courts, where all claims were routinely submitted on the grounds of *shiqāq*, even if wives principally complained about non-maintenance, or brought police and hospital reports certifying that they had been subject to domestic violence (Carlisle 2007).

8   There are also cases in which the ruling records that the wife voluntarily renounced her entitlement to dower in return for the divorce. This is not necessary under the terms of the *shiqāq* provision.

9   The ruling does not mention under what legal provision this petition was made and I cannot find justification for it in the Moudawana (2004).

10 It is interesting to note the gendered nature of the terms by which judicial compensation is awarded. While that due to ex-wives is described as *mut'a*, the pre-reform term describing awards sometimes made to ex-wives post-repudiation, amounts awarded to ex-husbands are described as *tawid* (direct compensation).

References

Buskens, L. (2003) 'Recent Debates on Family Law Reform in Morocco: Islamic Law as Politics in an Emerging Public Sphere', *Islamic Law and Society*, Vol. 10, No. 1, pp. 70–131.

Carlisle, J. (2007) '*Asbab l'il-Darb Ktir Basita*: The Legality of Claims of Violence during Judicial Divorce Cases in Damascus', *Hawwa*, Vol. 5, Nos 2–3, pp. 239–61.

El-Mekkaoui, R. N. (2009) *La Moudawana (La Code de la Famille): Le Referential et le Conventionnel et Harmonie La Dissolution du Mariage*, Bouregreg, Rabat.

Fakhury, I. (2009) *Al-'Amal Al-Qada'i Al-Usri Al-Juz' Al-Thani: Al-Talaq Al-Shiqaq* (The Work of the Family Court Judiciary, Second Part: Divorce for Discord) Dar Al-Afaq Al-Nashr wa Al-Tauzi', Casablanca.

Kouzzi, S. and S. Willem Bordat (2009) 'Legal Empowerment of Unwed Mothers: Experiences of Moroccan NGOs', International Development Law Organization (IDLO), Rome.

Ligue Democratique des Droits des Femmes (LDDF) (2006) *Rapport Annuel: 2006 Reseau des Centres* (Annual Report 2006: Network Centres), LDDF Assistance, Rabat.

Mir-Hosseini, Z. (2000) *Marriage on Trial: A Study of Islamic Family Law,* I. B. Tauris, London and New York, NY.

Ousra (2010) 'Quand les Hommes Fêtent Leur Divorce!' (When Men Celebrate Their Divorce!), April, pp. 76–8.

Wuerth, O. (2005) 'The Reform of the Moudawana: The Role of Women's Civil Society Organisations in Changing the Personal Status Code in Morocco', *Hawwa*, Vol. 3, pp. 309–33.

Zeidguy, R. (2007) 'Analyse de Jurisprudence' (Legal Analysis), in M. Benradi, H. Alami M'chichi, A. Ounnir, M. Mouaqit, F. Zohra Boukaissi, and R. Zeidguy (eds), *Le Code de la Famille: Perceptions et Practique Judiciaire* (The Family Code: Perceptions and Legal Practice), Friedrich Ebert Stiftung, Bonn.

Zohra Boukaissi, F. (2007) 'Du Déroulement des Audiences à la Section de la Justice de la Famille près de la Tribunaux de Première Instance de Rabat' (The Conduct of Hearings at the Justice Section of the Family Court of the First Instance in Rabat), in M. Benradi, H. Alami M'chichi, A. Ounnir, M. Mouaqit, F. Zohra Boukaissi, and R. Zeidguy (eds), *Le Code de la Famille: Perceptions et Practique Judiciaire,* Friedrich Ebert Stiftung, Bonn.

7
Organizing to Monitor Implementation of the Maria da Penha Law in Brazil

●●●

Silvia de Aquino

The first Brazilian federal law addressing domestic violence against women was approved in August 2006. Law No. 11.340/2006 is also known as the Maria da Penha Law (LMP) in reference to the case of Maria da Penha Fernandes, a Brazilian woman who suffered threats and aggression from her former husband throughout their marriage. Fearful of what might happen, she did not separate from him. In 1983 she survived a murder attempt by him which left her paralysed by several hard blows to her spine. Her husband escaped punishment, claiming that her injuries had been caused by an attempted robbery, not by him. Two weeks later, Maria suffered another murder attempt as her husband tried to electrocute her in the bath. There was evidence that these crimes had been planned. Her husband had tried to purchase a life insurance policy for Maria, of which he would be the beneficiary, just a few weeks before the murder attempt (AGENDE 2006a).

But how was the LMP introduced? What of the efforts undertaken by feminist activists who lobbied for this law? And how are they monitoring its implementation? This chapter will address these questions by examining the work of the Maria da Penha Law Observatory, which was established in 2007. Set up by a consortium of twelve research and non-governmental organizations, the observatory aims to monitor the implementation of the LMP, raise awareness about the new code, and gather relevant information regarding implementation of the law so as to enhance current policy measures for combating violence against women.

First, I will review the efforts of feminist movements and activists that have led to the introduction of the law. Second, I will outline the activities of the observatory, reporting and analysing preliminary findings from the advocacy and research work that I undertook along with other observatory colleagues. Finally, I will reflect on the implications of the findings in a brief conclusion.

Feminist activism and the LMP

In 1998, Maria da Penha Fernandes, together with representatives from CEJIL-Brasil[1] (Centro para Justiça e o Direito Internacional – Centre for Justice and International Law) and CLADEM-Brasil[2] (Comitê Latino-Americano e do Caribe para a Defesa dos Direitos da Mulher – the Latin American and Caribbean Committee for the Defense of Women's Rights), entered the offices of the Inter-American Commission of Human Rights to present a petition against the Brazilian state, based on the Convention of Belém do Pará (the Inter-American Convention on the Prevention, Punishment, and Eradication of Violence against Women).[3] The petition pointed out that, in spite of being sentenced, the aggressor was not arrested. In 2001 the Inter-American Commission on Human Rights declared the Brazilian state responsible for negligence, tolerance, and omissions related to domestic violence, making the Maria da Penha case the first in which the Belém do Pará Convention was implemented (Sociedade Brasileira de Direito Público 2001). Based on this decision, the Inter-American Commission recommended that the Brazilian state pay the victim compensation. Other important recommendations included the drafting of a law addressing violence against women. The following is an excerpt from the Commission's finding on the case:

> The impunity that the aggressor and ex-husband of Senhora Fernandes enjoyed and still enjoys is against the international obligations that

the Brazilian state has voluntarily taken on by ratifying the Belém do Pará Convention. The lack of punishment for those responsible in this case is effectively the state showing its acceptance of the violence that Maria da Penha suffered. The negligence on the part of the Tribunal and the Brazilian justice system directly contributes to aggravate the violence against Senhora Maria da Penha Maia Fernandes. Furthermore, as was demonstrated earlier, this is unfortunately not an exclusive case but part of a systemic inequality. This is about tolerance of a system that does not attempt to address the roots and the psychological, social and historical factors that maintain and encourage violence against women. (Organização Dos Estados Americanos 2001: 12–13)

The document concluded that:

This violation against Maria da Penha is part of a general pattern of negligence and lack of efficiency on the part of the state in terms of processing and sentencing aggressors; the Commission thus considers both the obligation to process and sentence aggressors as well as the obligation to act to prevent these degrading practices. This lack of general judicial efficiency in combination with a discriminatory practice help create the very environment that allows the existence of domestic violence, as there is no socially perceived evidence of the will and effectiveness on part of the state, as a representative of society, to punish acts of this type. (Organização Dos Estados Americanos 2001: 13)

In other words, the document highlighted the failure of the state and legal system to uphold women's rights and proposed recommendations to address this failure. This document was of great importance in the history of a political mobilization led by Brazilian women's and feminist movements to address violence against women. And of course this would not have been possible without the relentless fight by Maria da Penha and the organizations that fought by her side in this process.

But it is also important to recognize and contextualize the approval of the Maria da Penha Law (LMP) as an event that is directly linked to this political process. For the past thirty years in Brazil, feminist and women's movements have organized sustained and vigorous resistance to violence against women. These women dared to confront the military dictatorship of the 1970s and early 1980s. We must not forget that the expression 'violence against women' itself carries a special political significance for these movements, as unfortunately there is a certain type of violence that persists, of men against women. It is a phenomenon that is neglected historically and rarely even recognized as violence. This situation remained unaddressed until the second wave of feminist and women's movements – revolutionary movements providing radical social criticism, drinking out of the same spring as liberation groups as diverse as the Black and 'Hippy' movements. The second wave feminist movement went to the core of the oppression lived by women in an effort to eliminate it.

Women gathered in groups to talk about issues that mattered to them. They mobilized against the idea of 'legitimate defence of honour' in cases where women were murdered by their male partners.[4] The feminist movement also pushed for the creation of the SOS Services, centres for women who were victims of violence. At the beginning of the 1980s the first of these centres were established in Brazilian state capitals such as São Paulo, Rio de Janeiro, and Belo Horizonte in the southeastern region.

In the decade that followed, Brazil witnessed political changes that created conditions for re-democratization. For instance, the first direct elections were held at the state level in 1982 for the governors' seats. For some sectors of the feminist movements, this was also a chance to try to influence the state directly by making proposals for public policies. This created some dissent within the movements because some of the more radical activists did not think that working with the state was a viable option in terms of changing gender relations. Didn't the state itself function through patriarchal institutions and parameters? However, in spite of these internal differences, there was still a great emphasis on pressuring the Brazilian state to recognize its responsibility to guarantee women's rights and implement public policies accordingly. This process led to the creation of the first public service institution addressing violence against women in São Paulo in 1985: the Women's Police Station. Later on, Reference Centres for Women and Shelters for Women were also established. According to the Special Secretariat for Policies for Women (SPM), the Reference Centres for Women are:

> the strategic space in which the national policy addresses violence against women and seeks to break the violent situation and to construct citizenship through global action and an interdisciplinary approach (psychological, social, legal guidance, and information)....
> The Reference Centres should exert an important role in articulating the services, government agencies, and NGOs within the network of care to women in situations of social vulnerability, women who are suffering gender violence. (SPM 2006: 2)

The Shelters for Women, according to the same document, 'are safe places that offer comprehensive care and sheltered accommodation to women at risk of death due to domestic violence. The services they offer are confidential and temporary until users meet conditions necessary to resume the course of their lives' (*ibid.*: 8).

Through this political process of struggle, marked by a remarkable creativity, feminist and women's movements brought about some important changes and won significant victories.[5] Violence against women was no longer a hidden, private issue, but a serious public concern for policy makers. This change was achieved through successfully publicizing the problem of violence and highlighting the intrinsic link between the personal and the political. As part of their struggle to combat violence against women, feminist movements also succeeded in highlighting the connection between a democratic society and the recognition of women's rights. This entailed emphasizing the link between women's rights and human rights. These connections are reflected in the positions and arguments of Brazilian feminist theorists, as I illustrate below:

> In Brazil, as indeed in most countries, women experience situations of violence (physical, sexual, emotional, and institutional), devaluation of domestic work and employment, maternal mortality,

exclusion from positions of power and policy making, among other situations. With this observation, we can say that the reality of women jeopardizes Brazilian democracy, embarrassing its scope and horizons.... Democracy presupposes the reception of the differences ... presupposes, as feminists say, 'equal rights and the right to difference'. (Rodrigues 2005)

Building democracy means to assert rights and freedoms, fight against secular traditions, and have the courage to change history. The experience of women around the world demonstrates that the construction of female citizenship faces arduous obstacles, such as sexism and patriarchy in the existing political institutions and society in general. Therefore, ensuring the human rights of women from all walks of life, colours, creeds, ages, sexualities, abilities – within a vast diversity – is one of our greatest democratic challenges. (Campos 2010)

Feminist and women's movements have crossed three major thresholds in their struggle to overcome violence against women (Barsted 1994; Barsted and Hermann 1999; MacDowell Santos 2008; Pandijiarjian 2006; Pasinato and MacDowell Santos 2008). The first of these came when public policy proposals to combat violence against women culminated in the establishment of institutional services for female victims of violence, such as the Women's Police Stations in 1985. These specialized police stations are public services linked to the Department of Public Safety. Their main task is to investigate crimes committed against women. Currently there are 475 Women's Police Stations (DEAMs) in Brazil. In addition to the Women's Police Stations there are 68 shelters (Casas Abrigo), 146 reference centres (Centros de Referência), 56 specialized public defence hubs, 19 specialized prosecution hubs, 8 centres addressing human trafficking, and 7 services for addressing perpetrator accountability (SPM 2010).

Victories in terms of normative legislative texts mark the second threshold of fundamental change. These include the federal constitution of Brazil, which was passed on 5 October 1988. The following articles in the federal constitution are particularly illustrative of the progress made:

- The recognition and the guarantee of equality between men and women: 'men and women are equal in rights and obligations in the terms of this Constitution' (Article 5, Paragraph 1, Federal Government of Brazil 1988).
- The recognition of the responsibility of the state in terms of intra-familial violence: 'The state assures familial assistance to all those who are part of family, creating mechanisms to curtail violence in their relationships' (Article 226, Paragraph 8). (AMB 2000; CLADEM 2000; Gonçalves 2005: 33; Pinto 2003; Pitanguy 2002)

These advances were won by hard organizing work to co-ordinate the efforts of the women's and feminist movements, together with the National Council of the Rights of Women (CNDM) and the Councils on Women's Rights at the state and municipal levels. Discussions and proposals from these groups took the form of a document entitled 'Carta das Mulheres Brasileiras aos Constituintes' (Letter of the Brazilian Women addressed to the Constituent Members), which was delivered to the President of the National Congress at the Assembléia Nacional Constituinte (National Constituent Assembly). Although the text of the Brazilian federal constitution does not refer explicitly to the issue of violence against women, various Brazilian state constitutions have done so. These include the states of Amapá, Ceará, Distrito Federal, Mato Grosso do Sul, Paraná, Rio de Janeiro, Rio Grande do Sul, Sergipe, Pará, São Paulo, among others (Pandijiarjian 2006: 92). The constitution of the state of Bahia (Bahia Assembléia Legislativa 1989) is an interesting example. Its Chapter XIX, entitled 'The Rights of Women', includes Article 281:

> It is the responsibility of the state government to combat and to prevent violence against women through the following mechanisms:
>
> I – The creation and maintenance of Women's Police Stations for the protection of women in all the municipalities with more than 50,000 inhabitants;
>
> II – The creation and maintenance, directly or through conventions,

of legal, medical, social, and psychological services for female victims of violence.

At the international level, support came from the Convention on the Elimination of all Forms of Discrimination against Women (CEDAW), adopted by the United Nations in 1979. The adoption of this convention was the product of pressure from the women's and feminist movements at the first UN Conference on Women which took place in Mexico in 1975. This document, which included in its content promises to 'eliminate discrimination and assuring equality between men and women', was ratified by Brazil in its entirety in 1994 (AGENDE 1979).

In that same year, as mentioned previously, the Convention of Belém do Pará was approved by the Organization of American States (OAS)[6] and ratified by Brazil in November 1995. The Convention of Belém do Pará is similar to CEDAW in a number of articles, but it also has some fundamentally different legal points, including a definition of violence against women and indicators of how and where this violence is manifested. It is also worth noting that the text holds the state responsible for protecting women from violence, whether in public or in private. The text of the convention stipulates that this responsibility should be translated into concrete actions to prevent and combat this violence. Moreover, the state is obligated to make every effort to investigate any violation of women's rights, which also brings with it the responsibility to guarantee the existence of adequate resources for the due punishment of the aggressors and compensation for those affected (AGENDE 2006b).

Finally, the third major threshold was crossed when Brazilian feminist and women's movements successfully lobbied for the passing of the LMP on 7 August 2006. The LMP is based on the terms of the federal constitution of Brazil, CEDAW, and the Convention of Belém do Pará. These documents are cited at the beginning of the LMP, and this formal link between the law and these earlier legal instruments was a huge victory for the feminist movements. In addition, the LMP considers domestic and familial violence against women as a violation of human rights and defines it as follows:

> any action or omission based on gender which causes death, injury, physical, sexual and psychological suffering and moral or property harm within the household, understood as the permanent living space for people with or without family ties, including the aggregate sporadically; in the family, understood as the community formed by individuals who are or consider themselves akin, joined by natural ties, by marriage or by expressed will; in any intimate relationship of affection, in which the perpetrator shares or has lived with the victim, regardless of cohabitation. (Law 11.340/ 2006, Article 5)]

Other major changes introduced by the LMP (Federal Government of Brazil 2006) include:

- Definition and classification of domestic and familial violence against women into physical, psychological, sexual, and moral;
- Determination that domestic violence against women is independent of sexual orientation;
- Prohibition of enforcement of monetary penalties, and fines. This means that the penalty for guilt should be imprisonment rather than a fine (Law 11.340/ 2006, Article 17);
- Specific procedures to be undertaken by the police authority in relation to women victims of domestic and familial violence;
- Prohibition of female disputants being forced to undertake the task of delivering the summons to the offender;
- Permitting arrest and detention for flagrant aggression (prior to an act of violence taking place), dependent on the perceived risk to the woman;
- Victims to be notified of legal processes, especially in relation to the admittance and release of the offender from prison, and to be accompanied by a lawyer or advocate during all legal proceedings;
- The judge to be allowed to order a minimum safe distance to be kept between the aggressor and the victim, their families, and witnesses. The judge may also prohibit any contact by the aggressor with the abused, their families, or witnesses;

- Promotion of studies and research, statistics, and other relevant information with a gender and race or ethnicity perspective, relating to the causes, the consequences, and the frequency of domestic violence and familial violence against women – these materials to be included in a nationwide systematization and standardization of data, with periodic assessment of results of the measures adopted;
- Promotion of educational programmes that disseminate ethical values of unrestricted respect for human dignity, cognizant of perspectives including gender, race, and ethnicity;
- The law obligates the government, at the federal, state, and municipal levels, as well as within the justice system, to be fully involved in its implementation. In addition, it stipulates the creation of specialized Courts (*Juizados*) of Domestic and Familial Violence against Women.

This last point is considered particularly important by women's and feminist movements because it was the very first time that a Brazilian federal law involved the justice system in efforts to address violence against women. Article 14 of the LMP stipulates that:

> Special Courts for Domestic and Familial Violence against Women, bodies … with civil and criminal liability, *may be created* in the Federal District and Territories *by the Brazilian states* for the process, trial and execution of the causes resulting from the practice of domestic and family violence against women. (Federal Government of Brazil 2006, my italics)

The creation of these new courts is particularly significant because the justice system in Brazil has always been (until the introduction of the LMP) the most resistant sector to the demands made by women's and feminist movements in regard to the issue of women's access to justice (Barsted and Hermann 1999).

Thus several major structural impacts produced by the feminist struggles – socially, politically, and culturally speaking – helped create the space for the introduction of a law addressing familial and domestic violence against women, the LMP. This does not mean, however, that the success of this process is complete. There remains the challenge of the effective implementation of the law and a sound monitoring of this process.

The Maria da Penha Law Observatory and the issue of implementation

The Maria da Penha Law was an honourable victory for the feminist and women's movements, but effective implementation is still an issue. The movements developed campaigns with this in mind – like the 16 Days of Activism against Violence against Women Campaign, held in 2006. This campaign adopted the LMP as its theme (see 16 Days of Activism Campaign 2008). The Articulação de Mulheres Brasileiras (AMB - Articulation of Brazilian Women) soon took things further. The AMB

> is a non-partisan political articulation, which enhances the feminist struggle of Brazilian women nationally and internationally [and] ... has as its goal action-oriented social transformation and building of a democratic society, with reference to the feminist political platform (built by the Brazilian women's movement in 2002). In this context, AMB is focused on five priorities: mobilization for the right to safe and legal abortion; action to end violence against women; confronting the neoliberal policy; the organization of movements; and the fight against racism.... In Latin America, the AMB integrates the Marcosur Feminist Articulation Committee with the Women's Continental Social Alliance. (INESC no date)

In 2008 the AMB organized two videoconferences with the participation of representatives from feminist and women's movements from all over Brazil in order to publicize and discuss the law. In their campaign for the LMP, the Salvador Women's Forum and the Group for the Articulation of the Network for Assisting Women Victims of Violence used 'before and after' information in a flyer to raise awareness of issues related to the implementation of the law.

It is in this context that the Observatory of the Maria da Penha Law was created to monitor the law's implementation. The establishment of the observatory resulted from an initiative entitled 'Construction and Implementation of the Maria da Penha Law Observatory' presented by a consortium of organizations in April 2007 to the Special Secretariat of Policies for Women, which is responsible for 'public policies that contribute to improving the lives of all Brazilian women and that reaffirm the Federal Government's commitment to women. Establishing partnerships with various bodies across the whole sweep of federal government, the Special Secretariat confronts social, racial, sexual, ethnic, and disabled women's inequalities' (Federal Government of Brazil 2003). The consortium brings together 12 organizations,[7] amongst which are research centres and NGOs with representatives from the five different regions of Brazil. The work of the observatory, which was initiated in September 2007, was planned over a period of two years to develop various activities to raise awareness of the LMP; identify challenges and advances in the effectiveness of its implementation; and collect useful information for women's movements and for public institutions responsible for policy making.

The Observatory of the Maria da Penha Law is unique in that it focuses on implementation. As research members of the observatory, essentially we are trying to construct a monitoring methodology. This is a pioneering task, as Brazil is a country where there is a considerable distance between what happens at a legislative level and the law's actual implementation, a gap that affects women most. The organizations involved in the observatory are currently in the process of refining the strategic indicators, which were developed during the first year of work. We have designed and administered two questionnaires which were undertaken at Women's Police Stations and Specialized Courts for Domestic and Familial Violence against Women. These field sites were selected because of the strategic roles that they play in solving cases of domestic and familial violence against women.

Women's Police Stations are the first and the most consolidated public service addressing violence against women. They are police departments under the authority of the Public Security Departments, and are located in each Brazilian state. Their main task is to investigate crimes committed against women (de Aquino 2006). We undertook the questionnaire with two professionals based at the Women's Police Station in Salvador. One of the interviewees directed the Investigation Sector at the station and had been a member of the station team since the beginning of its operation in October 1986. The other was the Chief Officer. The objective of the questionnaire was to obtain information on the institution's working conditions, the nature of the services provided, and details of the content provided by the police register database. It is through the police register 'that the police or judicial authority is informed of a crime, providing a range of data (names of officers, victims, witnesses, traces, instrumentalities and proceedings of crime, etc.). It is also a valuable means of monitoring the legality of police actions. The police register can be conceptualized as an orderly and thorough record of events that require police intervention' (Universo Policial 2009).

As for the specialized courts, they have 'the jurisdiction for processing, trial and execution of civil suits and criminal cases arising from the practice of domestic and familial violence against women' (Article 71, Federal Law No. 11.340, 7 August 2006). The courts are assisted by a multidisciplinary team consisting of psychosocial, legal, and health professionals. The role of this team is to 'provide information in writing to the judge, the prosecutor and the public defender, in reports or orally in open court, and to work to develop guidance, referral, prevention, and other measures aimed at the victim, the offender, and family, with special attention to children and adolescents' (Federal Government of Brazil 2006). Applying the questionnaire to the Specialized Courts of Domestic and Familial Violence against Women, in Salvador, however, was not possible since this service had not been installed during the period when we were doing fieldwork. This is because, although it was officially established on 27 November 2007, the special court in Salvador did not begin operation until a year later on 18 November 2008. At the time of the writing of this chapter, 4,805 cases had been processed in the Salvador specialized court (Law of the Judicial Organization of the State of Bahia no date; Violence Against Women Portal 2008; Vermelho Portal 2010). Nevertheless, the Northeast Regional Coordination of the Observatory (based at NEIM/UFBA) undertook efforts to build a relationship of dialogue and exchange of experiences with the Department of Justice through contacts with the Prosecuting Counsel, Public Defender, and the Court of Justice. Cooperation with these legal institutions enabled us to identify practice in the fields of public safety and justice; and to learn about the register records, police investigations, and later the legal proceedings covered by the LMP. Identification of these procedures was achieved through workshops especially organized for this purpose.

Since the observatory is composed of five coordinating bodies located within the five Brazilian regions, we thought it would be essential to gather information nationwide to construct a kind of 'portrait' of police stations and courts. Therefore, the two previously mentioned questionnaires were also applied in four Brazilian state capitals: Belém (northern region), Brasília (midwest region), Rio de Janeiro (southeastern region), and Porto Alegre (southern region). In what follows, I will report on some of the preliminary findings from fieldwork carried out in Salvador (northeastern region), but I will also link these results to those presented in the reports produced by the other regional coordinators of the observatory.

First, we found that the numbers of crimes registered at the Women's Police Station in Salvador had gone down between 2006 and 2007. This was also the case in other Brazilian cities, such as Brasília. The figures compiled on the Women's Police Station in Salvador provide information for some initial conclusions (see Table 7.1). The declining figures are disturbing in the light of the fact that less than half of the women who suffer from violence report it. One issue that might be contributing to the decrease in

Table 7.1 Women's Police Station, Salvador, Bahia, Brazil – analysis of 4,863 register records (January–August 2008)

Years/Offence	2000	2001	2002	2003	2004	2005	2006	2007	until June 2008
Rape	89	55	61	55	44	50	36	43	18
Moral violence[a]	925	726	595	425	364	418	536	520	254
Threats	2,512	2,718	2,781	2,123	2,422	2,530	2,983	3,029	1,179
Physical violence	2,750	2,536	2,390	2,039	2,133	2,313	2,137	2,436	1,129
Vias de fato[b]	4,034	3,590	3,081	2,950	3,345	3,107	2,986	2,595	891
No. of crimes registered	10,760	9,884	9,107	7,769	8,481	8,583	8,982	8,875	3,555
Police inquiry	36	46	38	54	35	27	30	328	227
Preventive measures	0	0	0	0	0	0	1	122	52
Arrested in the act	8	6	3	4	3	5	10[c]	38[d]	22

a Moral violence is any act of slandering, defamation, and/or breaking out into invective against a person.
b Vias de fato refers to situations when physical violence is reported, but there is no material evidence of it.
c Four of these cases are related to the LMP.
d All of these cases are related to the LMP.
Source: Women's Police Station, Salvador/Brotas (author's figures)

the numbers of reported violence cases is the way in which police officers at the Women's Police Stations have been presenting the new law to the public. We have information – gleaned through contact with care services, and feminist and women's movements – indicating that police officers usually emphasize the possibility that, through the process of the LMP, the aggressor may be imprisoned, whereas research has indicated that women who come to the Women's Police Stations, in general, expect the problem to be solved through mediation by the police officer handling the case. In other words, few women seek a radical action such as having their aggressors imprisoned, since they fear the implications of such a punishment in terms of their safety. Ironically, the growing perception that the new law aggressively punishes perpetrators may have made some women less willing to report violence committed against them, reducing the number of reported cases. These results highlight the need for continuous training of police officers – among other professionals – for proper law enforcement. They also indicate the importance of a comprehensive public policy that pays attention to the multiple protection needs of women victims of domestic violence, and incorporates efforts to raise awareness about women's rights.

Second, since the promulgation of the LMP in 2006, 62 specialized courts have been established in Brazil (see Table 7.2). Despite this being an insufficient number given the size of Brazil, it is notable that the number of specialized courts is almost the same as the number of shelters for women at risk of death (66 shelters). This is a significant achievement since the shelters, unlike the specialized courts, are services that have been demanded by the feminist and women's movements since the beginning of the 1990s. Moreover, although Article 14 in the LMP stipulates that specialized courts should be set up, the law does not obligate the state government or the state court to implement this article, and since Brazil is a federal republic, the federal government cannot dictate to the state government how to use its own budget. Accordingly, the creation of specialized courts is the responsibility of state governments and state courts.

The growing number of specialized courts thus points to successful lobbying for these courts at the state level.[8]

In fact, the creation of specialized courts has proven to be absolutely necessary for the implementation of the LMP. Historically, the justice system of Brazil has resisted calls for a dialogue regarding the role of the legal system in protecting the rights of women. In particular, feminists have a historical concern with the issue of impunity for those who are accused of committing violence against women. Before the establishment of the specialized courts, the measures taken by the legal system in cases involving violence against women reflected the failure of state concern to guarantee the rights of women. With the LMP, the Brazilian legal system has become an integral formal part of care services for women victims of violence, as shown in Table 7.2.

Table 7.2 Care services for women victims of violence in Brazil

Services/ Regions	Reference centres for women	Women's Police Stations	Shelters for women at risk of death	Specialized courts	Services by region
North	12	35	8	14	69
Northeast	22	63	15	6	106
Central West	7	39	7	9	62
Southeast	55	192	24	26	297
South	17	67	12	5	101
Total	113	396	66	60	635

Source: Special Secretariat for Women's Policies, information organized by the Maria da Penha Law Observatory Northeast team.

Third, there is an indication from court cases that the number of re-offences of violence has fallen, as observed for instance in Rio de Janeiro and Cuiabá. But this decrease in numbers is not necessarily good news for women. We have information, through our partners working in the observatory, that sometimes judges press women to make settlements with their alleged aggressors, which is often not in the interest of the women. For instance, an agreement would be arranged by the judge that the plaintiff would agree not to go out by herself, or go to a night school, as long as the man agrees not to hurt her anymore. Such practices on the part of judges indicate that we need to do more research that goes beyond statistical data in order to be able to truly assess the effectiveness of the new legal system.

Other flawed legal practices resulted from poor knowledge of the LMP on the part of some of the members of the justice system, which had a negative impact on female disputants. This problem is illustrated by the case of Eloá, which was brought before the Superior Court in October 2008. Eloá was a fifteen-year-old girl who had ended a relationship with her boyfriend. Her boyfriend refused to accept her decision and kidnapped her. He kept her prisoner for four days and during this time beat her severely and repeatedly. He also threatened to kill her. This went on until the police invaded the apartment where she was held captive. Unfortunately, by then Eloá had already been killed by her ex-boyfriend. Neither the police force nor the justice sector representatives who were involved in this incident perceived it as a case of 'violence against women'. The young man was treated as someone who had never been violent before and it was assumed that it was a case of his being put under severe emotional stress. He was even treated as a potential suicide case. That this could be a case of domestic violence never even came up in the proceedings. In other words, the Brazilian Superior Justice Court at the time did not perceive relationships between boyfriends/girlfriends as being intimate relationships, and thus they were considered to be outside the jurisdiction of the LMP. This demonstrated poor knowledge of the law on the part of the Superior Justice Court. However, as a result of emails sent by the feminist and women's movements and a document delivered by the Maria da Penha Law Observatory, the Superior Court reversed its decision, and acknowledged that violence against women occurring within relationships between lovers and ex-lovers also falls under the jurisdiction of the LMP.

Of course, building one's capacity and knowledge of the law is a task that confronts not only members of the justice system, but us too, as feminists and members of the observatory. Not all of us had knowledge or experience in the legal field, although we all had considerable expertise in the area of violence against women. Undertaking the task that we had assumed necessitated that we learned the basics of the technical language and procedures of the legal system. In fact, the intervention of the feminist movements in the Eloá case resulted from a successful process of collective capacity building on the part of feminists and members of the observatory.

Our continuing work in monitoring the implementation of the LMP includes the need for further information. We need to find answers for questions such as: How many processes are related to the LMP? What happens within these legal processes? How long do the processes take to be concluded? What types of decisions are taken? How many processes are followed through to the end? How many processes derive from accusations made at the Women's Police Stations? Our experience shows us that without the specialized courts this information is quite difficult to find – and if our objective is to define a methodology for the monitoring of the law, answers to these questions are essential, and we need to get them.

Concluding remarks

The observatory is working in a context in which successes, failures, and contradictions coexist. There are certainly successes, but they still need to be consolidated. We have services, but they are inefficient and unequally distributed over the country. At the time of conducting our research there were 396 Women's Police Stations, 113 reference centres, 66 shelters, and 60 specialized courts, but they are still not consolidated as public policy. That is, there are no coordinated actions to ensure that these institutions function (more effectively) as instruments to reduce and/or overcome social inequalities (Barsted 1994) that are shaped by gender, class, and ethnicity. These coordinated actions should stem from principles and norms based upon the guarantee of a life without violence for women.

There are federal and state government policies for women, but their effectiveness and transformative power are limited. Substantive legal forms to address domestic violence are still vulnerable to changes in federal, state, and local government that may lead to the dismantling of services for which activists have lobbied so painstakingly, and to the diminishing of opportunities for further positive change. We need to extend the concept of a network of care for women to all relevant policy areas. Carreira and Pandijiarjian (2003) define this concept as follows:

> We call network services to face gender violence the articulation between institutions and government departments and organizations and civil society groups aimed at expanding and improving the quality of care, the identification and referral of cases existing in the communities, and the development of prevention strategies. (Carreira and Pandijiarjian 2003: 21)

Such a network should include government sectors, public services, organized civil society, research centres, and NGOs in a permanent process of coalition building and partnership. Its work should be driven by the objective of generating knowledge, and providing information and skills 'to advance the inclusion, citizenship and equality rights of women' (DAWN 2006). In that sense, identifying and sharing best practice is necessary so that the best care possible is provided to the target audience. In short, establishing networks of care is essential for the processes of formulation, implementation, maintenance, and evaluation of public policies addressing violence against women.

These are some of the important changes needed and the challenges we face as part of our current situation. So, *companheiras*,[9] the struggle continues … and we should pursue all the paths still unexplored or waiting to be ventured upon. The efforts to analyse public policies addressing violence against women are functioning in only a few places such as the big cities. These efforts, thus far, have rarely included collecting information on the opinions of the women who are the target of these policies. In addition, we still need information and reflection on the impact of the specialized services on women who are victims of violence. There is also a great need for systematic studies that analyse public policies over a longer period of time, in terms both of their content and their implementation. We also need to understand better the conditions in which these policies are implemented and how the processes of policy making and implementation are shaped by gender, race or ethnicity, and social class. This would inform the formulation and implementation of better public policies for the prevention of violence against women (Diniz 2006; MacDowell Santos 2008; Pasinato and MacDowell Santos 2008). Defining indicators for a system of monitoring that will generate reliable information in relation to the implementation of the LMP will support many of these tasks and objectives. These are some of the challenges we are currently facing.

Notes

1 'The Center for Justice and International Law (CEJIL) is a non-governmental, non-profit organization that protects and promotes human rights in the Americas through the strategic use of the tools offered by international human rights law. CEJIL offers advice and free legal representation to victims of human rights abuses – and to organizations that defend their causes – when justice proves impossible to achieve in their own countries' (CEJIL, no date).
2 The Latin American and Caribbean Committee for the Defense of Women Rights 'is a women's organization and a women's organizations network ... that supports organizations and individuals committed to the defense and promotion of Women's Rights through different activities such as formulating legislative proposals, researching, training, litigating, teaching at universities, informing, communicating and exercising solidarity actions' (CLADEM, no date).
3 The convention is a binding treaty inspired by the United Nations Declaration on the Elimination of Violence against Women (1993). It was adopted during a Special Session of the General Assembly of the Organization of American States (OAS) on 9 June 1994. To

date, it has been ratified by 29 countries. The Convention includes provisions referring to a number of concrete measures that state parties agree to carry out with all appropriate means and without delay; another series of measures and programmes that states parties agree to undertake and implement progressively; the need to take into account the plight of particularly vulnerable groups of women, including migrants, refugees, and women who have been targeted by reason of their race or ethnic background; and the reporting and redress mechanisms under the Convention (ICCLR no date). A full-text version can be accessed on the Inter-American Commission of Women (CIM) website (no date).

4 The Supreme Court of Brazil declared the legal argument of legitimate defence of honour invalid in 1991 (Sociedade Brasileira de Direito Público 2001).

5 Obviously, there were also limits and challenges. I am not thinking of these movements within a linear process with a specific goal, nor am I thinking of the feminist movement as a sort of ethereal entity existing somehow above women who inspire it, or as being free of both internal and external contradictions.

6 'The OAS is a forum that represents the countries of the American continent. It seeks to strengthen peace and security in North, Central, and South America, promoting cooperation on economic, social, and cultural issues' (AGENDE 2006b).

7 The organizations that are working with NEIM/UFBA, as members of the consortium, are: AGENDE Brasília/DF; NEPeM/UNB (Núcleo de Estudos e Pesquisas sobre a Mulher – Women's Studies and Research Nucleus), Brasilia; CEPIA, Rio de Janeiro; NEPP-DH/UFRJ (Núcleo de Estudos de Políticas Públicas em Direitos Humanos – Public Policies Studies in Human Rights Nucleus), Rio de Janeiro; Coletivo Feminino Plural (Feminist Plural Collective), Rio Grande do Sul; THEMIS (Assessoria Jurídica e Estudos de Gênero – Judicial Advice and Gender Studies), Rio Grande do Sul; NIEM/UFRGS (Núcleo Interdisciplinar de Estudos sobre a Mulher e Relações de Gênero – Women's Interdisciplinary Studies and Gender Relations Nucleus), Rio Grande do Sul; and GEPEM/UFPA (Grupo de Estudos e Pesquisas Eneida de Moraes sobre Mulheres e Relações de Gênero – Eneida de Moraes Reseach and Study Group on Women and Gender Relations), Pará. This is the reference group that assumed the task of feeding the observatory with data from all regions of Brazil. We also work with the following partners: Rede Feminista de Saúde, Rede Nacional Feminista de Saúde, Direitos Sexuais e Direitos Reprodutivos (National Feminist

Network on Health and Sexual and Reproductive Rights), Rio Grande do Sul; REDOR (Rede Feminista Norte e Nordeste de Estudos e Pesquisas sobre Mulheres e Relações de Gênero – North and Northeast Feminist Network on Research and Study of Women and Gender Relations); and CLADEM/Brasil.

8 These figures illustrate the context in which we conducted the fieldwork. Currently there are 147 courts on domestic and familial violence against women in Brazil (SPM 2010).

9 The term *Companheiras* means companions in the struggle.

References

16 Days of Activism Campaign (2008) '16 Days of Activism against Violence against Women Campaign', http://www.campanha16dias.org.br/Ed2008/index.php (accessed 19 November 2008).

AGENDE (Ações em Gênero, Cidadania e Desenvolvimento – Actions in Gender Citizenship and Development) (1979) 'Convention on the Elimination of All Forms of Discrimination against Women (CEDAW)', http://www.agende.org.br/convencoes/cedaw/cedaw.php (accessed 13 October 2006).

—— (2006a) 'Sobrevivi... O Relato do Caso Maria da Penha' (I Survived... The Story of the Maria da Penha Case), http://www.agende.org.br/docs/File/convencoes/belem/docs/Caso%20maria%20da%20penha.pdf (accessed 13 October 2006).

—— (2006b) 'The Convention of Belém do Pará', http://www.agende.org.br/convencoes/belem/belem.php (accessed 13 October 2006).

AMB (Articulação de Mulheres Brasileiras – Articulation of Brazilian Women) (2000) *Políticas Públicas para Mulheres no Brasil: Balanço Nacional Cinco Anos Após* (Public Policies for Women in Brazil: National Status after Five Years), AMB, Beijing and Brasília.

Bahia Assembléia Legislativa (Bahia Legislative Assembly) (1989) *Constituição do Estado da Bahia* (Bahia State Constitution), http://www.mp.ba.gov.br/institucional/legislacao/constituicao_bahia.pdf, Assembléia Legislativa, Salvador.

Barsted, L. L. (1994) *Violência Contra a Mulher e Cidadania: Uma Avaliação das Políticas Públicas* (Violence against Women and Citizenship: An Assessment of Public Policies), CEPIA Working Paper 1, CEPIA (Cidadania, Estudo, Pesquisa, Informação, Ação – Citizenship, Study, Research, Information and Action), UNIFEM, and Ford Foundation, Rio de Janeiro.

Barsted, L. L. and J. Hermann (1999) *O Judiciário e a Violência Contra a Mulher: A Ordem Legal e a (Des)ordem Familiar* (The Judiciary and

Violence Against Women: The Ordered and Disordered Family), CEPIA Working Paper 2, CEPIA, Rio de Janeiro.

Campos, C. H. de (2010) 'Democracia e Direitos das Mulheres. Zero Hora' (Democracy and Women's Rights. Zero Hour, online edition), 16 January, (http://zerohora.clicrbs.com.br/zerohora/jsp/default2.jsp?uf=1&local=1&source=a2779332.xml&template=3898.dwt&edition=13917&section=1012) (accessed 1 April 2010).

Carreira, D. and V. Pandijiarjian (2003) 'Vem Pra Roda! Vem Pra Rede! Guia de Apoio à Construção de Redes de Serviços para o Enfrentamento da Violência Contra a Mulher' (Come to the Hub! Come to the Network! Guide to Building Support Network Services to Combat Violence Against Women), Rede Mulher de Educação (Women's Education Network), São Paulo, http://www.redemulher.org.br/publicacoes/vempraroda.pdf.

CEJIL (Center for Justice and International Law) (no date) http://cejil.org/en/cejil/cejil (accessed 1 April 2010).

CLADEM (Comitê Latino Americano e do Caribe para a Defesa dos Direitos das Mulheres – Latin American and Caribbean Committee for the Defense of Women's Rights) (2000) *Questão de Vida: Balanço Regional e Desafios Sobre o Direito das Mulheres a Uma Vida Livre de Violência* (Life Questions: Regional Status and Challenges against Women's Right to Live a Life Free from Violence), CLADEM, Oxfam, and Ford Foundation, São Paulo.

—— (no date) http://blog.world-citizenship.org/wp-archive/829 (accessed 1 April 2010).

DAWN (DisAbled Women's Network) (2006) 'Family Violence against Women with DisAbilities', DAWN, Ontario, http://dawn.thot.net/violence_wwd.html (accessed 1 April 2010).

de Aquino, S. (2006) 'Análise de Delegacias Especiais de Atendimento à Mulher (DEAMs) em Funcionamento no Estado da Bahia, em uma Perspectiva de Gênero e Feminista' (Analysis of the Functioning of the Women's Police Stations in Bahia State from a Gender and Feminist Perspective), PhD thesis, Federal University of Bahia, Salvador.

Diniz, S. (2006) 'Violência Contra a Mulher: Estratégias e Respostas do Movimento Feminista no Brasil (1980–2005)' (Violence Against Women: Strategies and Responses by the Feminist Movement of Brazil), in S. Diniz, L. P. Silveira, and M. A. Liz (eds), *Vinte e Cinco Anos de Respostas Brasileiras em Violência Contra a Mulher (1980–2005): Alcances e Limites* (25 Years of Brazilian Response to Violence Against Women: Scope and Limitations) Coletivo Feminista Sexualidade e Saúde (Feminist Collective on Health and Sexuality), São Paulo.

Federal Government of Brazil (1988) *Federal Constitution of Brazil*, http://www.planalto.gov.br/ccivil_03/Constituicao/Constituicao.htm (accessed 1 April 2010).

—— (2003) 'Special Secretariat of Policies for Women', http://www. presidencia.gov.br/estrutura_presidencia/sepm/sobre/ (accessed 1 April 2010).

—— (2006) 'Maria da Penha Law', http://www.planalto.gov.br/ccivil/_ ato2004-2006/2006/lei/l11340.htm (accessed 1 April 2010).

Gonçalves, T. (2005) 'Violência Contra a Mulher'; 'Nós Merecemos Respeito'; 'Diga não à Violência Contra a Mulher'; 'Projeto Gênero, Raça e Cidadania no Combate à Violência nas Escolas' (Violence Against Women; We Deserve Respect; Say No to Violence Against Women; Gender, Race and Citizenship Project Combatting Violence in Schools), PhD Working Papers, Núcleo de Estudos Interdisciplinares sobre a Mulher (Women's Interdisciplinary Studies Nucleus) (NEIM/ UFBA), Salvador.

ICCLR (International Centre for Criminal Law and Criminal Justice Policy) (no date) 'Convention of Belém Do Pará - Five Years Later', http://www.icclr.law.ubc.ca/Site%20Map/Programs/Con vention_of_ Belem.htm (accessed 1 April 2010).

INESC (no date) 'AMB' (Articulation of Brazilian Women), http://www. inesc.org.br/biblioteca/textos-e-manifestos/manifesto-da-articulacao-das-mulheres-brasileiras (accessed 1 April 2010).

Inter-American Commission of Women (CIM) (no date) http://www.oas. org/cim/english/convention%20violence%20against%20women.htm (accessed 1 April 2010).

Law of the Judicial Organization of the State of Bahia (no date) http:// www.tjba.jus.br/site/arquivos/nova%20LOJ%20e%20alteracoes.pdf (accessed 1 April 2010).

MacDowell Santos, C. (2008) 'Da Delegacia da Mulher à Lei Maria da Penha: Lutas Femininas e Políticas Públicas Sobre Violência Contra Mulheres no Brasil' (Women and the Maria da Penha Law: Feminist Struggles and Public Policy on Violence against Women in Brazil), Centro de Estudos Sociais (Social Studies Centre), No. 301, Coimbra University, https://estudogeral.sib.uc.pt/dspace/bitstream/10316/11080/1/ Da%20Delegacia%20da%20mulher%20%C3%A0%20Lei%20Maria%20 da%20Penha.pdf.

Organização Dos Estados Americanos, Comissão Interamericana de Direitos Humanos (2001) 'Report No. 54/01, Case 12.051: Maria da Penha Maia Fernandes', 4 April http://www.sbdp.org.br/arquivos/ material/299_Relat%20n.pdf (accessed 1 April 2010).

Pandijiarjian, V. (2006) 'Balanço de 25 Anos da Legislação Sobre a Violência Contra as Mulheres no Brasil' (Status of 25 Years of Legislation on Violence Against Women in Brazil), in S. Diniz, L. P. Silveira, and M. A. Liz (eds), *Vinte e Cinco Anos de Respostas Brasileiras em Violência Contra a Mulher (1980-2005): Alcances e Limites* (25 Years of Brazilian Response to Violence Against Women: Scope and Limitations),

Coletivo Feminista Sexualidade e Saúde (Feminist Collective on Health and Sexuality), São Paulo.

Pasinato, W. and C. MacDowell Santos (2008) 'Acesso à Justiça para Mulheres em Situação de Violência: Estudo Comparativo das Delegacias da Mulher na América Latina (Brasil, Equador, Nicarágua, Peru)' (Access to Justice by Women in Situations of Violence: Comparative Study of Women in Latin America), http://www.observe.ufba.br/_ARQ/bibliografia/ MAPEO_Brasil[1].pdf, Núcleo de Estudos de Gênero (Gender Studies Nucleus)/Pagu, Unicamp, Campinas and São Paulo.

Pinto, C. R. J. (2003) *Uma História do Feminismo no Brasil* (A History of Feminism in Brazil), Editora Fundação Perseu Abramo, São Paulo.

Pitanguy, J. (2002) *Democracias, Ciudadanía y Estado em América Latina en el Siglo XXI: Análisis de Género de los Caminos Recorridos Desde la Década del 80 y Futuros Posibles* (Democracy, Citizenship and the State in Latin America in the 21st Century: Gender Analysis of the Routes Taken since the 1980s and the Possible Future), Seminário FLACSO–PRIGEPP, Rio de Janeiro, http://www.cepia.org.br/Textos_online/FLACSO.pdf.

Rodrigues, A. (2005) 'Mulher e Democracia' (Women and Democracy) (online), July, http://www.cfemea.org.br/temasedados/detalhes. asp?IDTemasDados=94 (accessed 3 November 2010).

Sociedade Brasileira de Direito Público (Brazilian Society of Public Law) (2001) 'Relatório Anual 2000' (Annual Report 2000), http://www. sbdp.org.br/arquivos/material/378_Relatorio%20anual%202000.pdf (accessed 1 April 2010).

SPM (Special Secretariat for Policies for Women) (2006) 'Terms of Reference', http://200.130.7.5/spmu/docs/TERMO_DE_REFER ENCIA_2006_Centro_e_Casa_Abrigo.doc, (accessed 1 April 2010).

—— (2010) http://www.sepm.gov.br/noticias/ultimas_noticias/2010/03/ not_dia_mulher_2010 (accessed 25 July 2010).

Universo Policial (2009) 'Bulletin of Police Records', http://www. universopolicial.com/2009/09/boletim-de-ocorrencia-policial.html (accessed 25 September 2009).

Vermelho Portal (2010) 'Violência Contra a Mulher é Tema de Debate na Câmara de Salvador' (Violence Against Women and Themes for Debate in the Salvador Assembly), 15 July, http://www.vermelho.org. br/ba/noticia.php?id_noticia=133370&id_secao=58 (accessed 1 April 2010).

Violence Against Women Portal (2008) http://www.violenciamulher. org.br/index.php?option=com_content&view=article&id=1315:salv ador-tera-vara-contra-violencia-domestica-em-novembro-vermelho- 230908&catid=13:noticias&Itemid=7 (accessed 1 April 2010).

8

Implementing Domestic Violence Legislation in Ghana
The Role of Institutions
Takyiwaa Manuh and Angela Dwamena-Aboagye

In 2007 Ghana finally passed a Domestic Violence Act (Act 732 of 2007) following a campaign of more than six years by gender rights advocates to persuade the state to recognize and criminalize the pervasive practice of gender-based violence in Ghanaian society. A national study conducted by the Accra-based Gender and Human Rights Documentation Centre (Gender Centre) revealed high rates of violence against women and girls in communities and households around the country, with the attendant severe health, social, and economic consequences (Coker-Appiah and Cusack 1999). One in three of the women and girls surveyed had experienced physical, psychological, or emotional abuse; 20 per cent stated that their first experience of sex was by force, while 33 per cent had been fondled or touched against their will. The levels of psychological and economic abuse were also high; 20 per cent of the women in the survey had been prevented from seeing family or friends by male partners, while 10 per cent had had their earnings taken from them, and 8 per cent had been prohibited from going to work, trading, or making money. A parallel study commissioned by the then national machinery for women, the National Council on Women and Development, confirmed that 72 per cent of respondents reported that wife beating was a common practice in their communities (Pappoe and Ardayfio 1998). Eight per cent of the female respondents in the study reported having been raped before, and 6 per cent had been defiled. However, 95 per cent of the respondents failed to

203

report the violations. Analyses of the data suggested that much of the violence could be traced to perceptions of women's and men's roles and positions in marriage, family, and society (Manuh 2009). Men were considered the 'heads', 'guardians', and 'keepers' of women and girls, and had the right to punish and chastise them for acts ranging from disrespect to sexual impropriety or infidelity (Adomako Ampofo and Prah 2009).

The studies were influential in naming the problem of gender-based violence in Ghana and drawing public attention to it as a contravention of women's human rights. It is also a contravention of the constitution and its equality provisions, and of Ghana's signature and ratification of important continental and international treaties and conventions such as the African Charter on Human and People's Rights, the Protocol on the Rights of Women in Africa, the Declaration on the Elimination of Violence against Women, and the Convention on the Elimination of all forms of Discrimination against Women (CEDAW), all of which commit states to bringing their national laws into conformity with international and regional human rights instruments and standards by enacting and enforcing legislation. Signing or ratifying the convention or protocol implies that a nation is committed to its goals, at least to the extent that it should enact and enforce laws against violence towards women.

This chapter will focus on the implementation challenges that are undermining the effectiveness of the new Domestic Violence Act. In the first section, we will provide contextual information about the Act through a brief description of the process of lobbying for the Act, the actors who were involved in this process, the challenges encountered, and the factors that led to success in passing the legislation. In the second section, we will describe the legal and policy framework of the Act, and how it is related to a number of other acts. Following this we will provide a description of the process of implementation in terms of the steps that are undertaken from the moment that a crime of domestic violence is reported, and the work of the different agencies that are involved. In the third section, we will examine some of the serious implementation challenges. These challenges can be grouped into contextual challenges relating to inadequate understanding of gender-based violence as a 'real' crime, media trivialization and sensationalizing of domestic violence, and societal interference with legal and other processes; the limited scope and range of services and lack of specialized services; coordination and funding issues; and the quality of services provided. The chapter will also shed some light on women's experiences with this new legal measure. As the chapter makes clear, the greatest challenges for the effective implementation of the law and for the future remain the political will to enhance the capacity of all institutional stakeholders with the mandate to implement the law; the allocation of the necessary budgetary support; a robust monitoring and evaluation mechanism that ensures compliance and sanctioning for recalcitrant institutions; and the continued advocacy of civil society organizations (CSOs) at various levels, from the community to the national.

Contextualizing the Domestic Violence Act in Ghana

On 21 February 2007, Ghana's Parliament passed the much-awaited Domestic Violence Bill (DVB), which had been the subject of heated debate since its proposal in 2003. The process leading to the passage of the law involved not only introducing new legislation, but also confronting a social system that tolerates various forms of violence against women and girls within the context of existing gender relations and especially in the domestic sphere. Thus, between February and March 2002, the media reported that four married women were killed by their husbands on suspicion of infidelity (Boateng 2002). During a protest march by Sisters Keepers, a loose coalition of NGOs formed to confront violence against women, some marchers, including the two authors, were assured by male bystanders that so long as women continued to 'step out of line', they would be '[physically] disciplined by their partners as was proper in "our culture"'.

Much of this so-called culture revolves around marriage and

other forms of conjugality and the rights that men acquire within them. Marriage is viewed as a necessary and desirable social status for both men and women in Ghana, although perceptible changes are under way; the reported age at first marriage is increasing, especially for women, while the proportion of persons who have never been in union has also been increasing (GSS 2009). While several complementarities between the genders exist in different Ghanaian communities, the various systems of customary law under which the majority of marriages and partnerships are contracted do not view women and men as equal partners (Manuh 2009), and constitutional guarantees of equality and non-discrimination have not succeeded in eradicating such views. A prime example is the perceived 'right' of husbands and partners to 'correct' both actual and perceived transgressions of their wives, such as disobedience or 'stepping out of line'. Such correction can take the form of beating, although it is expected that a reasonable man would 'exercise moderation (sic) in beating his wife so as not to hurt her' (Nukunya 2003: 47). In addition, while both parties in a relationship have the right to sexual satisfaction, and unreasonable refusal to engage in sexual relations can be a ground for divorce, over time a husband's right to sexual satisfaction has come to be viewed as paramount. Women's refusal to submit to the demands of husbands or partners can lead to physical chastisement and or emotional abuse. Such a position was reinforced by the provisions of Section 42(g) of Ghana's Criminal Code, 1960 (Act 29), inherited from British jurisprudence, which accepted the use of force in marriage on the basis of the supposed consent given upon marriage.

To a large extent, views about and practices within marriage that subordinate women to men have remained unchallenged in Ghanaian society; when women are physically assaulted or sexually abused within conjugal relations, this is not regarded as unusual. As a consequence, many women tolerate and remain in abusive relationships and do not complain publicly about their ordeals because such issues are considered 'private', although they may complain to family members or their pastors, who usually counsel them to be patient or to behave better. Boas (2006: 5) cited a 2004 newspaper report about a Ghanaian judge who stated his opinion that '(i)t is un-Ghanaian for a man to be sentenced into imprisonment because he slapped or pushed his wife', noting that this opinion was shared by others in the country.

But Ghana is also a signatory to CEDAW and has ratified it. Ghana also signed on to the Beijing Platform for Action (1995) and the Solemn Declaration on Gender Equality adopted by the African Union in 2004, all of which called for the passage of laws criminalizing gender-based violence. Several women's rights organizations were established in Ghana during the 1990s, to build support for the promotion and protection of women's rights and women's full citizenship (Manuh 2007; Tsikata 2009), following the country's return to multiparty democracy after several decades of military rule. These organizations included the International Federation of Women Lawyers (FIDA), the Gender Centre, Women in Law and Development Africa (WiLDAF), Women's Initiative for Self-Empowerment (WISE), the Ark Foundation, and NETRIGHT. The work of these organizations led to the establishment of the Women and Juvenile Unit (WAJU) within the police service in 1998, specifically to deal with violence against women and girls, and to report on the incidence and types of crimes against them. The findings of the national study (Coker-Appiah and Cusack 1999), as well as the serial killings of women in 1999–2000, and other reported femicides led to a mobilization by women's and other civil society organizations to end the impunity and promulgate legislation against it. Women's CSOs organized protests and marches against the murders and the increasing reports of gender-based violence, and strategized on the way forward.

Following a change of government in 2001, women's CSOs prepared a private member's bill in consultation with the Office of the Attorney-General, for the enactment by Parliament of anti-domestic violence legislation. The bill was laid before Parliament in 2003 but generated a lot of controversy. Its supporters and gender activists were portrayed as purveying foreign ideas that threatened Ghanaian cultural beliefs and practices, in particular the sanctity of marriage and men's rights within it. The bill was subject to an unprecedented nationwide consultation on the grounds that its provisions had serious implications for family life and gender relations. The National Coalition on Domestic Violence Legislation was formed by individuals and human rights organizations, and organized a nationwide consultation to win support for the passage of the bill from 2003. The coalition faced several challenges, including the hostility of the then Minister of Women and Children's Affairs,[1] who should have spearheaded the passage of the bill. It also had to address the widespread view that the bill would endanger marriages as a result of the inclusion of a provision on marital rape that would allow women to 'threaten and dominate their husbands and lead to the disintegration of marriages' (Dovlo 2005, cited in Boas 2006: 11).

Several strategies were adopted by the coalition, including a pictorial campaign entitled 'Faces of Violence', a collection of pictures of abused women which projected the 'voices' and 'faces' of real victims of abuse in the press, to raise awareness of the issue and engender public support. It also commissioned a documentary on domestic violence, produced newspaper articles, and led several discussions on radio and television, while some newspapers followed and reported on the progress of the bill and the arguments of its proponents and opponents. The coalition conducted educational campaigns in all ten regions of Ghana and organized meetings with religious and traditional leaders, and also with media personnel, to sensitize them and ensure their support. It also lobbied and organized meetings with MPs and political party representatives. A crucial factor that facilitated the passage of the law was the replacement of the Minister of Women and Children (MOWAC) by a younger female colleague with a background in policy analysis and advocacy, which led to helpful change in the positions taken by the Ministry. Above all, it was the responsiveness and flexibility shown by several women's CSOs and the coalition in engaging with broad sections of the

Ghanaian population and their leaders, at the same time as they maintained a principled position on the bill, that led to its passage.

The legal and policy framework on domestic violence in Ghana

The legal regime on domestic violence in Ghana consists of the recently passed Domestic Violence Act, the Criminal Code, the Criminal Offences (Amendment Act), and the Children's Act. The policy framework for the Act is also guided by the National Policy and Plan of Action for the Implementation of the Domestic Violence Act.

The Domestic Violence Act (Act 732 of 2007)

The Domestic Violence Bill was passed by the Ghanaian Parliament in February 2007. In May 2007, it was given presidential assent and it entered into the statutes as Act 732 of 2007 (DV Act). Its purpose is stated as 'an Act to provide protection from Domestic Violence particularly for women and children and for connected purposes'. It aims to offer a holistic and effective legal framework for addressing domestic violence in Ghana; to provide broad redress for cases of domestic violence, sanctions on perpetrators, and protective remedies for victims; and to improve Ghana's compliance with its legal obligations under international human rights standards.

The law, which is in three parts, prohibits domestic violence within an existing or previous relationship, and defines it as including physical, sexual, economic, and emotional abuse, including harassment. It also defines a domestic relationship as a family relationship, akin to a family relationship, or a relationship in a domestic situation that exists or has existed between a complainant and a respondent, and provides that a single act can amount to domestic violence. There are provisions on the filing of complaints to the police, police assistance, and arrests by the police. The second part of the Act makes provision for protection orders and procedures to activate these. The final part covers miscellaneous provisions including the relationship of the Act to the Criminal Code; the promotion of reconciliation by the court; psychological and rehabilitative services for victims or perpetrators; publication of proceedings; criminal charges and protection; civil claims for damages; regulations; and interpretation.

While the Act did not explicitly repeal Section 42(g) of the Criminal Code 1960 (Act 29) that justifies the use of force in marriage, it provides that: 'The use of violence in the domestic setting is not justified on the basis of consent.'

The Act also establishes a 'Victims of Domestic Violence Support Fund'. The fund is to be applied towards the basic material support of victims of domestic violence; tracing the families of victims of domestic violence; the rescue, rehabilitation, and reintegration of victims of domestic violence; the construction of reception shelters for victims of domestic violence; and their training and capacity needs. These funds are to be raised from voluntary contributions by individuals, organizations, and the private sector, and a budget approved by Parliament, as well as money from sources approved by the Ministry of Finance.

A Domestic Violence Management Board (DVMB), a multi-sectorial board which includes representatives of CSOs, is to oversee the implementation of the Act. The DVMB is supported by a Domestic Violence Secretariat, which acts as an administrative, technical, and implementing body. Key implementing institutions specifically mentioned in the Act are the police, social welfare officers, courts (the District Court and the Family Tribunal), health personnel, clinical psychologists, and alternative dispute resolution mechanisms. In the Miscellaneous Clause, mention is also made of shelters.

Related Acts: The Criminal Offences Act and the Children's Act

Because domestic violence is only treated as a misdemeanour by the Act, attracting not more than two years' imprisonment or a fine of 500 penalty units upon conviction, aggravated incidents of violence within domestic relationships such as rape and other aggravated assaults need to be prosecuted under the Criminal Offences Act (Act 29) of 1960. There are also other forms of violence perpetrated against children within a domestic relationship which may fall within the DV Act, or the Children's Act of 1998. These may include betrothal, early marriage, and other cruel, inhuman, degrading treatment or punishment. Where children are involved in domestic violence incidents, the DV Act urges referral of their issues to the Family Tribunal, as specified under the provisions of the Children's Act.

The National Policy and Plan of Action for the Implementation of the Domestic Violence Act

After the passage of the DV Act, the government was persuaded, mainly by civil society organizations working in the area of violence such as the National Advocacy Partnership (NAP) Project Working Group, whose aim was to advocate for a coordinated policy framework for addressing violence against women and children in Ghana, and the National Coalition on Domestic Violence Legislation in Ghana, to initiate and adopt a national policy framework with a plan of action to ensure a coordinated and integrated approach to implementation of the DV Act. After a process of consultations, a National Policy and Plan of Action (NPPA) to Implement the Domestic Violence Act (Act 732), 2009–2019, was adopted by MOWAC in 2008.

The resulting national policy is based on the principles of prevention, protection, safety, and provision, now adopted as part of strategic policy objectives. These principles were gleaned from sources such as the 1992 UN Recommendation 19 on Violence Against Women, the 1995 Beijing Declaration and Platform for Action document, and the 1993 UN Declaration on Violence Against Women (DEVAW). They are seen as necessary for fashioning effective approaches for addressing violence against women (Government of Ghana/MOWAC/ Department of Women 2008: 12) and underpin the overall goal of Ghana's national policy, which is 'to ensure an integrated effective and efficient approach to dealing with the problem of domestic violence in Ghana' (*ibid*.: 11). The policy recognizes the reality that the scope of domestic violence requires more than governmental action, and pledges to ensure 'effective co-ordination of multi-agency action to combat domestic violence in Ghana' (*ibid*.: 11). It further states that the government will promote public–private partnerships and multidisciplinary solutions, and facilitate the mobilization of resources to ensure that the necessary administrative arrangements are made for the implementation of the Domestic Violence Act.

An important statement in the NPPA, which was a result of a series of consultations and lobbying from the civil society organizations, is as follows:

> Government recognizes that victims/survivors of other forms of violence against women, sexual and gender-based violence, and violence against children not covered by the DV Act, require similar services as those of domestic violence and that in most cases the same institutions and service providers cater for all these categories of victims/survivors. Government will therefore take appropriate measures to avoid discrimination against victims/survivors of other forms of sexual and gender-based violence, violence against women, and violence against children in the provision of services and application of standards. (*Ibid*.: 11)

The NPPA's strategic policy objectives consist of promoting the prevention of domestic violence; enhancing victim/survivor safety and empowerment; ensuring the protection of victims/survivors of domestic violence; enhancing service provision for victims/survivors; and ensuring the accountability of abusers. The NPPA is also to ensure the responsiveness and accountability of systems, the coordination within and between institutions and other actors handling domestic violence, and to promote community involvement/participation.

In relation to its stated principles, the policy broadly outlines steps to prevent domestic violence and re-offending: community, regional, and national coordination in response; involvement of society stakeholder groups such as the youth, media, and opinion leaders, among others, in prevention and protection; mass public education and sensitization; training for service providers in counselling and safety planning, temporary shelter provision, police protection for victims/survivors, and investigation and prosecution of offenders; arrangements for children involved in domestic violence incidents; medical and psychological screening and development of protocols and standards for service providers; mobilization of financial and other resources; and institution of effective systems of monitoring and evaluation.

Implementing the Act: contextual and institutional challenges

A number of contextual and institutional challenges and gaps have been exposed in the implementation of the Act. These include the inadequate understanding of the gendered nature of domestic violence, inadequate funding, lack of clear perspectives in violence prevention work by state agencies, ambivalence in attitudes towards perpetrators, and media treatment of domestic violence. These are discussed in turn.

Inadequate understanding of the gendered nature of domestic violence

Specific parts of the content of the DV Act show that it is a largely negotiated document with compromises to ensure that certain sections of the populace do not feel threatened. Although the Act is primarily the result of years of work led by women's rights organizations, it covers all victims and perpetrators, irrespective of sex. The gendered nature of domestic violence was largely toned down by the drafters of the legislation when courts were given the mandate to promote reconciliation and refer cases for settlement by an alternative dispute resolution method (Section 24 (1)). That the Act was passed without the section that sought to repeal the criminal code provision allowing force in marriage due to consent by the parties also implies a 'watered–down' law as a result of compromises made to calm anti-feminist sentiments.

It is obvious that the very 'watered–down' nature of the Act will feed the inclinations of enforcement institutions to avoid as much as possible the prosecution of perpetrators, and to blame victims and undermine the seriousness of sexual assault complaints within marriage.[2] As noted above, before the passage of the Act, women's rights organizations spent a lot of time trying to convince the public and law enforcement personnel of the need to see domestic violence in its different manifestations as a criminal act for which perpetrators had to be held accountable, and that this required state intervention in the so-called private/domestic sphere to address this issue. Thus the passage of a largely negotiated and watered-down Act does not serve the purposes of sending a strong message about zero tolerance for domestic violence acts and strong institutional accountability in enforcement. Current information on trends in the work of the Domestic Violence and Victim Support Unit (DOVVSU) and general lack of prosecution of domestic violence offences bear this out. Women are still blamed for violence by families and the institutions that should support them. There is inadequate understanding of the nature and dynamics of domestic violence and its root causes, which are primarily patriarchy, power and control, cultural beliefs and perceptions of women's status, and gender socialization. Women's lack of voice, especially in political spaces, and women's general lack of economic means, all under-mine their access to necessary services. These are important issues in considering the gendered nature of violence. Men still have more options in the Ghanaian context to get out of abusive situations or to find alternative means of consolation; men's motives and use of violence differ from women's, and men have more resources at their disposal than women in Ghana. It is clear that state institutions will continue to respond to gender-based violence with their 'cultural blinkers' on – women and girls have more to lose than men and boys in such situations (Cusack and Manuh 2009).

Funding challenges and shifting donor agendas

The Government of Ghana gives little budgetary support to domestic violence work. MOWAC's allocation, which is usually less than 1 per cent of the national budget, is expected to finance its work, including funding the Domestic Violence Management Board and its secretariat. Since the DV Act was passed in 2007, the Dutch Embassy in Ghana has practically shouldered funding for its plan of action, choosing which items it wishes to support. Limited support has also been given by the Unitd Nations Population Fund and, more recently, the UK government's Department for International Development in Ghana, but for very specific items on the plan. The question is, what happens to domestic violence implementation should the Dutch shift their interest to a new agenda? Another factor undermining implementation is that NGOs providing critical services to survivors do not receive any funding from the government for their work. Research has shown that money for women's rights work is dwindling globally. Ghana's primary NGOs – including WiLDAF-Ghana, WISE, FIDA-Ghana, the COMBAT Project of the Gender Centre, and the Ark Foundation, Ghana, which all provide direct services to survivors – are facing a financial crunch and are cutting down services in some of the communities they serve.

No clear direction on domestic violence prevention work

There is no clear strategy for addressing *prevention* of domestic violence in the country, even though the NPPA makes references to public awareness raising and training of different sections of state institution personnel. A serious zero tolerance for domestic violence strategy would actively seek the collaboration of the Information Services Department and the National Commission for Civic Education at national and decentralized levels, promoting mass sensitization drives as part of their regular work. With such a strategy, the media, especially the state media, would from time to time be 'flooded' with zero tolerance messages, animations, and programmes. Since the DV Act was passed, there has been no such concerted effort, ostensibly through lack of funds and delays in procurement processes, for publishing information, education, and communication materials. Meanwhile, domestic violence continues unabated.

Ambivalence in how to handle perpetrators

As noted above, domestic violence is often not regarded as a 'real crime' or a 'serious crime' like robbery or murder, even by the very agencies mandated to deal with it, and the situation in Ghana is no different. Thus there is no clear position on how to handle perpetrators of domestic violence. First, there is not a single formal perpetrators' programme in the country. Second, the perception that men (who usually represent the majority of offenders) are 'breadwinners' for their families breeds a certain reluctance to prosecute and imprison them for their acts of domestic violence. The Act requests judges, as an alternative to sentencing or in addition to sentencing, to refer offenders to counselling or for psychiatric evaluation where found necessary. While perpetrator treatment or counselling may be necessary for some cases, it is trite knowledge that most offenders choose to use violence selectively; most have neither mental illness nor substance addictions, and their violence is simply a display of their power over the victim (Awotwi *et al.* 2001: 10).

Media trivialization and sensationalism

Although the print and audio-visual media have improved reporting cases of domestic violence in terms of incidents covered, sensationalism and trivialization of cases still character-ize such reportage. Male media presenters on some radio stations routinely blame women for being abused or exploited. On some radio stations inappropriate laughter often accompanies reports of sexual assaults. Newspapers continue to emphasize the 'culturally undesirable' attributes of murdered women (for example, suspicion of adultery), leading to victim blaming – 'she made me do it!' (Gadzekpo 2009). Gadzekpo's analyses of the editorial pages of some major newspapers such as the *Daily Graphic, The Mirror,* and *The Ghanaian Chronicle* in terms of their coverage of gender-based violence issues brought out the discourses framing news reporting of violent crime in Ghana. As she concludes, the kind of coverage in the newspapers in question requires a reappraisal of news traditions that 'favour event over context, and framing strategies that advertently or inadvertently maintain the status quo and prevent readers from understanding the wider dimensions of complex gender-based victimization such as domestic violence' (Gadzekpo 2009: 283). This is a challenge that different news media need to confront as they re-examine their representational and news strategies. The general media culture of objectifying females in domesticated roles, or in hyping product sales in advertising, contributes to undermining women's autonomy, bodily integrity, and rights, especially within the family setting. However some newspapers occasionally publish informed and gender-sensitive articles, and a few journalists working for the news weekly *Public Agenda* have been recognized by the women's rights' coalition, NETRIGHT, for their coverage of gender issues in Ghana.

Other challenges facing the institutions mandated to deal with domestic violence include the scope and capacity of services; coordination issues; the diverse nature of domestic violence and capacities needed within one agency to address these differences simultaneously; family and societal interference with processes; and survivors' perceptions of the efficacy of institutions.

Limited scope, range, and capacity of services

There are police stations and police sub-divisions in every district in Ghana, together with offices of the Department of Social Welfare (DSW). Offices of the Commission of Human Rights and Administrative Justice (CHRAJ), a constitutional body, also exist in about 80 of the 130 districts in Ghana. Health posts are also available in districts and some communities. In spite of the spread of these services however, many survivors, especially in the rural areas, find it difficult to access them, because of long distances or poverty. Community health posts and district offices of the DSW and CHRAJ usually have limited human, logistical, and financial resources. Most personnel also lack the requisite skills to handle survivors and their multifaceted problems. NGOs that have built capacity over the years in service provision are also few and far between, compared to the population requiring services. Survivors, particularly women, may come to these service centres with bruises from physical battering, with little or no money, sometimes accompanied by their children and not knowing where to go. They may need temporary shelter, money for food, and medical treatment as immediate pressing needs, but further assessment may reveal lack of economic resources or income-generating activity; little or no life skills or education; non-maintenance of the children by their father; and a number of issues all needing response – shelter, medical treatment, legal support, training, and economic empowerment among others. With limited resources at the disposal of responding institutions, it is a challenge to provide the survivor with adequate services. As both an advocacy and service provider NGO, the Ark Foundation has for close on seven years organized what is called Practitioners' Case Management meetings for service providers in both the NGO and state sectors in Accra and Koforidua, in the Greater Accra and Eastern regions of Ghana respectively. These case management meetings represent an attempt to get service providers to discuss challenges in responding to survivors, in referring cases to one another, and to improve practice. It is from these meetings that these challenges have become apparent and have been a source of concern to organizations trying to respond, regardless of the contextual and institutional limitations.

The critical condition of social services in Ghana

Social services exist primarily to improve the living conditions of citizens and address vulnerable groups within the population. In Ghana, work with vulnerable groups such as children, the aged, people with disability, or women living in poverty is broadly the mandate of the DSW under the Ministry of Employment and Social Welfare. It is trite knowledge that the DSW is one of the least adequately funded agencies within the national budget, although it is saddled with legal responsibility for a broad range of people. Its staff capacity and resources are thinly stretched, contributing to the perception of its ineffectiveness in the eyes of the public. The DSW is the first point of call for reporting abuse of children of any kind, according to the Children's Act (although it appears the public prefer to go to the police first). Under the DV Act, the DSW is to prepare social enquiry reports about violence-affected families for the courts; ensure the safety of children; and report cases of abuse for investigation to the police. Project reports from an NGO on the status of the implementation of the DV Act, as well as DSW personnel feedback at a government assessment forum for partners, show that officials of the DSW are unable to execute their mandate adequately (Ark Foundation/NAP Project 2008; 2009). For example, the 2009 'Monitoring Implementation of the Domestic Violence Act and Related Legislation Report' states that although DSW officers in Kumasi were generally aware of the provisions of the DV Act, their understanding and practice were mainly limited to addressing non-maintenance of children (Ark Foundation/NAP Project 2009: 36). Personnel of the DSW also reported, in a forum organized by MOWAC, that they face challenges in their ability to execute their mandate under the DV Act (MOWAC 2011). It is obvious the DSW needs major re-engineering and resourcing to be able to perform its tasks under the DV Act and related legislation.

Coordination issues

An effective system for addressing DV and gender-based violence has certain minimum requirements: it should be survivor-centred; its structure should be carefully planned and coordinated from national policy levels through to the decentralized levels; and there must be clear leadership at all levels of coordination, clarity of roles among coordinating and collaborating agencies, and a system of accountability and reporting. Binding inter-agency protocols should be adopted to ensure standardization and reduction of trauma. Certification may become necessary for practitioners, and a good referral system should be instituted at the levels of direct service provision for survivors, including the development of common referral documents to ensure tracking of survivors. Case management at inter-agency level should become a routine part of the system, and case review meetings should be held. An effective system will have data systems, funding, training for service providers on a regular basis, hotlines and service directories, as well as a good monitoring and evaluation framework (Dwamena-Aboagye 2010). However, a recent forum held to assess the work done so far to implement the DV Act shows that the country has a long way to go in providing an acceptable minimum standard of response (MOWAC 2011). Most of the features outlined above are not yet present, and MOWAC and the DV Management Board need to tackle the challenges and gaps in the current response system systematically.

Societal interference, family/kinship ties, and sense of 'helplessness'

Kinship ties in Ghana are quite strong. The culture of belonging to a family or community, in spite of challenges arising from migration and the economic stratification of society, affect to a large extent the decisions that are made when domestic violence occurs. Chiefs, MPs, religious leaders, and family members of complainants and alleged offenders often interfere with cases, asking for their withdrawal and for amicable settlement at home. While this is not peculiar to domestic violence offences, this area is targeted the most because of the general perception that DV cases are essentially private family matters that should be dealt with outside the purview of the state. Unfortunately, survivors are pressured into dropping cases or risk facing ostracism from their family, religious, or other groups.

Challenges of handling diverse but related cases of violence

Relevant implementing institutions specified in the DV Act are confronted with several capacity and logistical challenges as a result of their broad mandate. A DOVVSU office, for example, handles child abuse, all sexual and gender-based violence, human trafficking, commercial sex work, criminal abortions, and complaints that women or children have been subjected to harmful traditional practices. This has implications for effective response and sensitivity in handling survivors, and ensuring effective investigations and prosecution. Specialized skills and kits are required for handling sexual assault survivors, for example, but these are currently unavailable except at the Police Hospital in Accra.

The institutions

Institutions working on domestic violence in Ghana range across government ministries and agencies, a specialized unit of the police service, the courts, a constitutional body, and women's civil society organizations. This sub-section analyses their roles, operations, and achievements so far, and also the challenges that they face.

Ministry of Women and Children's Affairs (MOWAC)

The Ministry of Women and Children's Affairs (MOWAC) is the lead ministry responsible for coordinating all domestic violence matters nationally. The Domestic Violence Management Board (DVMB) is the nerve centre for coordination and has the Minister of Women and Children's Affairs as chairperson, and the Chief Director of the Ministry as Secretary to the Board. MOWAC therefore plays the critical role of leading and providing policy direction on DV implementation. Its specified roles include the establishment of a data management system, together with data collection and information sharing on domestic violence. It also hosts and chairs the DVMB and mobilizes resources from its budget and from donors for implementing the DV Act. MOWAC collaborates with the Ministry of Justice to create and maintain legislative instruments (LIs) on the DV Act, and with all other ministries to ensure protection, safety and support for survivors of domestic violence, as well as protection for individuals who prevent such occurrences. It also liaises with CSOs and private sector actors on domestic violence programmes.

In the NPPA, the DV Secretariat is the management board's operational arm. It provides administrative and technical support for the work of the board and ensures a decentralized system of coordinating DV work. Coordinating Committees are set up at the regional, district, and community levels. This implies a high level of capacity and political clout to ensure especially that all relevant ministries, departments, and agencies play their expected roles, and to coordinate the implementation of their tasks (Government of Ghana/MOWAC/Department of Women 2008: 28).

Challenges facing the DVMB

The first DVMB was sworn in under the New Patriotic Party (NPP) Government in 2008 and started work. However, the Government of the National Democratic Congress (NDC) came to power on 7 January 2009, and dissolved all government boards. A new DVMB was constituted. New faces representing the institutions were sworn into office, with CSOs managing to retain only one of their former representatives. Work began afresh with the new NDC minister, who, a little over a year into the work, was moved to a new ministry in a cabinet reshuffle. A new MOWAC minister had to begin the process again. Disruptions in leadership have had the effect of slowing down implementation of the DVMB's work considerably. The current staffing and technical capacity of the DV Secretariat has been identified as an impediment to the effectiveness of its work (MOWAC 2011: 12). Most staff have been seconded from MOWAC's Department of Women, whereas the NPPA had envisaged that an Executive Secretary to lead implementation would be hired in a competitive recruitment process (Government of Ghana/MOWAC/Department of Women 2008: 52).

While a number of activities listed in the NPPA short-to-medium-term plan have been implemented successfully – including the setting up of the DVMB and the secretariat; provision of equipment; some training for media personnel; commencement of a shelter renovation project; and piloting of a district coordinating committee in one region of Ghana (MOWAC 2011) – bureaucratic bottlenecks within the civil service have delayed other important procurement activities –

such as the selection of consultants to prepare training manuals for service providers; a national communication strategy on domestic violence; and the construction of a prototype shelter for survivors of domestic violence.

As a government ministry, MOWAC receives less than 1 per cent of government budgetary allocations for all its activities, and the government's contribution to DV work is woefully inadequate. The main support for DV work under MOWAC comes from one donor agency. This relationship, though fruitful, is challenged by the risk of shifting donor interests and of submitting to the donor's own interest in specific activities.

The board meets only four times a year to give direction to the secretariat. But the amount of work envisaged by the Act and the NPPA, and the infrequency of its meetings, undermines effective supervision and follow-up of critical actions. Important matters identified in the NPPA such as access to medical services, reviewing alternative dispute resolution (ADR) systems, ensuring appropriate perpetrator programmes, and working with the judiciary to improve access to justice, have so far not been addressed by the board, and all these issues have the potential to undermine the effective implementation of the Act.

The Act enjoins the Attorney-General and Minister for Justice to collaborate with the Minister of Women and Children's Affairs to ensure the adoption of a legislative instrument to operationalize and regulate certain aspects of the Act. These include the management of shelters, education and counselling for survivors and perpetrators, training for service providers, and forms required by the courts (protection and occupation orders) (Section 41 of the DV Act). This process has been delayed, leading to police refusal to prosecute accused persons under the Act. However, a committee set up by MOWAC at the end of 2011 has submitted proposals for drafting the LI to the Attorney-General's department.

The Police and the Specialized Domestic Violence and Victim Support Unit (DOVVSU)

Under the Act and the NPPA, the police are to receive, document, and respond to domestic violence reports; assist victims to get to medical facilities; assist bailiffs to enforce protection orders; and ensure prosecution before the courts.

At a recent seminar in Accra,[3] an officer from the national headquarters of the DOVVSU of the Ghana Police Service, outlined achievements and challenges of the DOVVSU as a specialized police unit for handling violence against women and children since its inception in late 1998, some of which are captured below.

The DOVVSU has contributed to breaking the silence about domestic violence in Ghana, and it has recorded over 95,000 cases that can be further categorized into different types of violence. Thus it is helping to providing reliable data on a hitherto 'silent' crime, and fostering cooperation between state and non-state actors in assisting victims. However the DOVVSU faces several challenges as regular police personnel often do not refer gender-based violence cases to DOVVSU offices because they do not regard them as 'real' offences like murder or robbery, but 'trivial' domestic issues.

Currently the DOVVSU has only 98 offices and desks country-wide in a country with 13 police regions, 195 divisions, and 722 stations and posts. It is further marginalized within the police hierarchy, which displays ambivalence concerning its status as a specialized police unit. Trained officers of the DOVVSU can be transferred at will to other police units without reference to the skills they have built up for handling sexual and gender-based violence. Since its establishment in late 1998, the DOVVSU has been coordinated under four different police departments – the Welfare Department, Criminal Investigation Department, Human Resource Department, and Administration. Its specialized status has therefore not been conceptualized or recognized fully.

Overall, the police service does not provide adequate in-service training on domestic violence for its personnel, and outdated police procedures and formal internal protocols for addressing domestic violence and referrals to other institutions are used. Police personnel do not have adequate investigative skills, including crime scene management to aid evidence gathering and so build dockets that yield a high rate of successful prosecutions. There is also a lack of staff members with adequate specialized skills for handling child offences and sexual assaults, and police personnel undertake counselling and mediation in many instances without requisite skills.

The Department of Social Welfare

Staff of the Department of Social Welfare prepare social enquiry reports on cases, provide counselling services, work with the police, refer victims to health facilities, and profile victims and abusers. They are also to help in drawing up protocols for the establishment of shelters. However, the department is poorly funded, and it does not have enough staff and capacity to deal with the myriad issues under its mandate.

The courts

Under the Act, District Courts deal with the criminal aspects of domestic violence and also rule on applications for protection or occupation orders. They are also required to refer cases involving protection of children in domestic violence situations to Family Tribunals, refer cases for ADR, and also refer victims and abusers for counselling, psychiatric care, or psychological profiling.

Outstanding issues identified under the NPPA for the courts to address so as to contribute to effective implementation of the DV Act include adopting simple forms to facilitate access to the courts to obtain a protection or occupation order; reforming the rules of evidence for child victims of domestic violence to make it easier for them to give evidence in cases; and organizing training for judges and other court officials. In addition, the courts are to ensure that the safety of complainants is not compromised in the process of promoting reconciliation through the use of ADR in cases of domestic violence.

Through an initiative from the Chief Justice of Ghana, the first specially designated court for gender-based violence was set up as a pilot in Accra, following the passage of the DV Act. The court has so far handled several cases of domestic violence prosecuted under the Criminal Offences Act and the DV Act. Women's rights organizations have been actively involved in monitoring the work of courts in handling gender-based violence since the passage of the Act. The findings recorded in two different project reports[4] assessing the work of the courts in handling cases of violence against women and children and the implementation of the DV Act revealed the following issues and challenges.

In the majority of cases, the perpetrators are male and the victims are female. A significant number of cases are withdrawn by complainants for economic reasons, under pressure from families, after court adjournments, or in reaction to social stigmatization. Sometimes cases are heard in open court, causing embarrassment to survivors, who are also intimidated by the environment in court rooms where they often face unfriendly court officials and bullying from defence lawyers. A majority of the cases directly falling under the ambit of the DV Act are not being prosecuted using provisions of the Act because prosecutors claim it is easier to charge offenders under the Criminal Offences Act. Police prosecutors at the courts lack prosecutorial skills and the knowledge of the law, deficiencies which undermine successful prosecution. However, it was also claimed that judges and magistrates handling domestic violence cases are now familiar with the content of the DV Act, a situation that was not the case two years after the Act was passed.

The Ministry of Health

Personnel of hospitals under the Ministry of Health are mandated by the Act and the NPPA to identify, assist, and treat survivors of domestic violence, and refer them to other service providers. They are also to ensure that free medical care is provided for victims;[5] that a victims' charter on free medical care is displayed; and that identified cases of domestic violence are reported to the police. Health personnel may also be required to carry out psychological profiling of abusers.

Challenges facing the Ministry of Health include lack of sensitization and training of medical personnel on domestic violence; inadequate social welfare services at hospitals for referral purposes; the inability of the government to determine how free medical care provision under the Act is to be operationalized; and the general unwillingness of health personnel to report cases to the police. The Victims' Charter has not been adopted, and the Ministry of Health has yet to adopt protocols for handling domestic violence cases.

Legal aid and alternative dispute resolution systems

Ghana has a Legal Aid Board that has offices in all ten regions. Some of the cases it handles, especially on maintenance of children and inheritance issues, help to protect the rights of survivors. However it is ill-resourced and lacks the support of lawyers willing to undertake *pro bono* cases. Due to economic constraints, many survivors are thus unable to access legal services especially concerning civil aspects in domestic violence cases.

ADR systems, particularly informal ones, abound in Ghana. People prefer to have religious and traditional authorities, family members, and even friends as a first point of call in settling disputes, including cases of domestic violence. They usually turn to formal systems – police, courts, and NGOs – when the informal ADR processes break down. However, formally established ADR practice is increasing in Ghana, and courts are able to refer parties when this is deemed appropriate, for speedy resolution of disputes. An Alternative Dispute Resolution Bill was published in 1998, and new High Court Civil Procedure Rules were adopted in 2004. The judiciary has also promoted ADR on their own account at the beginning of each legal term, in an attempt to speedily resolve outstanding cases through out-of-court settlements. Many judges, magistrates, and lawyers have been trained in ADR techniques and there are plans to expand ADR to all courts in Ghana. The state is also providing training in recognized ADR techniques to traditional authorities – chiefs and queen-mothers – and to pastors. However objections have been raised about the role of traditional authorities in dispute resolution, and factors such as conflicts of interest and bias, particularly towards women, have been cited. But it is countered that the training provided to mediators reorients traditional authorities from showing bias when they adjudicate a dispute (AfriMAP *et al.* 2007).

Under the DV Act, courts are required to promote reconciliation in cases that are not aggravated or do not require a sentence of more than two years (Section 24 of DV Act). Women's rights activists have warned that the processes for recommending use of ADR should be carefully monitored to ensure that the safety of survivors is not compromised, and that survivors are not pressured into participating in such ADR processes; and that the courts file proper records of terms of settlement, which could be referred to in case of subsequent offences by the perpetrator.

Obviously there needs to be close monitoring of ADR in resolving DV cases. It is important that all ADR practitioners to whom cases are referred should undergo training to equip them to handle domestic violence cases in view of the socio-cultural challenges relating to domestic violence issues.

The Commission on Human Rights and Administrative Justice

The Commission on Human Rights and Administrative Justice (CHRAJ) has the mandate to protect human rights. With offices spread across the country, it provides some access to justice for survivors. However, like most state institutions, it lacks adequate resources to prosecute its mandate. CHRAJ officials also need skills and capacities to be able to handle domestic violence and other sexual and gender-based violence cases effectively, frequently in collaboration with other state and non-state agencies.

Survivors' perceptions of services received from state institutions

In 2007 the Ark Foundation, under the National Advocacy Partnership Project, undertook a survey to assess the availability and coordination of services in responding to violence against women and children. Survivors gave their views about the nature and adequacy of the services they received from state institutions such as the police (DOVVSU), the Department of Social Welfare, district courts, and health institutions. Generally, survivors appreciated the services offered, but had many complaints and suggestions. Formal systems need higher levels of sensitivity to survivors who wanted to speak and to be listened to. Referral processes between agencies need to be reviewed and improved, as survivors require redress and other complementary services such as legal and financial assistance and child support. Survivors frequently did not complete formal complaints because they could not afford the fees that doctors charged to document the abuse in police medical forms. And although the law waived these medical fees, doctors continued to require them in exchange for signing medical reports.

Survivors also stressed that perpetrators should be made accountable for their actions. Where some form of network exists, such as COMBAT – a community response programme to violence against women that was set up in 2001 by the Gender Centre and its partners under the Nkyimkyim Project (Coker-Appiah and Cusack 1999), and which has been piloted in 21 rural communities in Ghana – survivors reported a better response to their issues. Informal response systems consisting of family and religious leaders are also important to survivors, although they also often exerted pressure on survivors to drop complaints.

Civil society organizations

Apart from the formal institutions indicated above, CSOs, primarily NGOs and faith-based groups, have roles to play to ensure the successful implementation of the Domestic Violence Act. In the NPPA, women-led organizations, having provided leadership in putting domestic violence on the national agenda, are to continue playing key roles in response to domestic violence, especially in the areas of sensitization, training, advocacy, and service provision. The Coalition on Domestic Violence

Legislation in Ghana is to continue its critical advocacy for implementation of the DV Act and related laws and policies.

Challenges confronting CSOs in ensuring effective roles in implementation include lack of funding for services provision and training, and the limited scope of operation, as most CSOs are urban-based and do not have offices in rural parts of the country. There are also inadequate specialized skills and personnel to respond to survivors' multifaceted needs, or to the risks involved especially when interacting with irate partners and spouses of survivors. CSOs also operate within a largely informal referral system that does not ensure proper tracking of cases and the accountability of agencies to one another.

Conclusion

Joining a growing list of countries in Africa and elsewhere, Ghana has passed domestic violence legislation, both in fulfilment of its treaty obligations and in response to pressure from women's rights organizations, and it has thus broken the silence and denial around the abuse of women and children. The process for passing the Act was not without controversy as much resistance was manifested – and, ironically enough, supported by the Minister of Women and Children's Affairs who was expected to shepherd the Act through Parliament. However the difficulties in the passage of the Act pale in comparison with the everyday work of ensuring its implementation. This chapter has presented the legal and policy framework guiding domestic violence work in Ghana, and reviewed the contextual and specific institutional challenges and weaknesses that need to be addressed for effective enforcement of a law that aims to enhance the personal security and human rights of women, girls, and other victims of violence.

The limited understanding of the gendered nature of domestic violence by the several agencies mandated to perform functions under the Act, limited availability and reach of specialized services, including those offered by DOVVSU, and the lack of funding, are of concern. Through these limitations, the reform that has been achieved is whittled down and the status quo is protected. As Smith observes:

> Men may no longer have a legal right of chastisement, but if men who beat their wives are rarely charged, let alone prosecuted, and penalties are small even if a man is convicted, then his *de facto* power over his wife amounts to almost the same authority men always historically had. Similarly, a woman may no longer be legally required to remain with a husband who beats her, but if she has nowhere to go, no income or employment opportunities and children to support, then her restriction is almost the same as it was in the past. (2010: 15).

We have seen that several challenges remain for the effective implementation of the law in the Ghanaian context. First, political will must be demonstrated to enhance the human and financial capacity of all institutional stakeholders with the mandate to implement the law, especially the DV secretariat and the management board, because of their overall management and coordinating roles. Other equally important considerations are allocating adequate budgetary support towards implementation; developing an appropriate monitoring and evaluation system; ensuring coordination and continued collaboration between state and NGO service providers; and adopting a survivor-centred approach as an integral part of the ethos of building an effective response system. Finally, continued advocacy by CSOs – from community through to national levels – will be vital to ensure state accountability to its obligations to prevent domestic violence, provide services, protect survivors, and hold perpetrators accountable for their actions. Only when these obligations are accepted and fulfilled can Ghana begin to boast that it has tackled the issue of domestic violence.

Notes

1 In 2001, the government of the New Patriotic Party (NPP) established the Ministry of Women and Children's Affairs in place of the National Council on Women and Development as the new machinery for women and children in Ghana. A minister of full cabinet status was appointed,

who was expected to formulate policy to promote and protect women's rights in Ghana.

2   The law-making and reviewing circumstances were curious. Women's rights organizations' advocacy to include the repeal of Section 42(g) of the Criminal Code, Act 29 of 1960 in the DV Act, was unsuccessful. However, in the process of statutory revision of Ghana's laws by Justice V. C. R. A. C. Crabbe, the Statutory Law Commissioner, after the DV Act was passed, Section 42(g) was declared unconstitutional and outmoded, and was struck off the criminal legislation of Ghana!

3   The presentation was made on 25 January 2012 by a senior officer from the national DOVVSU office. This was at a forum organized by the Coalition on Domestic Violence Legislation in Ghana in Accra.

4   Between 2007 and 2008, a monitoring project was undertaken by the Ark Foundation, Ghana, which among other things examined the administration of trials of cases of violence against women and children in three courts, especially regarding the behaviour of court officials and judges towards the complainants. Another project was conducted by WiLDAF-Ghana in 2010, assessing the implementation of the Domestic Violence Act at the courts. See Ark Foundation/NAP Project 2009 and WiLDAF-Ghana 2010, on the Domestic Violence Act, 2010.

5   Sections 8(1c), 8(2), 8(3), and 8(4) of the DV Act refer to the provision of free medical care for victims.

References

Adomako Ampofo, A. and M. Prah (2009) '"You May Beat Your Wife, But Not Too Much" – The Cultural Context of Violence against Women in Ghana', in K. Cusack and T. Manuh (eds), *The Architecture of Violence against Women in Ghana*, Gender Studies and Human Rights Documentation Centre, Accra.

AfriMAP, Open Society Initiative for West Africa, and The Institute for Democratic Governance (2007) *Ghana Justice Sector and the Rule of Law – A Review*, OSIWA, Dakar.

Ark Foundation/NAP Project (2008) 'Monitoring Implementation of the Domestic Violence Act and Related Legislation Reports', unpublished reports, The Ark Foundation, Accra.

——— (2009) 'Monitoring Implementation of the Domestic Violence Act and Related Legislation Reports', unpublished reports, the Ark Foundation, Accra.

Awotwi, E., A. Dwamena-Aboagye, M. Giordano, and K. Polich (eds) (2001) *Working with Survivors of Gender-Based Violence*, the Ark's CRC-

WISE Collaboration Project, Ghana.

Boas, H. (2006) 'Lessons from Ghana: The Challenges of a Legal Response to Domestic Violence in Africa', ABA Commission on Domestic Violence, Boalt Hall School of Law, Law Student Writing Competition.

Boateng, C. (2002) 'Gender Violence and the Ghanaian Press: A Content Analysis of Coverage in *The Daily Graphic, The Mirror* and *The Ghanaian Chronicle*', unpublished MA thesis, School of Communication Studies, University of Ghana.

Coker-Appiah, D. and K. Cusack (eds) (1999) *Violence against Women and Children in Ghana*, Gender Studies and Human Rights Documentation Centre, Accra.

Cusack, K. and T. Manuh (eds) (2009) *The Architecture of Violence against Women in Ghana*, Gender Studies and Human Rights Documentation Centre, Accra.

Dwamena-Aboagye, A. (2010) 'How Should an Effective Response System to Gender-Based Violence Look Like in Ghana?', paper presented at Coalition for Domestic Violence Legislation in Ghana Conference, Accra, 25 November.

Gadzekpo. A. (2009) '"She Made Me Do It!": Discursive Frames and Representations of Spousal Murder in the Ghanaian Press', in K. Cusack and T. Manuh (eds), *The Architecture of Violence against Women in Ghana*, Gender Studies and Human Rights Documentation Centre, Accra.

Government of Ghana/MOWAC/Department of Women (2008) 'National Policy and Plan of Action to Implement Domestic Violence Act (Act 732), 2009–2019', MOWAC, Department of Women, Accra.

GSS (Ghana Statistical Service) (2009) *Ghana Demographic and Health Survey, 2008*, Ministry of Health, Accra.

Manuh, T. (2007) 'Doing Gender Work in Ghana', in C. Cole, T. Manuh and S. Miescher (eds), *Africa after Gender?* Indiana University Press, Bloomington, IN.

—— (2009) 'Understanding the Ghanaian Context for Gender-Based Violence', in K. Cusack and T. Manuh (eds), *The Architecture of Violence against Women in Ghana*, Gender Studies and Human Rights Documentation Centre, Accra.

MOWAC (2011) 'Assessing the National Domestic Violence Policy and Plan of Action to Implement the Domestic Violence Act', MOWAC/Domestic Violence Secretariat Partners' Forum, Accra, February.

Nukunya, G. K. (2003) *Tradition and Change in Ghana: An Introduction to Sociology*, Ghana Universities Press, Accra.

Pappoe, M. and E. S. Ardayfio (1998) 'The Dimension and Consequences of Violence against Women in Ghana', Study Reports I and II, NCWD, Accra.

Smith, P. (2010) 'Feminist Philosophy of Law', in E. N. Zalta (ed.), *The Stanford Encyclopedia of Philosophy (Fall Edition)*, http://plato.stanford.edu/archives/fall2010/entries/feminism-law/.

Tsikata, D. (2009) 'Women's Organizing in Ghana since the 1990s: From Individual Organizations to Three Coalitions', *Development*, Vol. 52, No. 2, pp. 185–92.

WiLDAF-Ghana (2010) 'Court Watch Report on Domestic Violence Act', WiLDAF, Accra.

About the Contributors

●●●

Silvia de Aquino was a professor of gender studies at Federal University of Bahia (UFBA) from 2009 to 2013, where she taught on gender and power relations, gender relations and diversity in contemporary society, and gender and violence. She has also been an associate researcher at the Center for Interdisciplinary Studies on Women (NEIM/UFBA) since 1996. Among other projects, de Aquino has worked with the Maria da Penha Law Observatory and as part of the Pathways of Women's Empowerment Research Consortium. Her research focuses on violence against women, particularly public policies to prevent it and the efforts of feminist movements of the 1970s and 1980s to address it.

Jessica Carlisle has done socio-legal research on courts and legal practices in Syria, Egypt, Libya, and Morocco. During her academic career, she has worked at the School of Oriental and African Studies (SOAS), the International Institute for the Study of Islam in the Modern World (ISIM), the Centre for Migration Law, and the Van Vollenhoven Institute. Much of her previous fieldwork has been on the application of personal status law and the organization of family life in the Middle East and North Africa. Recently she has also conducted projects focusing on the practice of criminal law, narratives about corruption, and property disputes.

Susanne Dahlgren is a lecturer in development studies at the University of Helsinki. She has worked as a post-doctoral fellow at the Helsinki Collegium for Advanced Studies with the project 'Spatial Moralities, Islam and the Public Sphere in the Middle East', after which she received a five-year Academy of Finland Research Fellowship with the project Rights in Law and at Home: Islamic Shari'a as Formal and Informal Legal Practice. Dahlgren is the author of *Contesting Realities: The Public Sphere and Morality in Southern Yemen*.

Angela Dwamena-Aboagye is a lawyer and the Executive Director of The Ark Foundation, a women's human rights NGO in Ghana, which established the first shelter for battered women in that country in 1999. She is currently undertaking a PhD in the Akrofi-Christaller Institute for Theology, Mission and Culture. She has won a number of prestigious national awards for her work in promoting women's rights and empowerment, including the Millennium Excellence Award in 2010. Her interests are young women's leadership development, working with survivors of sexual and gender-based violence, and women's mental health advocacy.

Takyiwaa Manuh is a retired professor of African studies at the University of Ghana, where she also served as the Director of the Institute of African Studies from 2002 to 2009. She now works as an independent researcher and consultant. Manuh was convener of the West African hub of the Pathways of Women's Empowerment Research Programme Consortium (2007 to 2011), and has also led and initiated other research programmes. She has published extensively in books, monographs, and journals on African development, women's rights and gender equality in Africa, contemporary African migrations, and African higher education systems.

Sohela Nazneen is a professor of international relations at University of Dhaka and a lead researcher at the BRAC Development Institute, BRAC University. Her research focuses on institutional analysis of gender, particularly in the areas of governance, rural and urban livelihoods, and feminist movements. She is currently leading research on gender and political settlement in selected South Asian and sub-Saharan African countries for the Effective States and Inclusive Development RPC. She has worked as an international consultant for the United Nations Development Programme, the Bill and Melinda Gates Foundation, and other development agencies. Her forthcoming co-edited volume (with Maheen Sultan), *Voicing Demands: Feminist Activism in Transitional Contexts*, includes many contributions by the Pathways team.

Arzoo Osanloo is an associate professor at the University of Washington's Law, Societies, and Justice Program. She is currently working on a new project that considers the Islamic mandate of forgiveness, compassion, and mercy in Iran's criminal sanctioning system, jurisprudential scholarship, and everyday acts among pious Muslims. Formerly an immigration and asylum/refugee attorney, Osanloo researches and teaches on the intersection of law and culture, including human rights, refugee rights and identity, and women's rights in Muslim societies. Her geographical focus is on the Middle East, especially Iran. She has published in numerous edited volumes and journals and is the author of *The Politics of Women's Rights in Iran*.

Nahda Shehada is a senior lecturer of gender, culture, and development at the International Institute of Social Studies, Erasmus University, where she teaches advanced sociology, feminist theories, and cultural studies. Shehada is interested in the anthropology of Islamic law, both in the Middle East and Europe. She is currently coordinating a research project entitled 'Islamic Family Law in Palestine: Text and Context', in cooperation with Zurich and Bern universities, and also involved with another project, 'Comparative Sexualities and Politics'. Shehada is chercheure associée at the Laboratoire d'anthropologie urbaine and has worked as a researcher at the Institute for the Study of Islam in the Modern World and at Bern University.

Index

238